JFK and LBJ

JFK and LBJ

The Last Two Great Presidents

GODFREY HODGSON

Yale UNIVERSITY PRESS ⮌ New Haven and London

Yale University Press books may be purchased in quantity for
educational, business, or promotional use. For information,
please e-mail sales.press@yale.edu (U.S. office) or
sales@yaleup.co.uk (U.K. office).

Set in Minion Roman type by Integrated Publishing Solutions,
Grand Rapids, Michigan.
Printed in the United States of America.

Library of Congress Cataloging-in-Publication Data

Hodgson, Godfrey.
JFK and LBJ : the last two great presidents / Godfrey Hodgson.
pages   cm
Includes bibliographical references and index.
ISBN 978-0-300-18050-3 (cloth : alk. paper)   1. Kennedy, John F. (John Fitzgerald),
1917–1963.   2. Johnson, Lyndon B. (Lyndon Baines), 1908–1973.   3. United States—
Politics and government—1961–1963.   4. United States—Politics and government—1963–1969.   5. Presidents—United States—Biography.   I. Title.
E842.H58 2015
973.09′9—dc23
2014045527

A catalogue record for this book is available from the
British Library.

This paper meets the requirements of ANSI/NISO Z39.48-1992
(Permanence of Paper).

10 9 8 7 6 5 4 3 2 1

In Memoriam

HARRY C. McPHERSON JR.

Friend and teacher

Contents

Preface   ix

INTRODUCTION   A Parting of the Ways   1

Part One: The Actors

CHAPTER ONE   Life Is Unfair   27

CHAPTER TWO   One Brief Shining Moment   69

CHAPTER THREE   Doctor Fell   83

Part Two: The Actions

CHAPTER FOUR   Rumors of War, Rumors of Peace   107

CHAPTER FIVE   Other Americas   134

CHAPTER SIX   Surpassing Kennedy   150

CHAPTER SEVEN   No Umbrella Man   180

Conclusion   217

Notes   231

Acknowledgments   261

Index   263

Preface

Why are the lives of these two "almost great men," John F. Kennedy and Lyndon B. Johnson, worthy of attention thirty and forty years after their respective deaths? Why, to make it personal, did I decide to write this book?

First, from my days as a young White House correspondent I have been convinced that JFK, for all his style and charm, his good intentions, and his real achievements, was overrated, and that LBJ was not merely underrated but deprived of his due reputation as not only the more liberal but in many ways the more effective president, the greatest since FDR.

I still think the comparison between JFK and LBJ tells us something about how vulnerable public opinion in a democracy is to deceptive stereotypes. I have long been astonished by the way in which the Washington press corps, in spite of (or perhaps because of) the access it has to the White House, unequaled in other large democracies, has demonstrated its ability to get presidents and other major figures *wrong*. In my political lifetime, most prominent Washington journalists (not all, of course) fawned over John Kennedy, snubbed Lyndon Johnson, idolized Henry Kissinger, and patronized Jimmy Carter. They called George Herbert Walker Bush, an unusually gifted athlete who had been twice fished out of the Pacific in crashed fighter aircraft, a "wimp." With

Ronald Reagan they achieved the remarkable feat of first ridiculing him as a mere cowboy actor; then failing to appreciate his instinctive political skills; and finally adopting the inflated estimate of his historical stature promoted by conservative ideologues and publicists, as if—to take a single example—the fall of Communism in Eastern Europe was caused, rather than simply registered, by a speech Ronald Reagan made in Berlin. (With the late Phillip Whitehead, I spent a year, 1988–89, making a series of documentaries about Reagan. I came to have great respect for Reagan's political gifts as well as gratitude for his friendliness. I still think his contribution to the collapse of Communism has been wildly exaggerated.) To this day many people attribute to Jack Kennedy virtues he did not possess, and charge Lyndon Johnson with political vices of which he was innocent. If American government has failed the nation and the world in the past fifty years, which it surely has in many specific ways, some of the blame must lie with the way the nation has been misled about personalities and policies.

Long after serious historians had abandoned Thomas Carlyle's somewhat shallow model of hero worship, the whole gamut of American media, from blockbuster commercial biographies through radio and television to the routine of Washington reporting and especially the work of Washington columnists, has focused on the personality of presidents at the expense of serious understanding of what is really happening and why.

The concept of "greatness" in political leaders is elusive. It nevertheless seems to me, looking back on their presidencies after an interval of almost half a century, that John F. Kennedy and Lyndon B. Johnson were the two last undeniably great presidents—with the contestable exception of Ronald Reagan—great in their goals and, in spite of grievous failures, in their achievements.

If "we shall not look upon their like again," we should perhaps ask ourselves why. The eight men who have succeeded them—Nixon, Ford, Carter, Reagan, Bush senior, Clinton, Bush junior, and Obama—certainly did not lack ability as individuals, even if some were conspicuously abler than others. What has changed, it must be concluded, is not the human caliber of the men who have been elected president so much as the political and perhaps the cultural context of their efforts.

Franklin D. Roosevelt, on the whole the most successful president of the last hundred years, was able to govern by his skillful use of four once-powerful intermediary forces in the system: the Congress, the permanent government, the party, and the media. Each has become either wholly or partially unavailable to modern presidents. It has become steadily more difficult for them to count on assistance from Capitol Hill, and in Barack Obama's time it has been almost wholly impossible. His Republican opponents have shown no willingness to compromise, let alone to help him, and his own party has been scarcely more effective as a tool of presidential power.

The permanent government—the elected and unelected servants of the federal government—while perhaps its members are more powerful than they are perceived to be, if only because their actions are not generally regarded by the news industry as having much interest, has not been able to bring recent presidents much succor.

The cohesion and the effectiveness of the two great political parties fluctuates, but even at their height, they have in recent decades been far from able to support any president with anything like the massive organized political weight that FDR received from the "Roosevelt coalition," divided as it was, in the Democratic Party.

As for the media: the media industry, as a provider of entertainment and a generator of revenues, has never been more powerful or more profitable. But the old news industry—as exemplified in the well-tailored front ranks of those Kennedy press conferences I attended in the early 1960s—is a shadow of its former self. Its advertising revenues, as opposed to those of the great conglomerates that have largely taken over the news industry, have shrunk. Those who run the news departments of the television networks and the great national newspapers still live in the hope that they will once again be able to generate revenues that will enable them to rebuild their diminished news-gathering operations. We must wish them well, but this has not yet happened. New technologies, new media, social media—each of these has been prayed to, like a rain god, to bring refreshment to parched fields. But for all their attempts, with their bloggers and tweeters and spinmeisters of every species, presidents have not succeeded in getting through to the people to an extent that is remotely comparable to the effect of FDR's skillful fireside chats.

Indeed, the whole political system, for all the truly oceanic tides of money that flow through it from those who believe they can use it to favor their ideas and their interests, seems to be in decline. People continue, for example, to refer to the U.S. Senate as "the greatest deliberative assembly on earth," although it has largely ceased to deliberate and—since many senators spend more time in their offices than on the Senate floor—can only rarely be described as an assembly at all. American democracy, we are still constantly told, is a model for the world. In truth, it is hardly a model for most Americans. Its institutions cannot attract the awe that is spread before the Super Bowl, the Oscars, or the Augusta Masters golf tournament.

The buses still come to the capital, parked in their dozens along the National Mall in Washington, bringing neatly turned-out young Americans to see their government at work. Yet when they get back home, how much will these young people retain of the reverence and the trust their grandparents had for the institutions of their government?

For almost two generations now, an ideology that is perhaps inaccurately called conservative has derided government. It is not therefore surprising that government no longer draws into its service men and women as idealistic as those who served the New Frontier and the Great Society. The reasons for the change are many, and change itself is not only inevitable but healthy and welcome. One reason the glory has departed is perhaps that Americans no longer turn to government with the hope that both John Kennedy and Lyndon Johnson truly did inspire. Sadly, if hope has diminished, in part it is because of the failings and failures of the two heroes we are about to autopsy.

JFK and LBJ

Introduction

A Parting of the Ways

On the evening of November 22, 1963, I went out to Andrews Air Force Base near Washington to meet the plane that was bringing back from Dallas the murdered President Kennedy and his newly sworn-in successor, Lyndon Johnson. The previous day I had returned from a short vacation in Jamaica and was having lunch with a friend, the *Guardian*'s correspondent Richard Scott, so that he could fill me in on what had happened while I was away. There was a radio on in the restaurant and with half an ear I heard, "The president has been shot." Moments later the announcer said it was serious. I left Richard at the table and jammed myself into a pay phone booth. People pounded on the door, everyone needing to call someone in reaction to the news, while I phoned the *Observer* in London, which immediately packed a reporter on a plane to Dallas. (I did not know that in London at that same moment a television news team was sending my second wife, whom I was not to meet for another two years, to Dallas on the same errand.) Then I hailed a cab and went out to Andrews.

As the plane taxied to a stop, Robert Kennedy, who had been hiding in a truck to take cover from the news media, dashed past the waiting reporters and up the steps into the aircraft. On the way to console his sister-in-law, he rushed past the new president, brushing aside his outstretched hand.

I found myself standing next to Kennedy's—now Johnson's—national security adviser, McGeorge Bundy. I knew him slightly, and we spoke in undertones as John Kennedy's casket was lowered from the tail end of the plane. His widow followed, his blood, famously, still staining her smart pink suit.

Then Johnson came down the steps right in front of us. He said a few words, with dignity. He needed God's help, he said, and ours. Bundy stepped forward, and I saw that he was carrying a sheaf of manila folders, which he handed to the new president. I have no idea what was in those folders: I imagine Bundy was handing to Johnson the Kennedy White House's hasty appraisal of the situation at this critical moment, in the world and in Vietnam. Lyndon Johnson, like the tragic hero of an epic, was being handed his own fate, for Vietnam was to be his nemesis.

JFK and LBJ, John Fitzgerald Kennedy and Lyndon Baines Johnson, were linked together and at the same time torn apart in that tragic moment as one succeeded the other at the apex of world power. When Air Force One landed at Andrews, misunderstandings and fierce resentments between the Kennedy and Johnson staffs on the aircraft had already created a situation that made the succession almost unbearably tense. We will have to look more closely at the troubled history of the relationship between two fiercely loyal political tribes.

There was little love lost between the two men, and even less between the "charismatic hordes" of their rival tribes of followers.[1] The relationship fascinated those who knew them both, especially those who worked with and for them before Kennedy's death and afterward. We shall look in depth at the details of their differences. But fascinating as that contrast is, this is not a matter of mere gossip or a biographer's random character speculation.

The contrast between John Kennedy and Lyndon Johnson raises one of the oldest questions that have troubled historians. In 1841 the Scottish historian and philosopher Thomas Carlyle set forth in his book *On Heroes, Hero-Worship and the Heroic in History* what has come to be called "the great man theory of history."[2] Carlyle the moralist thought that the supreme task of historians was to study the lives of heroes of superhuman stature—his examples included Jesus and Mahomet, Luther,

Alexander the Great, and Napoleon—because their study would enable lesser mortals to discover the hidden hero in themselves.

Among academic historians the great man theory has long gone out of fashion. Subsequent generations of scholars have insisted that the doings of great men are little more than froth on the top of deeper currents of human history. Marxists saw the tides of history as moved by economic and class conflict. Other historians—"Namierites" and the *Annales* school, for example—have focused on the interactions within and between elites, or studied "mentalities" and *la longue durée*, the "long view" of social and political development.[3] The great French historian Marc Bloch poured elegant scorn on the kind of history that was interested only in kings, presidents, and military commanders.[4] Most professional historians now insist that history should not be mainly about rulers and battles but should reflect the circumstances and the mindset, the struggles and the fate of "ordinary people." More popular works do present the lives of the Founding Fathers and other heroes. Indeed, it is striking how in the United States a handful of political heroes—the Founding Fathers, Abraham Lincoln, the two Roosevelts, for example—attract a monumental, often hagiographical style of biography that largely went out of fashion long ago elsewhere, while professional historians in the United States focus on narrow issues in a far more skeptical manner. Twentieth-century dictators from Stalin, Mao, and Hitler to their vicious little imitators, the Pol Pots and Kim Jong-Ils, Saddams, and Ghaddafis, have enforced official hero worship within their domains. In free societies spontaneous hero worship has tended to be reserved for the long dead.

John Kennedy is the exception. Few men in politics have ever received so much unforced hero worship as he did immediately after his death. In the 1960 presidential election Kennedy won 49.7 percent of the popular vote, a whisker under half. After his death, 65 percent of those polled, a whisker under two-thirds, told pollsters they had voted for him![5] His fame was sung by talented biographers, including the magisterial and devoted historian Arthur M. Schlesinger Jr. and the president's gifted speechwriter Ted Sorensen.[6] His reign was compared to Camelot, the legendary court of King Arthur, by the court journalist Theodore White.[7] We shall have to ask why Kennedy, alone of all the talented men who have occupied the White House since FDR, has attracted this post-humous apotheosis.

Lyndon Johnson was not so fortunate. His White House intellectual, the Princeton historian Eric Goldman, was a decent enough historian but scarcely carried the rhetorical guns of a Sorensen or the reputation of a Schlesinger.[8] His favorite journalists, men like William S. White, seemed in comparison with "Teddy" White mere sycophants. His biography, still far from finished, became the life work of a writer, Robert Caro, who scarcely conceals his low opinion of his subject.[9]

With the passing of time, however, the almost hagiographical tributes to Kennedy and Camelot were succeeded first by an orgy of conspiracy theory about the assassination and then by prurient, though undeniably intriguing, investigation of Kennedy's ill health and frenzied womanizing. These contradicted in a startling manner the early emphasis on his "vigor" and the idyllic character of his marriage and family. With a certain perverse symmetry, the pendulum has swung back in Lyndon Johnson's favor. A number of writers, such as Robert Dallek, Irving Bernstein, and Randall Woods, have praised his political skill and legislative achievements.[10]

Considering the voluminous literature that celebrates, denounces, or assesses both Kennedy and Johnson, it is remarkable that so few writers have attempted to look at them together. The only book I know that includes "JFK and LBJ" in its title is a thoughtful essay on "the influence of personality upon politics" written by a *New York Times* editor, Tom Wicker, in 1968, before Lyndon Johnson announced that he would not run for reelection.[11]

A modern Carlyle, it occurred to me, might find much merit in studying the lives of these two heroes together. For, different as they were, they were both in their contrasting ways undeniably great men, at least in the sense that in their lifetimes they were both formidably powerful and extravagantly admired, and indeed both did achieve truly great accomplishments. Of the eight men who have succeeded Lyndon Johnson in the White House, only Ronald Reagan could be claimed as their peer, and that judgment would be both ideologically motivated and highly contentious.

The relations between JFK and LBJ, though an important and interesting element in this book, are not its main theme. That will be an assessment of what they set out to achieve and how far they succeeded. The book also examines the conventional view of the two men to suggest that Kennedy's qualities, though real, have been exaggerated, and Johnson's underestimated.

John F. Kennedy and Lyndon B. Johnson were both great presidents because of their ambitions and their achievements, even if the one was cut short before he could do more than a fraction of what he wanted to attempt and the other was frustrated and discredited by the disaster of Vietnam: as Wicker put it, Lyndon Johnson came into office seeking a Great Society in America and found instead "an ugly little war that consumed him."[12] Ugly, one might agree, but not so little.

John Kennedy incarnated the confidence and ambition of the United States as it entered its epoch as a new political model for the world. Some of the praise lavished on him seemed exaggerated even at the time. Reviewing the two massive biographies by Schlesinger and Sorensen for a small, conservative British journal in 1966, I wrote that "one could not live as a foreigner in Washington, during the Kennedy years, without being irritated into irrational outbursts by the mood which Schlesinger evokes with naïve accuracy: 'The future, everywhere, looked bright with hope. . . . It was a golden interlude . . . never had girls seemed so pretty, tunes so melodious.'"[13]

Yet "even the ranks of Tuscany could scarce forebear to cheer":[14] "There was a quality about Kennedy as a man," I went on, "that was undeniable. He was intelligent, he was brave and he was generous. Skeptical, even philosophically pessimistic as he was, he believed that men can improve their life through political action, and that they must do so."[15] I would not change that verdict today.

Johnson did not receive many accolades from admiring journalists or historians in his lifetime or after his death. When I wrote a profile of him on the day after Kennedy's death, I summed him up: "He is a man who invites a certain cynicism. His virtues are hidden behind his slightly raffish façade. He has a subtle intelligence, and yet an utter lack of intellectuality. He will make a very American President of the United States."[16] I was angrily called to order by some of Kennedy's admirers for daring to give Johnson even such limited praise.[17] Yet Johnson was a man of historic dimensions. He was the culminating figure of the New Deal—and he meant to be more than that. His lifelong ambition was to fulfill and surpass the social democracy of the hero of his youth, Franklin Roosevelt, and in an astonishingly short time, that is just what he did.

Both Kennedy and Johnson achieved great things. Both ultimately failed. Paradoxically, Kennedy, the supposedly dashing young idealist, deliberately put off his more ambitious projects until the political conjuncture might be more favorable. Johnson, the supposedly cynical political operator, went hell for leather at an unprecedented menu of bold reform with little apparent concern for the possibility of failure. A further irony of their historical relationship was that Johnson's successes were made easier by Kennedy's death.

This book aims to illuminate two counterfactual questions. Would Kennedy, if he had lived, been able to achieve the titanic domestic reforms—the Civil Rights Act, Medicare and Medicaid, immigration reform, federal aid for elementary, secondary, and higher education, and much more—that are Johnson's monument? And would Kennedy, if he had lived, have made Johnson's mistake of committing American power and America's reputation to an unwinnable war in order to demonstrate American "resolve"? We know that Johnson did make that mistake, and we must conclude that he made it not, indeed, out of respect for Kennedy's memory—he was too pragmatic a politician and too proud a man for such quixotism—but out of his calculation that if he was to do what he dreamed of doing, he must first win election in his own right. If he was to do that, he calculated, he must first not fail to carry out what he thought people would see as Kennedy's legacy.

Those two questions, it seems to me, justify a retelling of this tale of heroes, hero worship, and history because, half a century later, the consequences of Kennedy's wars and of Johnson's legislative revolution are still with us. The proper role of government in American society and the appropriate conduct for America in a complex and angry world are still at the top of the agenda of American politics.

The story of the Kennedy and Johnson administrations, their bright hopes and tragic failures, was the hinge on which momentous outcomes turned. The seven years from John Kennedy's inauguration in 1961 to Richard Nixon's victory at the polls in 1968 saw transformations

in American life as great as or greater than those in any other comparable period, arguably not excluding even the years of the Civil War or
the less than four years of World War II. Among them, without exhaust-
ing the creative ferment of those troubled years, we can list: a historic
confrontation with deep-seated racial injustices that were the delayed
consequences of slavery; the fulfillment of the New Deal and its replacement as America's public philosophy by a new conservatism; changes in
immigration law that would eventually end the historic predominance
of people of European stock in the American population; the rise and
partial success of a newly confident feminism; and a political involvement in the Middle East that has already had far-reaching consequences
and may yet have even more.

The uplifting rhetoric of Kennedy's inaugural address, the trumpet, as he called it, summoned Americans to "bear the burden of a long
twilight struggle, year in and year out, 'rejoicing in hope, patient in trib-
ulation'" in a struggle against "the common enemies of man: tyranny,
poverty, disease and war itself."[18]

This was, no doubt, a cold war summons. Kennedy had won election in large part by denouncing the slackness of the previous administration's posture in the face of an aggressive and militant Soviet Union.
He and his speechwriter Ted Sorensen, the master of an almost Augustan
style of elevated rhetoric, full of alliteration and suchlike tropes, summed
up what Kennedy and many of his generation despised in the Eisenhower administration, its supposed "lack of effort, lack of initiative, lack
of imagination, vitality and vision."[19]

No doubt the tyranny he meant was that of Communism, and the
war he had in mind was the conflict with the Communist powers and
their allies. Yet in fairness he intended something more than a cold war
call to arms. He went on to speak of his hopes of an alliance to "assure a
more fruitful life for all mankind." No doubt that was a rhetorical flourish. But Kennedy's immense appeal, not least to the young, to the highly
educated, and to those who cherished an ambitious vision of America's
destiny, did not come merely from the idea that he would contest the
Soviet Union more vigorously. As the outpouring of grief after his death
demonstrated, he appealed to deep seams of idealism in many kinds of
Americans.

There was in that great speech no hint whatsoever that the United

States might be imperfect in any serious way. America would help the world but would itself scarcely need any help. There is a ringing sentence of St. Augustine: *Securus judicat orbis terrarum,* the Christian world "judges and is not judged."[20] So too, for Kennedy and his victorious wartime generation, "tempered by war, disciplined by a hard and bitter peace," the United States would judge and would not be judged.[21]

Kennedy called on Americans, as everyone knows, to ask not what their country could do for them but what they could do for their country. It is less well remembered that he also wanted foreigners, "fellow citizens of the world," to ask not what America would do for them, but to ask what "together we can do for the freedom of man."[22]

Not a word, in that bold statement of his project, about the drab compromises and urgent decisions of domestic politics. He did not so much as mention the humdrum tasks that would be needed to bring the "freedom of man" to the African American citizens of the Deep South and the northern ghettos.[23] Still less was there any inkling that there might be limits—military, financial, or political—to America's guarantee of freedom to the world. Indeed, part of Kennedy's appeal lay precisely in his affirmation of a new American style, a sense of omnipotence, or at least optimism, that was special to those of the "great generation" who, like him, had fought as young men and women in World War II and—with some help, it is not always remembered, from the British empire and the Soviet Union—conquered Nazi Germany, fascist Italy, and militarist Japan. In an earlier account, JFK's personal chronicler, Teddy White, recalled the mood he encountered when he arrived as a correspondent in China in 1945: "All was free, room, food, liquor, girls—because we were Americans. The whole world belonged to America."[24] Theirs was a new and universal ambition: to make the world over in the image of America. It has had fateful consequences: some happy, some less so.

Already, in the brief thirty-four months of Kennedy's presidency, this optimistic confidence had been called into question. The civil rights revolution in the South was the first test. At first, neither President Kennedy nor his brother the attorney general, into whose portfolio it fell, fully grasped the momentous character of that challenge to racial supremacy. It was not just the regional customs of some eleven states and something between a quarter and a third of the population that were at stake;[25] so was the whole national political system on Capitol Hill. There the reality was not the formal contest between Democrats and Republicans but the steady imposition of limits to social and political change guaranteed by the conservative alliance between Democratic members of Congress from the one-party states of the South and conservative Republicans who largely represented midwestern and western business interests.

Early in my time in Washington, in 1962, as part of my policy of interviewing as many important people as would see me, I went to talk to Robert Kennedy in his cavernous office at the Justice Department. (Halfway through the interview, in token of Kennedy informality, our discussion was interrupted by the arrival of Kennedy's dog Brumas, a famous black Newfoundland, escorted by an attractive, but anonymous, young woman.) Rather naïvely, perhaps, I asked him why it was that the United States was the only major democracy in which the political divide between the two major parties was not an ideological contest between Left and Right or an economic conflict between haves and have-nots. To my surprise, the attorney general reached into a deep drawer of his desk—the drawer where many Washington politicians might have kept a bottle of bourbon whisky—and pulled out a battered shoebox full of five by eight filing cards on which he had taken notes, in his own handwriting, on this very subject.

He replied, as I remember his answer, that the United States was already so divided, by race, by section, by ethnicity, and by geography, that a further divide by class would tear the country apart. At the time what struck me most about this answer was surprise that the supposedly less intellectual of the Kennedy brothers, famed for his "hard-nosed" political effectiveness, should have thought so much about a theoretical question and taken the trouble to write down opinions on the subject from both practicing politicians and academics. Looking back after half a century, what I find more surprising is how swiftly Robert Kennedy was proven wrong.

The process had already begun when he spoke, but it accelerated rapidly after passage of the 1965 voting rights legislation. When I first went to Washington, if a foreigner asked me to explain the issues that divided Democrats from Republicans, I would explain that it all went back to the events of the 1860s—the Civil War and Reconstruction. Very soon afterward, I would have to say that, in order to understand the contemporary party divide, you must understand the events of the 1960s, both the civil rights movement, the drive of African Americans for justice and equality, and the resistance to that demand.

In 1962, there were conservative Democrats in plenty, especially in the South, and not a few liberal Republicans of the stamp of John Lindsay or Jacob Javits in the North. By the 1980s, enough southern conservatives had become Republicans, and enough African Americans had begun to vote (and overwhelmingly to vote Democrat) that you would indeed have to say that one of the two historic American political parties had become ideologically a party of the Right, the other of the Left; and therefore that broadly speaking the Republicans represented the haves and the Democrats the have-nots. That is even more true today, although the way political life is funded means that the have-leasts are not much represented in either party.

The Kennedy brothers and most of their advisers did not guess that within months, rather than years, the politics of race would come to preoccupy not only the states of the former Confederacy but the great northern cities as well. The same could be said of many of Johnson's supporters, though not of LBJ himself. Rioting would reveal the anger and misery that were the dark side of even the most glorious American cities: Los Angeles, the entertainment capital; Chicago and Detroit, the commercial and industrial capitals; New York, the intellectual capital; and the marble monuments of Washington, the political capital, itself.

Immediately before his death, Kennedy had been annoyed and embarrassed by the murder of the Diem brothers, America's Roman Catholic neocolonial proxies in South Vietnam. There is no reason to suppose that Kennedy wanted, let alone that he ordered, their assassination, though recent research has established that he knew more about the conspiracies that led to it than was acknowledged at the time.[26] His ambassador, Henry Cabot Lodge, his sinister French-Corsican-born Saigon CIA station chief, Lucien "Lou" Conein, and others among his officials were more or less deeply implicated in the plot that led to the assassinations. (Conein literally sat in the plotters' clandestine head-quarters and relayed their intentions to Washington.)[27] We will examine in detail in a later chapter the vexed question of whether Kennedy, if he had lived, would have committed the United States as deeply and irrevo-cably to war in Vietnam as Johnson actually did. There is no doubt, how-ever, that Kennedy did initiate that commitment, or that elsewhere—in Laos, the Philippines, and Indonesia, in Central Africa, Central Amer-ica, and the Caribbean—the "long twilight struggle" was not just a liter-ary trope. American men and many others fought and died, and Amer-ican money was spent, in many such twilight wars. If John Kennedy was shocked by the humiliating position he had been left in by the CIA's foolish attempt to overthrow Fidel Castro, he nevertheless continued to pursue comic opera assassination plots against Castro.[28]

The quarter of a century between the end of World War II and Kennedy's election had been the age of a "liberal consensus." This did not mean that everyone in American public life was a liberal: far from it. It did mean that most politicians went along with a vast, unspoken bar-gain, by which most (not all) Democrats adopted a conservative anti-Communist foreign policy, while most (again, not all) Republicans more or less grudgingly accepted the outlines of the New Deal, with its "lib-eral," or social democratic acceptance of government's role in seeking to achieve a measure of equality and justice in domestic policy.

Between 1961 and 1968 the liberal consensus, such as it was, was definitively shattered. In some respects, to be sure, Richard Nixon was a politician who—however conservative his temperament—had grown up with the assumptions of the consensus, shared some liberal instincts, and even boasted of some liberal achievements.[29] But his election did mark a historic watershed in political history. The Watergate episode, consequence and culmination of Nixon's paranoid willingness to do whatever he thought he needed to do to win reelection, delayed by eight years, until Ronald Reagan's 1980 victory, the fulfillment of the conser-vative ascendancy. But from 1968 that reversal of ideological fortunes was inevitable.

What was challenged in the Kennedy/Johnson years went far be-yond the political consensus. Deep assumptions of American social and cultural life were called into question, mocked, challenged, overthrown.

In particular, these years saw a rebellion against all forms and conventions of leadership and authority: in the White House, on campus, in the armed forces, in the pulpit, even in the home and in the bedroom. This bombardment of the nuclei of American civilization by the fast protons of racial, political, industrial, intellectual, and sexual rebellion transformed American society with the explosive force of many megatons. It also evoked a reaction that was at the heart of the new conservatism of the 1980s and the subsequent conservative ascendancy. In politics, as in Newton's third law of motion, every action has an equal and opposite reaction. In this case, the reaction proved even stronger than the original action.

If Kennedy's inaugural address was the clearest statement of the primacy he gave to international goals, the iconic representation of what Johnson stood for was neither his first pledge to Congress—"Let us continue"—or his own impressive 1965 inaugural, but the remarkable commencement speech he gave at Howard University on June 4, 1965, the boldest statement of the liberal dream first sketched by Johnson's personal hero, Franklin Roosevelt. The speech, of course, did not spring full-grown from Johnson's mind. Several gifted writers, including a Johnson staffer, Harry McPherson; a Kennedy speechwriter, Richard Goodwin; and a Kennedy admirer who briefly became a Nixon aide, Daniel Patrick Moynihan, contributed both ideas and polished phrases. But then Kennedy, too, owed a debt he was not overkeen to acknowledge to the eloquence Ted Sorensen and others, including Goodwin, lent him.[30]

In the Howard University speech Johnson moved imaginatively even beyond the two great legislative monuments he and Congress had fashioned, the Civil Rights Act of 1964 and the Voting Rights Act of 1965. It was not enough, he said, "just to open the gates of opportunity. All our citizens must have the ability to walk through those gates." In a sentence that can now be seen as the high-water mark of the evolving liberal enterprise that began with the New Deal, he defined an even more ambitious goal for the struggle for racial equality: "We seek not just legal equity but human ability, not just equality as a right and a theory but equality as a fact and equality as a result."[31]

Bold as that was, Johnson's vision of what he called "the Great Society" he sought to build in America was even broader and more elevated. It was not to be limited to civil rights or even to the grander, more elusive goals of racial justice and equality. In his speech at the University of Michigan in May 1964 he glimpsed a political ideal that would embrace not only the rebuilding of "the entire urban United States" and a universal grant of educational opportunity but an inchoate and perhaps incoherent but nonetheless passionately felt aspiration toward a good life that was spiritually as well as materially improved, "a richer life of mind and spirit."[32]

It was not long before that dream faded. By 1967, in a crossfire between the liberals in the Democratic Party on one side and the military and conservatives in both parties over the Vietnam War, and bumping up against the sheer cussed stubbornness of the social habits, intellectual assumptions, and political structures he wanted to change, Johnson's vision seemed unattainable, even perhaps to him. By early 1968, he was moving toward the fateful decision to withdraw from the presidency so as to leave himself free to concentrate on fighting, or at least ending, the war that had shattered his dream. The consequence was the loss of the 1968 presidential election, the end of the liberal era, and the arrival of the conservative ascendancy.

Yet just as Kennedy's style transformed the image that the United States would present to the rest of the world, and the image that Americans would have of their country, so Johnson too had caught a shaft of light. It illuminated a vision of the nation's destiny more ambitious and more humane than any of his predecessors since the self-deceiving Woodrow Wilson had dared to imagine.

Many Americans, after Lyndon Johnson inherited the presidency, could not take seriously his moral vision or his standing as a preacher of political morality. This was understandably especially true of those who had worshiped John Kennedy. Many others found his vision vitiated by an undeniable crassness in his personal style. They could not forgive, or even respect, a man who scratched his belly in public and insisted on issuing orders to his staff through an open door when enthroned on the toilet.

There was also the vexed matter of Johnson's "southernness." Jack Kennedy's loyal housecarl, Kenny O'Donnell, believed that his beloved

master saw Johnson's "identity as a Southerner who had never tried to
run for office out of Texas" as a major obstacle to picking him as his vice
president.[33] Robert Kennedy suspected Johnson's status as a southerner.
John Kennedy himself told Walt Rostow in 1960 that LBJ "has the most
legitimate claim to the nomination . . . but I do not believe a man with
his accent from that part of the country can be nominated."[34] Unmistakably, behind the petty jealousies of the Kennedy and Johnson staff aides,
there loomed the ancient rivalry between North and South.

The heirs, even the Catholic heirs, of abolitionist Boston despised
the heirs, even the liberal heirs, of the Confederacy. Many southerners in the mid-twentieth century had not forgotten the humiliation of
their defeat a century earlier. When Lyndon Johnson, newly chosen as
Jack Kennedy's vice presidential running mate, first visited the Kennedy
family home, Allen Duckworth of the *Dallas Morning News* drafted this
spoof introduction to his report: "Senator John F. Kennedy, at his Hyannis Port home, Saturday morning accepted the sword of Texas Senator
Lyndon B. Johnson and said 'The men may keep their horses.'" It was a
sardonic reference to the bitterest moment in the death of the Confederacy, when General Ulysses S. Grant allowed Robert E. Lee's men to
keep "their private horses" for the autumn plowing. So it was an implicit
warning against a good old southern boy being corrupted by northern
patronage.[35]

There was another, more immediate reason why it was understandable that Yankees should see Johnson as a southerner. Johnson's
main claim to political influence, his powerful performance as majority
leader in the Senate, owed a lot to his ability to ride herd on the powerful southern senators: John Stennis and James Eastland of Mississippi,
Harry Byrd of Virginia, Bob Kerr of Oklahoma, and above all Richard
Russell of Georgia. A specific factor in many northerners' perception of
Johnson as a southerner was his undeniably close relationship with Russell, the acknowledged leader of the southern senators. Southern senators gave Johnson an easier ride than they might otherwise have done
because they thought he might one day be president. Dick Russell did
not hide his conviction that the Civil War would not be over until a
southerner was elected president. Lyndon Johnson, Russell thought, was
the best prospect for that reconciliatory role.[36]

In truth, Johnson was far from a typical southerner. He came from Texas, a state where only a dozen counties out of more than 250 shared either the plantation economy or in full measure the Confederate passions of the Deep South.[37] Moreover, he grew up in a part of Texas, the Hill Country north and west of Austin, that was even less "southern" than the rest of the state. The Hill Country was largely settled by German pioneers, some of them refugees from the persecution visited on the partisans of the failed liberal revolution of 1848 in Germany;[38] the Johnson family cherished those maverick traditions. Johnson's aide Horace Busby, who knew his political instincts as well as anyone, stated flatly that Johnson did not think of Texas as a southern state.[39] Johnson was in many ways a westerner as much as he was a southerner. His political model was FDR and—in spite of all his business friends—he was more of a populist than a conservative. Unlike William Fulbright of Arkansas, Johnson did not sign the Southern Manifesto against desegregation. He refused to join the Senate's southern caucus. From Massachusetts or Manhattan, he might look like a southerner. (His accent did upset some northerners. On the fateful journey from Dallas Kennedy aides were offended by the fact that a Johnson aide, Cliff Carter, pronounced Kennedy as *Kinnedy*.[40] I remember sitting next to a Harvard faculty wife at dinner in Cambridge in 1964 who said that the new president might be a fine man, but she couldn't respect a president who couldn't pronounce the word *America*—in other words, one with a Texas accent!) But those who were closer to the man knew better. His close aides—Bill Moyers, Harry McPherson, Horace Busby, and George Reedy—all men of education and national perspective—understood that he was a westerner rather than a southerner insofar as he was a populist. Reedy, a middle western Catholic Democrat, said, "If ever there was a centrist in American politics, he was it," adding that there was in Johnson "a real streak of the sons of the wild jackass," as the western populists called themselves.[41] His father sat in the Texas legislature as a member of the People's Party. I like to think of LBJ as a grandson of the wild jackass.

If there was one area where Johnson can unhesitatingly be called a liberal,[42] it was on the issue of race. The Howard speech was no time-serving or hypocritical late conversion. Lyndon Johnson disliked racism all his life, from his experiences teaching Mexican children in Cotulla

in south Texas to his service with the National Youth Administration
and throughout his congressional career. That did not mean that he was
not ready to chaffer and deal and generally come on like a good ol' boy
when he thought he had to with southern colleagues in Congress who
certainly were racist. It did not mean that he did not want to be accepted
by men like Richard Russell of Georgia or Robert Kerr of Oklahoma,
who were more or less unashamedly racist. But the evidence is that—
however hard it was for New York and New England liberals to believe
it—Johnson's commitment to racial justice was earlier and far deeper
than that of the Kennedy brothers. Kennedy's admiring, if critical, biographer Richard Reeves went so far as to point out that "the only Negro
he spent time with was his valet for the past fourteen years," George
Thomas.[43] The contrast between Kennedy's master-servant relationship
with Thomas and the Johnsons' affectionate respect for their African
American cook, Zephyr Wright, is instructive.[44] This possibly reflected
a well-known cultural contrast between northerners and southerners
in their treatment of race: northerners theoretically believed in racial
equality but had little experience of individual African Americans;
southerners bitterly defended segregation but lived far closer to African
Americans, albeit in a defined hierarchy of superiority, enforced if they
saw it as necessary with cynicism and ruthlessness.

It would be hard to deny that until the civil rights movement burst
with urgency into the nation's consciousness in the summer of 1963, the
Kennedy brothers were far less aware of the fundamental importance of
race in the American polity than was Lyndon Johnson. As late as the Ole
Miss confrontation in October 1962, the record shows that both President Kennedy and his brother the attorney general (who later did totally
"get it" about race) could hardly bring themselves to take seriously a
brave black man's determination to enroll at Mississippi's all-white university. They went along with a collusive scheme for avoiding the issues
posed by the demand of an African American, James Meredith, to be
registered at the university. The scheme, cooked up by Mississippi governor Ross Barnett, proposed "a fake showdown at the gates of the campus. Two dozen armed U.S. marshals would support Meredith and Barnett would yield reluctantly to superior force." This scriptwriting broke
down only when Robert Kennedy drew the line at having the two dozen

federal lawmen all draw their guns. One gun would be enough, Kennedy thought; "the others [could] keep their hands on their holsters." The Kennedy brothers went along with this farce in the hope of avoiding confrontation until it was all too apparent that Barnett meant to cheat them. Even after the Mississippi students and segregationist thugs had launched a truck and a bulldozer against the handful of federal officials besieged in the Ole Miss Lyceum, twenty-eight federal marshals had been shot, and two bystanders had been murdered, the Kennedy brothers and their friends joked about the situation.[45] "We had riots like that at Harvard," the president said, in a particularly inopportune example of his (on other occasions attractive) taste for black humour.[46]

Ted Sorensen confirmed what was already clear to most—that it was not until the summer of 1963, after the events in Birmingham and the stand-off with Governor Wallace, when he "stood in the schoolroom door" to prevent two African American students registering at the University of Alabama in Tuscaloosa, that Kennedy grasped that the civil rights movement was an existential moment for his administration and his own reputation as well as for the entire nation's political future.[47] A recent careful study concluded that, while Kennedy would almost certainly have secured passage of the 1964 Civil Rights Act, and that by his personal example "he made racism unfashionable," nevertheless he missed a historic opportunity. He "abdicated his responsibility to lead the great social revolution of his age." He was "all too often tone deaf to civil rights," and essentially he remained a "bystander."[48]

As the nation reeled under the news of Kennedy's assassination, the dead president was lionized in the public mind. For a time he became the center of something like a cult. His death was compared to that of the gods and demigods of the ancient world—Adonis, Osiris, Balder—who had died in order that their people might live, and even to the life and death of Jesus. Isaiah Berlin wrote to his friend Arthur Schlesinger that there had probably been no such sense of loss at one man's passing since the death of Alexander the Great in 323 BC.

His successor attracted no such reverence. To many, he was suspect. At first the assumption was that Kennedy had been murdered by right-wing fanatics of the kind who had demonstrated against Adlai Stevenson in Dallas only weeks before Kennedy's death. In Washington, ill-natured jokes in the worst of taste circulated, on the lines of "Why is Lyndon Johnson not hunting deer this season? Because Lee Harvey Oswald has his rifle." (A subtler joke went like this: "Why does LBJ speak so slow? Because he thinks he's dictating to a stone mason.")[49] The Johnsons themselves assumed that such suspicions would circulate. Even the most serious and best-disposed worried that Johnson would not be up to the job, that he lacked Kennedy's style, his intellectual ability, his sophistication. The columnist Stewart Alsop, who was friendly with Johnson but a friend of Kennedy, wrote that "there was a feeling that LBJ was the usurper, that he was a Macbeth,"[50] and indeed later a crude satire based on the "Scottish play," *MacBird,* made a small fortune for its author, a University of California graduate student called Barbara Gershon.

Many influential journalists, like Ben Bradlee, then at *Newsweek,* Charlie Bartlett, and Joseph Kraft, were more or less close friends of Kennedy. Even reporters with no personal connection to Kennedy took it for granted that Kennedy stood for everything that was young, modern, sophisticated, and international, and that Johnson was a figure from an older, grosser, more provincial culture. This distinction reflected the idea that the executive branch of the government stood for modernity, efficiency, relevance, and cosmopolitan sophistication, while the Congress represented all that was archaic, bumbling, provincial, and ineffectual. "Teddy" White went so far as to say that his hero JFK was the protagonist in a drama with two historic antagonists, "the Communists abroad with their dogmas, and the Congress of the United States, with its dogmas, at home."[51] Such assumptions soon became the national mood.

Slowly, with courage as well as skill, Johnson set himself to reverse those judgments and prejudices. Even critics were reassured by his choosing, as the theme of his first televised address as president, "Let us continue." They were pleased that he kept on as many of Kennedy's White House staff as he could, though later it was pointed out that the result was that there were two White House staffs, wastefully duplicating each other and in several cases privately at loggerheads.

Johnson's most irreconcilable critics, initially, were the liberals, but for a time they were more than reassured, they were impressed by his spectacular legislative achievements.[52] They saw them as the fulfillment

of a liberal agenda that Kennedy either could not or would not risk trying to enact. After 1965, many liberals were progressively alienated by the
Vietnam War, which they called "Johnson's war," and by 1967, especially
after Martin Luther King denounced the war in his Riverside Church
sermon,[53] Johnson's reputation, in many liberal eyes, was lost beyond
repair. Yet after his abdication, and especially after Richard Nixon entered the White House, a crossover began between the reputations of
Kennedy and Johnson. While Johnson's star rose, Kennedy's waned.

The reasons for this reversal did not have much to do with the political achievements or failures of the two men. Johnson had never been
the hero of a cult of the kind that Kennedy had undoubtedly inspired.
His political and legislative achievements, on the other hand, came to
be valued, at least by liberals and Democrats. His stature was enhanced
rather than damaged by the sense that there was something crude about
his forcefulness. Joseph Alsop, a Georgetown neighbor and personal
friend of Kennedy, came to admire Johnson. When, in the early days
after the assassination, McGeorge Bundy admitted to doubts about
working for Johnson, Alsop told him that there was "something monstrous" about Johnson, but that "if you were working for a monster the
thing to remember was whether he was a beneficent monster."[54] It was as
a beneficent monster that Johnson was remembered by many more than
Joe Alsop.

The cult of Kennedy and Camelot attracted an extraordinary intensity of media attention. A whole publishing industry of speculations
about the causes of Kennedy's assassination obscured the memory of the
living hero. A steady drip of revelations about Kennedy's health and sex
life tarnished his reputation. Not an inconsiderable part of Kennedy's
appeal in his lifetime had been his image as a young, vigorous prince,
contrasted with the elderly, infirm Eisenhower, like Prince Hal compared to Henry Bolingbroke. One of the journalists' clichés in profiles
of Kennedy was affectionately to mock his pronunciation of one of his
favorite words, *vigor*. Gradually it became clear that so far from being
the youthful athlete to be contrasted with the jowly, middle-aged Nixon,
it was Kennedy who was the less healthy of the two. When he died,
Kennedy was afflicted with at least three potentially life-threatening
conditions—a painful back ailment, a malfunction of the adrenal gland

called Addison's disease, and a chronic venereal infection that resisted antibiotics. He also suffered from recurring stomach problems: Nixon lived to be eighty-five. Another part of Kennedy's appeal was the image of his family: the beautiful, cultivated young wife who could speak to Charles de Gaulle in correct French, the pretty children. Gradually it began to emerge that Kennedy was so compulsive and open an adulterer that, romantically affectionate though he was to his children's mother, his marriage was something of a sham; his wife preferred to withdraw to Glen Ora, her house in the Virginia hunt country, or go sailing in the Mediterranean with the Greek billionaire she later married, Aristotle Onassis. Whatever the precise nature of the relationship between the widow and the martyred prince had been, it became clear that at times John and Jackie's supposedly idyllic marriage had come close to breakdown, and that she retreated to Glen Ora in part because the sordid procession of paramours in the executive mansion was too painful to be endured.

It was nevertheless Jackie Kennedy who summoned Teddy White, the Kennedy clan's favorite journalist, and gave him the idea that her husband's brief time in the White House had been a reprise of the fabled reign of King Arthur, not as recorded in Malory's *Le Morte d'Arthur* but as recalled in her favorite Broadway musical.[55] The sacred memory of Camelot was not helped by the revelation that the tragic and beautiful widow found consolation in the arms of an elderly Greek gentleman who had been divorced from his wife when caught in flagrante delicto with the opera singer Maria Callas. There were even reports of Senator Edward Kennedy negotiating, in a robust manner, a more than comfortable financial settlement for his brother's widow with her new, immensely rich husband. Other scandals touched the hem of the garments of several Knights of the Round Table, not least the death of Mary Jo Kopechne in the car of the same senator. President Kennedy's own memory was smirched by serial revelations of his voracious sexual exploits, some undeniably damaging to his reputation.

By 1976, as we shall see, a biography by Joan and Clay Blair Jr., solidly researched, if hostile and by no means universally accepted as authoritative, even raised serious doubts about Kennedy's reputation as a war hero. "He was in effect," they concluded, "a 'manufactured' war hero," turned into one by his father's money and manipulation of the media."[56]

That may be an exaggeration. But twenty years after his death, the image of the shining prince, as portrayed in the biographies by Schlesinger and Sorensen, and indeed often associated with the mythology of sacrificed gods, could no longer be taken seriously. Later tragedies in the Kennedy family, notably the death of President Kennedy's son John, who crashed his Piper into the sea off Martha's Vineyard in 1999, evoked media extravagance. But now the emphasis was more on the tragic misfortunes of the Kennedy family than on its quasi-royal glory. By that point, the idea, once pervasive, that Jack Kennedy could be seen as the Adonis or the Osiris, let alone the Jesus, of an American cult of the king who dies for his people had become little more than a joke in bad taste.[57]

When Kennedy became president, he was taken for the standard-bearer of modernity, a man of eastern and international style, in contrast to Johnson, seen as the provincial with his roots in the log-rolling politics of Capitol Hill and the reactionary mores of the South. Yet by 1968, the last year of LBJ's presidency, Kevin Phillips was writing about the Kennedy heartlands as the "Rust Belt," contrasting it with LBJ's economically dynamic Sunbelt.[58]

Together John Kennedy and Lyndon Johnson guided the United States through the most intense period of social and political change since World War II, eight years that changed the nation and the world. It would be naïve to present those years of roiling turmoil solely through the lens of the contrast between JFK and LBJ. Both men surfed deep, fast-rushing breakers of social change that had been formed far out to sea, in the great events of the previous generation. Kennedy was formed more by World War II, Johnson, nine years older, more by the Depression and the New Deal. Both reflected, in their careers and ideas, those cataclysmic transformations of American life.

The eight years so abruptly shared between the two presidents witnessed nothing less than a metamorphosis of the national self-image. Brief as they were, their successive presidencies saw irreversible change in the relations of black Americans and white, men and women, in foreign policy and demographics, and in the tone and fundamental character of political life. To be sure, some of those changes were on their way when John Kennedy read his inaugural address, and many were not

complete when Lyndon Johnson went back to his ranch on the Peder-
nales River. No doubt much of that central characteristic of the ensuing
decades, the conservative ascendancy, was devoted to attempts to reverse elements of their legacy. Neither qualification should negate the
enduring impact of these two men.

Those years saw the end of the "Roosevelt coalition" in the Democratic Party between southern conservatives and the progressive intellectuals and labor unions of the North, just as it saw a transformation of
the conservative alliance. The Kennedy/Johnson civil rights legislation
triggered the metamorphosis of the Democrat/Republican relationship
into the now deep if asymmetrical polarization between liberals and
conservatives, blue and red—asymmetrical because Republicans have
become much more conservative than Democrats have become more
liberal. The widely perceived failure of the Kennedy/Johnson reforms
brought the end of automatic belief in the efficacy of government and
encouraged a new confidence in the superior effectiveness of the private
over the public sector. These changes, and the riots, violence, and assassinations of the period, saw the end of a certain civility in American
politics. They certainly fractured the unity Kennedy had celebrated in
1961 and Johnson in his turn had labored in vain to maintain. For better
and for worse, American political civilization in the twenty-first century
was engendered in the seventh decade of the twentieth.

Max Weber, in his famous essay on the different kinds of political authority, invented the (much-abused) concept of "charismatic"
authority. He did not mean by that word—as generations of political
journalists have assumed he meant—merely that certain political leaders, most notably John Fitzgerald Kennedy, possessed a magical quality
of charm or glamour that enabled them to attract followers and support
from the wider public. Weber's use of the word, as we shall see, was more
specific.[59]

My plan is first to sketch the personal and political style of the two
leaders in an effort to determine their motivations and priorities and to
look into the relationship between the two tribes who followed those
two very different leaders, JFK and LBJ. In the second part of the book,
I shall look at their respective achievements in domestic and foreign
affairs. All this will lay the groundwork for an attempt to answer two

counterfactual questions that still insist on answers, half a century after Kennedy became president and Johnson his uneasy and resentful vice president.

The first question, to repeat, is whether Jack Kennedy, if he had lived, would have escalated the war in Vietnam as Lyndon Johnson did in the spring of 1965. The second is whether, had he lived, Kennedy would have succeeded in persuading the Congress to pass the extraordinary program of legislative reform, including monuments of progress in civil rights, health care reform, education policy, and immigration law, that remain Johnson's monument, however tarnished or diminished by the disaster of Vietnam.

Neither question is easily answered. I may as well admit at the outset of this inquiry that my initial preconception was that the answers are respectively "Yes"—Kennedy would have escalated, and, whatever doubts he might have felt about doing so, he would have responded to the collapse of the American position in Vietnam much as Johnson did—and "No": Kennedy would not have passed two great civil rights statutes, Medicare, Medicaid, educational reforms, and the rest. But the questions are finely balanced, and there is much to be learned about American history and the nature of American political society in the attempt to answer them. But first we must try to sketch the elusive personalities of our twin subjects.

Part One
The Actors

O • N • E

Life Is Unfair

There is always inequity in life. Some men are killed in a war, and some men

are wounded, and some men never leave the country. . . . Life is unfair. . . .

Some people are sick, and others are well.

—*John F. Kennedy, press conference, March 21, 1962*

I met President Kennedy personally on only two occasions. One was at Easter 1963, when I accompanied the White House press corps to Palm Beach and we were invited to take a trip along the coast in the president's boat, *Honey Fitz*. The second time was more curious.

I was leaning in a somewhat loutish manner on a door in the West Wing of the White House, the door to what was then called the Fish Room linking that room to the entrance lobby, when the door opened suddenly and I fell heavily on a small man who was coming out. The small man was the new king of Morocco, Hassan II, who had been in to see the president in the Oval Office. If this incident had occurred in Rabat, no doubt I would have endured a terrible fate at the hands of General Oufkir, the king's chief torturer, and his experts. As it was, President Kennedy, who seemed not particularly fond of His Moroccan Majesty, was amused by his discomfiture. He invited me to accompany him and King Hassan to Blair House, the White House's official guesthouse, where the monarch was staying.[1]

So I walked slowly along the street, the Secret Service discreetly fanned out behind us, with the amused president and the ruffled king.

I desperately sought for some witty jest or brilliant aperçu that would bring me to the president's attention, but none came. We marched in a constrained silence a block or so before I could shrink into the lunchtime crowds, conscious of a professional opportunity wasted.

Other than that, I saw Kennedy one-on-one only at a White House children's party to which my little sons Pierre and Francis were invited, though I did get to know his brother Robert rather better. I also put a good deal of effort into getting to know as many of his lieutenants, spear-carriers, and gurus as I could, and to this day I am astonished, not to mention grateful, by how patient most of those busy and powerful men were with this—no doubt both cocky and naïve—young foreign journalist.

Where I really did acquire some sense of Jack Kennedy's personality and his political magnetism was at his press conferences. Over the twenty-one months from March 1962 to October 1963 I attended almost every one of these relatively frequent press occasions: they happened almost once a week. These were full-dress events, usually held not at the White House (the basement facility there was not opened until Nixon's time)[2] but in a large auditorium at the State Department. They were more than an important tool of Kennedy's presidential management; they were a revealing illustration of change in the news media and the nation. In Franklin Roosevelt's time, the reporters crowded round the president's desk in the White House's Oval Office, where the president, an amber cigarette holder jutting jauntily from his mouth, joshed and scolded the reporters like a football coach with his favorite players. Famously, for example, FDR arranged, as a pointed insider joke, for another journalist to present John O'Donnell,[3] the sometimes obstreperous correspondent of the *New York Daily News,* with an Iron Cross, the German medal of valor, to rebuke him for what FDR saw as excessively pro-German attitudes.

Kennedy's press conferences were less intimate and more theatrical than that. The president bounded onto the stage from the wings, in spite of what we later learned were his numerous physical ailments, usually in a smart navy blue suit, exuding an air of patrician style and glamour. He was carefully coached for these meetings with the fourth estate of the Republic and of the world. He was fed likely questions in advance by his jovial press secretary, Pierre Salinger, a half-French investigative reporter from San Francisco, who would also have taken the precaution of supplying reliable members of the press corps with the right questions to ask.

These were relatively hierarchical occasions, and their pattern reflected the oligopolistic character of the national news system that was evolving through the back door, as it were, as the 1950s moved into the 1960s. Few even of the big metropolitan dailies could afford either a network of foreign correspondents or a significant staff of experts on politics or business. So they bought in from national sources. They bought foreign news from news agencies, the Associated Press and UPI. They bought editorial comment from syndicated columnists, and they purchased cartoons—both of the political and the strip variety—from national suppliers.

At the same time, many readers of these diminished regional and local papers had begun to supplement their news diet by buying one of the national news magazines. By far the biggest circulation belonged to *Time,* which had a Republican orientation, albeit of a relatively internationalist flavor. *Newsweek,* more liberal, especially after it was acquired by the Washington Post Company in 1961, offered a cold war liberal alternative. Only *US News & World Report,* owned and edited by David Lawrence until he sold his shares to his employees, reflected the unapologetically conservative views of its boss.

The same "nationalization" of news media, the same concentration of the news industry in a handful of centers, primarily New York, was even clearer in television news. Before the emergence of CNN in Atlanta and Fox News in Los Angeles, the viewers' choice was essentially limited to the three national networks, whose head offices and main studio complexes were all within a few blocks of one another on Sixth Avenue in New York. Executive management and journalistic employees alike, though recruited from all over the nation, reflected New York style, values, and preoccupations.

John F. Kennedy ran for president and occupied the White House at a time when television news and its coverage of national and international affairs were changing dramatically. Between 1959 and 1961, CBS and NBC especially were sharply increasing the size and quality of their news divisions. They were poaching well-known reporters from newspapers. The process came to a head shortly before the end of the Kennedy administration. On September 2, 1963, CBS doubled the length of its flagship nightly news program from fifteen minutes to half an hour. Within a couple of weeks, NBC followed suit. (ABC, absorbed in exploring the commercial possibilities of televised sport, was slower to respond.) By doubling the length of the nightly national news, the networks took fifteen minutes of valuable prime time advertising from their own affiliate—that is, local—stations. Over the whole of Kennedy's political career, television news had been growing more influential, and he was to some extent both the cause and the beneficiary of that development.

More than most politicians, Jack Kennedy had grown up with the development of this new national, and corporate, news industry. His father had been an authentic Hollywood mogul. Jack Kennedy himself had covered the creation of the United Nations in San Francisco in 1945 as a reporter for the *Chicago Herald-American*. It was widely believed that Kennedy was the first national politician to have mastered the cool style so effective on television, and that this attribute had been decisive in his winning the presidential election in 1960. So when Jack Kennedy met the paladins of the new news media, he met them not as an old pol, nervous of reporters who might be derisive of his appearance or speech, but as one who was at ease with them, friends with some of them, and totally at home with the arts necessary to impress them all.

So a Kennedy press conference was a kind of celebration of the new news media and the new politics they were creating. Members of the leading news organizations—the TV networks, the AP, UPI, and a handful of foreign wire services such as Reuters, Agence France Presse, and TASS, the three news magazines, the *New York Times,* the *Washington Post,* and a scattering of columnists—sat in the front row. Most of the questions would come from those ranks. The rest of us, foreigners and provincials alike, would sit behind, though one or two licensed members of the awkward squad, such as the Texas freelancer Sarah McClendon or the occasional conservative columnist, would occasionally be recognized and more or less subtly mocked. I learned a great deal from attending those press conference, both about what my colleagues were working on and about the style and personality of the president, the jeune premier in this political soap opera.

I cherished at the time his subsequently famous remark, made at a dinner of American Nobel laureates at the White House, that no such collection of human genius had been assembled there since Thomas Jefferson last breakfasted there alone. Even at a less elevated level, Kennedy often managed to bat out a one-liner or witticism that was appreciated.

To be accredited as a White House correspondent, you had in those days, no doubt as a consequence of some ancient power struggle between executive and legislative branches of government, to seek out an office high on the Senate side of the Capitol building. By March 21, 1962, in the whirl of finding accommodation for myself, a wife, and two little sons (one of whom went down with a dangerously high fever), settling into an office, and introducing myself to sources and colleagues, I was not yet accredited. So I missed John Kennedy's very revealing answer to a question on that day, the answer I have placed as an epigraph at the head of this chapter. "There is always inequity in life," he said. "Some men are killed in a war, and some men are wounded, and some men never leave the country. . . . Life is unfair. . . . Some people are sick, and others are well."

When President Kennedy said that, he was probably thinking of physical tribulations. No doubt uppermost in his mind were those of his own family: his brother Joe's fiery death, his sister Kick's death in a plane crash, her husband's shooting by a German sniper, his sister Rosemary's mental condition and her lobotomy, and his own many wretched and painful medical problems.

For others, though, the unfairness could be seen to be on the other foot: it was unfair that the Kennedys were so rich, so privileged, so full of vitality and charm, young people who—no doubt thanks to their father's energy and shrewdness, not to mention a touch of ruthlessness on his part—were born with a whole canteen of silver spoons in their mouths.

I arrived in Washington too late, not only for that particular press conference but more important for the Kennedy presidential campaign of 1960. This event was widely seen as the beginning of a new era. It was also the critical career opportunity for a whole generation of talented political journalists. To have covered the successful campaigns of a new president is always a good career break. It was and perhaps still is quite usual at the *New York Times* or the *Washington Post,* for example, for the man, even occasionally the woman, who has covered the winning candidate to be sent to cover the White House. This was more than usually true of 1960. The golden aura in which the Kennedy administration was dipped owed much to the gilding of men like Theodore "Teddy" White, Charles Bartlett, Joseph Kraft, the Alsop brothers, Joe and Stewart, Ben Bradlee, and others, who found to their delight and professional satisfaction that a man of their generation, whom they considered a friend, now wore the purple.[4]

Kennedy was fortunate in the timing of his political career. He entered politics at a time when class resentment and suspicion of the rich was lower than either before or later. Millions of Americans did not envy the Kennedys, with their trust funds and their palaces in the havens of the rich: they fantasized about emulating them.

Perversely, perhaps, but naturally enough, at the age of twenty-eight, I was bored by what seemed to me the sycophantic tone of much coverage of the Kennedy administration. I was also irritated by the constant emphasis on the youth of a bunch of men who were at least a dozen years older than me.

Fifty years later, I look for reasons other than Jack's superlative talent and charm to explain the influences that shaped his politics. They included—I intuited then and I am now convinced—his age; the experience and aspirations of his generation; his wartime experience; his slightly awkward stance as the son of a very rich and famously ruthless capitalist offering himself as the champion of the underprivileged; his uncharacteristically sentimental interpretation of what it was to be Irish in Boston; and his thorough adoption of the conviction of the American establishment that it was the duty and destiny of America to defeat Communism and sponsor a new world order, one that would abolish colonialism, encourage capitalism, and sanctify American hegemony.

At first, when Jack Kennedy and his wife, Jacqueline, were in the White House, and even after his assassination, the prevailing attitude was admiration, even obeisance before the energy and the talent of the family. Journalists vied with one another to chronicle the glamour of the

Kennedy lifestyle, the homes on Cape Cod, at Palm Beach, and in the Virginia hunt country, the almost manic pursuit of victory at touch football, yacht racing, and everything else. They reveled in the compelling narrative of how two families of despised immigrants from East Boston became the first Irish Brahmins. After his death writers like Arthur M. Schlesinger Jr. and Theodore Sorensen, both of whom worked for JFK in the White House, and Theodore H. White, chronicler of the 1960s, contributed to the image of John Kennedy as a youthful philosopher-king or, as White put it, "restless, civilized, gay and witty, suffused in the talk of scholars, knowing his duty to translate their thinking into action."[5] Personal friends like Ben Bradlee, Red Fay, Kenny O'Donnell, and Dave Powers kept the flame alight with affectionate anecdote.

Then came an obsessive preoccupation with the assassination. Forests of books, proposing ever more unlikely conspiratorial theories, poured from the presses.

Later, after the disillusion with the Vietnam War, the Republican conservative victory in 1968, and the 1969 Chappaquiddick incident, a new tone took over. Edward Kennedy summoned his brother's paladins, including the deputy dean of Yale Law School, Burke Marshall, to help him talk his way out of responsibility for the death of a young woman drowned in his car in equivocal circumstances. For the first time, there was a broad hint of a sordid side to the Kennedy glamour.

After Joan and Clay Blair's 1976 book *The Search for JFK,* the legend was examined in a less uncritical vein. The Blairs stated bluntly, "Jack grew up in the shadow of a domineering, unscrupulous, absentee father, a devoutly religious absentee mother, and a bullying sibling, Joe Junior." They noted that apart from his political associates "most of his close pals" came from the same eastern prep school and Ivy League milieu and were dominated by him, in part because of his money. As to his relationship with the opposite sex, he grew up with "a chary, if not cynical," view of love and marriage. They pointed out that he "was lucky not to have been cashiered from the Navy" over his affair with the suspected Nazi sympathizer Inga Arvad, apparently one of only a handful of serious relationships with women in his entire life.[6]

Perhaps most damaging of all, the Blairs remorselessly unpicked the way Jack Kennedy's life had been turned by his father's public relations campaign into a Hollywood tale of heroism. They showed in detail how his undeniably brave conduct in the dark waters of the Solomon Islands had been massaged, with the help of Joe Kennedy's contacts and money, into the legend of PT 109. The impression was fostered, they said, that Jack was a dedicated and brilliant scholar, when at prep school he was "sloppy, lazy and uninterested" and at Harvard his much-publicized thesis was in fact "mediocre." So far from being a robust young athlete, his health was, almost from birth, "disastrously poor."[7]

The omissions and distortions in the record, the Blairs claimed, constituted "overwhelming evidence that shrewd manipulation of the media can make a man president of the United States." They concluded bleakly that "the American people seem all too glad to be given comic strip heroes to believe in."[8]

This negative school in biography reached its nadir with the British writer Nigel Hamilton's *JFK: Life and Death of an American President* (1988) and Seymour Hersh's *The Dark Side of Camelot* (1997).[9] Hamilton was particularly severe about the career and character of "the Founding Father" of Richard J. Whalen's more balanced biography.[10] "Born of ill-suited, unhappy parents locked in an emotionally blocked, socially quarantined, and maniacally competitive family, there was no way out" for Jack. Kennedy père was bluntly described by Hamilton as "the notorious stock-market swindler Joseph P. Kennedy" who had made his fortune "by a mixture of ruthlessness, fraudulence, and business acumen"; Hamilton did not hesitate to call Kennedy senior an anti-Semite and a coward. "Only the obsequious, the useful, and undemonstrative," Hamilton wrote, would be permitted in the family compound, "a motley gallery of second-raters, court-jesters, and hangers-on, men who would amuse or comfort, even pimp for the young."[11]

By the time Hamilton was doing his energetic research, much was known about Kennedy's health that punctured the image of the virile young prince whose youthful vitality had been routinely contrasted with the flaccid middle age of Richard Nixon. Hamilton boldly described as "venereal disease" the nonspecific urethritis or prostatitis that Kennedy seemed unable to get rid of.[12] He showed how from early childhood, so far from being an athlete, he had been a sickly child, plagued with digestive and other ailments. Later writers were unsparing in their detailed accounts of JFK's medical history, though some had the grace to admit that the obverse of Kennedy's illnesses was the courage with which he contrived to live an energetic life in spite of them.

By 1993 Richard Reeves could describe in detail JFK's Addison's disease (disorder of the adrenal glands), the back pain that drove him to sleep on a bed board in the White House and more than once involved surgery that almost killed him and that made him rely on the opium-based painkillers he was given by the shady Dr. Max Jacobson.[13] Ten years later Robert Dallek focused not just on the number and variety of the president's ailments but on the fact that his health problems did not prevent him being elected. "As we now know," Dallek wrote, "Kennedy feared that his Addison's disease, colitis, back troubles and prostatitis would be used against him in the 1960 campaign. . . . He worried that disclosure of his repeated hospitalizations in the 1950s and his reliance on steroids to combat Addison's disease, and on antispasmodics, painkillers, testosterone, antibiotics and sleeping pills to help him cope with collateral problems might block him from becoming president."[14] Indeed, the near panic caused in the Kennedy camp when, on the eve of his coronation as the Democratic presidential candidate at Los Angeles in 1960, Johnson supporters raised the question of his medical history suggests just how sensitive an issue this was.

Under the hammer blows of these less friendly biographers, Kennedy's reputation has been significantly damaged. In a 1975 Gallup poll 52 percent of respondents put Kennedy first among all presidents, ahead of both Abraham Lincoln and Franklin Roosevelt, and although his relative position subsequently fluctuated, he remained near the top in the public's estimation, though not in that of expert opinion. In 1988, for example, a group of seventy-five historians and journalists described Kennedy as "the most overrated public figure in American history," and a similar group in 2000 placed him a lowly eighteenth among presidents.[15]

So much has been written about the personal aspects of the Kennedy myth, about Camelot, and about the rather seamier underside of the Kennedy White House that a number of broader historical aspects of the brief Kennedy presidency and its long afterglow may be worth picking out.

Kennedy was the first president not just of the age of national media but of the age of national corporate business and national popular culture, whose centers were in Manhattan, Chicago, and Los Angeles, precisely the locations of Father Kennedy's principal operations. Kennedy's family business was centered in an office, run by his brother-in-law Steve Smith after Joe Kennedy's retirement, in the Pan Am building, looking up Park Avenue from its perch above Grand Central Terminal.[16] That was where the checks were written for private luxury and political expenditures, though all members of the Kennedy family were famous for their reluctance to use their own money in political campaigns. Another brother-in-law, Sargent Shriver, presided over the Merchandise Mart across the Chicago River from the Loop, at the time said to be the largest commercial building in America. Joe Kennedy had retired from movie production, but a third brother-in-law, Peter Lawford, was a charter member of the group of hard-living actors who called themselves the Rat Pack, led by Frank Sinatra himself. Through this connection, Kennedy had access not only to the favors of pretty ladies but to all the arcana of Hollywood. He grew up, in short, at an apex of the new national structure of power and cultural influence.

He was also the beneficiary of a short-lived consequence of the postwar prosperity: the apparent, albeit temporary, disappearance of social and economic class as an acknowledged concern of national politics. To be sure, since the days of the young Republic, from George Washington to the two Roosevelts, rich men had always entered politics and often thrived. But the issue of economic equality was always present. Briefly, between 1945 and the 1970s, that issue was less contentious because it was generally believed, both on the right and on the left—or at least by Democratic politicians who relied on the support of organized labor as well as by Republican politicians who represented the interests of corporate business—that economic inequality would gradually disappear, that out of the horn of plenty, economic rivalries could be bought off. "On the reefs of roast beef and apple pie," the German sociologist Werner Sombart memorably wrote, "socialistic utopias of every sort are sent to their doom."[17]

One by-product, or at least concomitant of this fading of class conflict from national politics was the decline of party. Jack Kennedy, promoted by his father and with his father's wealth in the background, was perhaps the first president who was not so much chosen by one of the two national parties as the beneficiary of a successful raid on the party's leadership.

The Kennedys fulfilled in many particulars Max Weber's portrait of the charismatic leader. This, Weber was at pains to explain, could be an inspired political or religious leader, or the leader of a band of robbers. In any case, his leader must possess charisma, or personal grace and charm. But this quality is morally neutral: he, or perhaps she, can be anyone from Ned Kelly or Spartacus to Mahomet or Jesus Christ. The charismatic leader does not, however, attract his followers, whom Weber called the "charismatic horde," by mere personal qualities. He must offer reward to his followers, in this world or the next.[18]

Jack Kennedy, to be sure, was elected to Congress as the official candidate of the Democratic Party in a Boston district, and he duly proceeded to become the Democratic candidate for the U.S. Senate from Massachusetts. But he became the Democratic presidential nominee in 1960, not—except in a formal sense—by a decision of the Democratic national nominating convention. That decision was to all intents and purposes taken before the convention met in Los Angeles, essentially because of Kennedy's triumphant procession through the primaries.

Kennedy had already come to the attention of news media, politicians, and the public by becoming a candidate for vice president in 1956.[19] That made him *papabile,* "popable," or "available," as the old political jargon had it. But essentially Kennedy was not chosen by the party. He captured the nomination with charm, money, and organization and by presenting policies with wide appeal. Like some bold band of robbers, galloping behind their charismatic chief across arid plains into some lush oasis, the Kennedys saw the prize, dared, planned, worked for it, and won.

They were helped in this victory by a certain historical conjuncture. Vast seismic movements were changing the United States in ways that helped Kennedy to seize his opportunity. The relative decline in the role played by religion in American politics made it possible for a Catholic to be elected, as had not been possible for Al Smith in 1928. There was, too, by the second Eisenhower term, a pent-up desire for change. It was not by accident that the late 1950s saw the publication of a small library of books calling for a vigorous, more active presidency.[20]

This generational wish for change was reinforced in the 1950s by the passing of the torch, as Kennedy himself put it, to a new generation "tempered by" war, specifically from the generation who had commanded in World War II, appropriately led and symbolized by General Eisenhower, to the more or less junior officers of his victorious army and navy. Members of Kennedy's cabinet and subcabinet were almost exclusively recruited from men with this experience. His secretary of state was Major, later Colonel, Dean Rusk from the China/Burma/India theater, born in 1909. His treasury secretary was Lieutenant Commander Douglas Dillon, USN, born in the same year as Rusk, one the son of a Georgia minister, the other the son of the founder of an investment bank. At the head of the Pentagon he placed Lieutenant Colonel Robert S. McNamara of the U.S. Army Air Force, born in 1916, who had introduced to the army the statistical techniques he had taught at Harvard before he became an executive at Ford.

The shattered face of his secretary of agriculture, Orville Freeman, former governor of Minnesota, was the badge of Freeman's combat service as a Marine in Pacific combat. His national security adviser, McGeorge Bundy, a Harvard dean, born in 1919, had served in army intelligence and was scheduled to land in the Japanese home islands if the war had not ended,[21] while his older brother Bill (born 1917) was one of the first Americans sent to learn cryptography at Britain's Bletchley Park,[22] where early steps toward inventing the computer were made by Alan Turing and his colleagues. President Kennedy's chief domestic adviser, Kenneth O'Donnell, born as late as 1924, served as a bomber pilot in the wartime Army Air Force before captaining the Harvard football team and working as a salesman and public relations adviser. At least two close aides had been prisoners of war: Nick Katzenbach, a bomber pilot shot down over Germany, and Fred Dutton, captured during the battle of the Ardennes Bulge. The war experience of many of these able but very different men was included at least some part in designing, critiquing, or administering victory. Chicago lawyer George Ball and Harvard economics professor John Kenneth Galbraith, for example, were both involved in the postwar strategic bombing survey. The sole officer who could be called "brass" and who was really close to the Kennedys —Bob named one of his sons after him—was Maxwell Taylor, born in 1901, former commander of the 101st Airborne and superintendent of

West Point; but Max Taylor, hero of a daring escapade behind enemy lines in Italy, could be seen as anti-brass, too, especially after his January 1960 book, *The Uncertain Trumpet*.[23] In it he severely criticized the previous generation of senior officers and proposed a doctrine of flexible response that appealed to Kennedy's radical streak.

The junior and not-so-junior officers Kennedy chose as his companions had risked much and achieved much. Their experience of life may have begun with the Depression, but from the last two years of the war on they shared the experience of victory and almost unbelievable American success in everything they touched. They had emerged from the war into a world where, if America's Soviet ally was going to be an enemy, America's rivals and competitors had all been ruined. American money, American dentistry, American entertainment, and the American Dream seemed incomparable. They were confident in their own abilities and at the same time determined that the country, and the world, must change.

It was for that they had fought. Lieutenant John F. Kennedy was an authentic war hero, even if his heroism had been skillfully publicized by his father and John Hersey's article.[24] Such a man was a natural leader of the brightest and the bravest of the wartime generation.

If historians and political journalists understood and in some cases resented the manipulations that had gone into creating the Kennedy legend, a far larger audience reveled in the compelling narrative of how two families of despised immigrants from East Boston surpassed the wealth and status of proper Anglo Boston. Several aspects of this legend distorted the truth. For one thing, though the Kennedy family did indeed start out as humble immigrants from Ireland, their penniless days were rather farther in the past than the legend suggested. As early as the generation of Kennedy's grandparents, they were already prosperous and marked out as political leaders. P. J. Kennedy, the president's paternal grandfather, left school at fourteen, but by the time he was thirty he owned three saloons in Boston, sources of political influence as well as revenue, and before long he owned substantial stock in a bank, the Columbia Trust Company. John F. Fitzgerald, "Honey Fitz," Jack Kennedy's maternal grandfather, to whom he was specially close, went to the prestigious Boston Latin School and (briefly) to Harvard. By his midtwenties he owned an insurance company. Later he also owned a newspaper and was a popular mayor of Boston. Immigrant struggles were three generations old when Jack Kennedy was growing up. Not for one moment did Jack Kennedy think of himself as an outsider in that way, but when it suited him he was not above claiming his kinship with the Boston Irish.

In Massachusetts and later all across the United States, the Kennedys were able to pull off an impressive political trick: to present themselves as the friend of the working man while at the same time impressing everyone with their wealth and their access to worlds of privilege to which most citizens could never aspire. In retrospect, we can see that they were the beneficiaries of a relatively brief moment when many Americans persuaded themselves that there was no such thing as social class in America. In the late nineteenth century, American literature and journalism were full of the contrast between barefoot poverty and silk-stocking wealth. In the Depression, no one hesitated to speak or write about the "working class." After the age of Kennedy and Johnson, class discourse would return. But for a brief interval, starting with the high wages of war industry and the Detroit contracts of the early 1950s, liberal intellectuals went to rather extraordinary lengths to persuade Americans that there was no such thing as class consciousness in America.

"Something has happened in the United States in recent years that has never happened before anywhere," wrote the later neoconservative pundit Ben J. Wattenberg. "The massive majority of the population of a nation is now in the middle class. . . . The head of the household may not be a doctor, lawyer, accountant or professor, but rather a lathe operator, steelworker, routeman or salesman."[25] Few lawyers or surgeons, even at the time, would have seen themselves as the social equals of lathe operators or foundrymen. Yet it became widely believed that American workers in general enjoyed the standard of living once enjoyed only by doctors, lawyers, and business executives.

This was always pure fantasy. Some believed it because they took pride in this (fictional) national achievement. Those who endlessly repeated it relied on blatant manipulation of U.S. Census reports and other statistics. For example, and it is only one example of a whole genre of political happy talk, in the 1970 census almost 10 million workers were

redefined, moved from the "blue-collar" category to "service workers."
They included waiters, porters, and gas-station attendants. Second, more
than 12 million working women (secretaries, typists, and sales workers,
many of them presumably married to blue-collar workers) were auto-
matically counted as white-collar workers. By such disreputable shifts
was the American public persuaded that social class divisions had been
abolished.[26]

The same sociopolitical legerdemain made it possible for the Kennedys in particular, with their trust funds, their expensive private edu-
cations, and their privileged lifestyle, to present themselves as just plain
folks, perhaps temporarily ahead of most Americans but on a path that
all, or most, would be able to follow. Jack Kennedy and the great majority of his political team belonged to what Tom Brokaw called the Greatest Generation:[27] they grew up in the Depression and fought in World
War II. Their experience was of an America effortlessly supreme, where
social equality did seem attainable.

There was a specifically Irish dimension to this trick. The Kennedys succeeded in portraying themselves as coming from the Boston
Irish working class, although over three generations they had moved out
of Charlestown, by way of upper-middle-class Brookline, to the multiple
residences of the polo-playing class. They continued to proclaim themselves loyal heirs of a Boston Irish Catholic political tradition that harbored ancestral hatred of British rule over Ireland while at the same time
drawing the maximum profit from Joe Kennedy's time as ambassador
to the Court of St. James and of his children's acceptance by the British
aristocracy.

Years after Jack's death I encountered an example of the latter
point. In 1989 I was invited to represent Great Britain at a meeting at
Harvard, set up ostensibly to study media coverage of Northern Ireland
but in reality to denounce British policy there, organized by Bob Kennedy's son, Congressman Joseph Kennedy. When I arrived, I mentioned
politely to the congressman that I had known his father. This was true;
indeed, I thought of Bob Kennedy as a friend. It did not, however, fit
the plan for the evening. Congressman Kennedy muttered something
grumpy and turned me over to the oratorical mercies of some Sinn Fein
supporters and a vociferous claque from South Boston.[28]

This inconsistency is summed up by the word *Lismore*. At the heart of Irish Boston's resentment of Britain was unforgiving hatred of the Ascendancy. That was the system of feudal landholding that allotted most of the richest land in Ireland to British, Protestant landlords, their interests protected by discriminatory legislation, by British resident magistrates, and ultimately by British redcoats. It condemned most of the Catholic—or, as they were called, the "mere"—Irish to landless labor or at best to renting the most marginal land. At the apex of this system lived the greatest of all the Ascendancy landlords, the Cavendish family, Dukes of Devonshire, owners not only of half a dozen palatial homes and estates in England but of the fairy-tale estate of Lismore, up the Blackwater River in the southeast of Ireland. Lismore was once owned by Sir Walter Raleigh. At its heart, by the 1950s, was a gigantic Victorian imitation of a medieval castle with hundreds of rooms, surrounded by tens of thousands of acres of tenanted farms, by gardens and vineyards, and by the finest salmon fishing in Ireland. Lismore was the very symbol of English colonial oppression. I do not know what the Cavendish employment policy was at Lismore, but on most such estates, all the responsible and better-paid jobs (stewards, butlers, farm and stable managers, and the like) were reserved for Protestants;[29] very likely the same was true at Lismore.

The Kennedys and their journalistic admirers loved to repeat the tale of their ancestors' desperate migration from New Ross. There was less talk of the fact that Jack Kennedy's sister Kathleen, known as Kick, married Billy Cavendish, Marquis of Hartington, who would have inherited this feudal paradise if he had not been hit by a German sniper's bullet late in World War II. But for that lethal fluke, the president of the United States, proud of his family's immigrant rise from rags to riches, would have had a sister ensconced as the chatelaine of the most glittering home of the family's hereditary enemy, the Protestant Ascendancy.

Two other influences contributed more than has often been noticed to the complex ragout of Jack Kennedy's political attitudes: Harvard and the Court of St. James. Jack's grandfather, as noted, briefly attended Harvard Medical School in 1884–85. His father was a Harvard baseball star. Jack himself and his three brothers all attended Harvard, with varying degrees of academic success. After his death, the hard core of his friends and supporters gathered to assuage their sorrow and plan their political survival at what came to be called "the Harvard lunch."[30] Harvard came to be seen, at least by its many critics, as the core of a liberal establishment, committed to equal opportunities for minorities of every hue, including the Irish. It had not always been so. Harvard did not admit women until 1999, when it fully integrated with Radcliffe College. (They had long been allowed at Radcliffe, an all-women's college on the Harvard campus.) Harvard's illustrious president from 1909 to 1933, Abbott Lawrence Lowell, was a vice president of the Immigration Restriction League. He deliberately reduced the number of Jewish students from 22 percent to under 10 percent and proposed a fixed *numerus clausus* of 15 percent. He also joined the movement to block the appointment of Louis D. Brandeis, the first Jew to sit on the Supreme Court. Although in many respects a reforming president, Lowell also tried to limit the number of Irish students. "What we need," was his rationale, "is not to dominate the Irish but to absorb them."[31]

The memoirs of "Tip" O'Neill, Speaker of the House of Representatives, who grew up in North Cambridge, a mile or two from Harvard Yard, make plain how Harvard was resented by its Irish neighbors. "It was at Harvard University in 1927," he begins his memoirs, "that I first decided to go into politics." No, he explained, he wasn't a Harvard man, but at the age of fourteen he got a summer job cutting the grass in Harvard Yard. One summer's day he saw "hundreds of young men standing around in their white linen suits . . . drinking champagne, which was illegal in 1927 because of Prohibition." "Who the hell do these people think they are," was his reaction, "that the law means nothing to them."[32] It was not only wealthy Brahmins who had a drink during Prohibition: there were even, wicked tongues have said, some Irish people who did too. But in Tip O'Neill's adolescence, class resentment was by no means dead.

When young Jack Kennedy arrived at Harvard, the rock-ribbed conservatives of an earlier generation were mostly gone. The rising intellectual stars were men like Arthur M. Schlesinger Jr., John Kenneth Galbraith, Don K. Price, and Samuel Beer. These men were not only more or less liberals; unlike Harvard luminaries of an earlier generation, strong in a revolutionary and republican tradition, they were more or less Anglophiles.[33] Indeed, JFK was at Harvard in an interval of Anglophilia between the traditional suspicion of the Yankee elite and a more recent indifference.

The softening of Harvard toward Britain was only a special case of a general development. By the New Deal 1930s, the American elite was in close and relatively sympathetic touch with its British equivalent. Traditional suspicion of Britain and anti-imperial convictions had been replaced in the American upper class by an attitude to Britain that was a mixture of affectionate contempt, irritation, and admiration. In the nineteenth century, Americans generally, including the Brahmin elite of Boston, later seen by many Americans and not least by their Irish fellow citizens as virtually indistinguishable from Englishmen, were suspicious of Britain, which they disapproved of as an imperial monarchy and feared as a potentially formidable commercial and even naval competitor. Even such an archetypal New England patrician as Henry Adams spent his years in London torn between resentment of what he saw as patronizing from the British aristocracy and a desire to be admitted to their society.[34]

Even before 1914, more and more Americans traveled in Europe, including the British Isles, and this traditional suspicion softened. World War I had an immense influence. Britain, France, and America found themselves allies against Germany, Austro-Hungary, and Turkey. Woodrow Wilson himself had close friends in Britain,[35] and his friend Colonel Edward House was well plugged in at the highest level of British political society.[36]

House and Walter Lippmann set up a research effort known as the Inquiry, which recruited many of the brightest young men (and a few women), mainly from Ivy League universities, to research the issues likely to arise in postwar diplomacy.[37] Many members of the Inquiry traveled with Wilson to Paris for the peace talks. After the peace, some even tried to set up a joint Anglo-American foreign policy research institution: it survived as two separate but friendly entities, the Council on Foreign Relations in New York and the Royal Institute of International Affairs ("Chatham House") in London. At the same time, friendly contacts in banking, business, and the law, not to mention competitive (and relatively expensive) sports like golf, tennis, and ocean yachting, brought the British and American elites together. The Times of London was bought

by one Astor, the *Observer* later by another, and a third Astor, the former
Nancy Witcher Langhorne of Virginia, was in 1919 the first woman to take
her seat in the House of Commons of the British Parliament.

One enduring survival of the interwar period was the loose group
of influential bankers and international lawyers who later came to be
called the American Establishment.[38] Many of them, like John J. McCloy
and Robert Lovett, were internationalist Republicans: others, like Dean
Acheson and Averell Harriman, were Democrats. When JFK became
president, it was from this group that he recruited many of the key
members of his administration. In fact, JFK offered Robert Lovett the
choice of the three top jobs in his cabinet—State, Defense, or Treasury—
but Lovett, not in good health, turned him down.[39] Establishment figures who did serve in key jobs in his administration included Dillon
at the Treasury, Dean Rusk, and McGeorge Bundy, national security
adviser to both Kennedy and Johnson, whose brother was married to
Acheson's daughter. All were Anglophiles, but one of the key ideas of
this American foreign policy establishment was that it was the proud
but sometimes painful destiny of the United States to supersede Britain
as the world's leading power. Before Pearl Harbor, these men were an
embattled minority. After World War II, theirs was the dominant view
of the world in American governing circles.

Jack Kennedy was the loyal son of his father, who, as an Irish An-
glophobe and an isolationist, by no means shared these instincts. But
the short years when Joe Kennedy was ambassador to the Court of
St. James had a disproportionate influence on Jack and indeed on his
whole family. While the ambassador had close contacts with British
conservatives, who feared Soviet Russia more than Hitler's Germany,
and his wife, Rose, was touchy at the smallest imagined social slight,
their children reveled in London society, which welcomed these open
and friendly young charmers. For Jack, though, London was not only
a series of exciting parties. It was also a base from which to explore a
Europe on the brink of catastrophe.

Jack Kennedy took something else from those prewar London
years. He became a Whig. It may seem a strange word to apply to an
American, and a Roman Catholic American of Irish descent at that.
Many of his close London friends, too, like the future Conservative

member of Parliament Hugh Fraser, were Tories. Nevertheless, one key to understanding John Fitzgerald Kennedy is to think of him as the twentieth-century American equivalent of a Whig: in the British, not the American, sense of the term.[40]

This is not to exaggerate the British influences on his political style. It is true that he spent a formative time as a young man in that last flowering of the old political London that rotated around the great Whig political families, their country houses, their clubs, and the London "season" of dinners and balls and sporting events, a world in which the young Jack Kennedy and his brothers and sisters were a triumphant success. It is true, too, that he often said that his second-favorite book was Lord David Cecil's life of the nineteenth-century British prime minister Lord Melbourne.[41] It was true, too, as I have noted, that the Kennedy siblings were linked by marriage into the very greatest of all the great Whig houses, the Cavendishes, Dukes of Devonshire.

Jack Kennedy was not, however, the heir of the English Whigs because of his brief London dancing "season" as a young man or his sister's marriage. Rather, his Whiggism derived from the fact he and those like him, the American elite of the generation that fought and triumphed in World War II, consciously saw themselves as the successors to the British empire. It was not Chatsworth and Lismore but Harvard that instilled the Whig ethos in the Kennedy brothers, and the essence of it was an attitude that acknowledged the social and political duties that went with privilege.

The name of Whig was first used in the civil wars of the three British nations (England, Scotland, and Ireland)[42] in the seventeenth century, wars that saw a challenge to the monarchy, the victory of Parliament, and the beheading of King Charles I; the establishment of a short-lived republic under Cromwell; and the return of the king's son as Charles II. In 1688 Charles II's brother, James II, who wanted to establish a Catholic autocracy on the French model, was chased off his throne by the Whig lords, who set up a constitutional monarchy, limited by the rule of law and the authority of Parliament.[43]

The name is an abbreviation of *whiggamores*, meaning horse thieves. During the great Civil War in England, the king's opponents were known as Parliamentarians or "Roundheads." But when the time came to put James II off his throne, the anti-Catholic, antiroyalist party (led by, among others, the ancestor of the Dukes of Devonshire) came to be called Whigs.

Through most of the eighteenth century the Whigs were the dominant party in English politics. Some saw themselves as the "Venetian oligarchy" of great noblemen with vast estates, masters of a system of political bribery and corruption that enabled them to control the House of Commons as well as their own House of Lords. Others, however, the "Old Whigs," not landed grandees but intellectuals, like the great philosopher of liberty, John Locke, and the "Commonwealthmen," such as John Trenchard and Thomas Gordon, who cowrote the influential *Cato's Letters,* took a more austere path. They played an important part in developing the radical, republican ideas that infused the American Revolution.[44]

The essence of Whiggism, and what connects it with the political style of John F. Kennedy, was that a cultivated elite shared a passion for "liberty" with the common people. Whigs like Charles James Fox, the wealthy and well-connected rake who once lost a great fortune on the turn of a single card at Almack's gaming club but who also championed both the American and the French revolutions, were the spiritual ancestors of the limousine liberals of the twentieth century. John Kennedy, statesman, intellectual, and man of pleasure, was a true descendant of Fox and his friends.

A strange thing that happened, or rather did not quite happen, at Kennedy's inauguration illustrates how much closer this son of Catholic Boston was to British Whiggism than to conventional traditions of American democracy. In his account of the ceremony, Arthur Schlesinger relates that the venerable New England poet Robert Frost had been invited to read a poem, "The Gift Outright," he had composed for the occasion. Because of the glare from the snow, Frost was able to read only the first three lines. The lines he could not read included these:

> It makes the prophet in us all presage
> The glory of the next Augustan age
> . . . .
> A golden age of poetry of power
> Of which this noonday's the beginning hour.

Now any historian would be careful of reading too much into lines that were never actually spoken (only admiringly quoted by a more or less official biographer). But attractive as is the golden aura of Augustan ages, they have not been democratic. The first Augustus destroyed the Roman Republic and replaced it with his own personal rule. And the Augustan Age of Whig England, rich as were its literary and architectural monuments, was ruled by a corrupt Parliament and an oligarchy whose wealth derived largely from rack rents and slavery.[45]

The young JFK spent his time in London (when he was officially his father's assistant but also supposed to be studying at the London School of Economics) researching a Harvard undergraduate thesis, which was later turned into a book with the title *Why England Slept*.[46] The most interesting element in *Why England Slept* was perhaps the young author's discussion of the idea that democracies, in comparison with autocratic governments, are by their nature ill-equipped to deal with foreign policy. The book was not especially critical of his father's appeasement policy. But the inspiration for JFK's interest in foreign policy was not the ambassador but his boss, Franklin Roosevelt.

JFK's Oval Office, like FDR's, was decorated with sailing ship models. JFK shared, perhaps even imitated, Roosevelt's passion for sailing. FDR too was a Harvard man. He had triumphed over physical ailments, even if JFK's back pain and adrenal problem were hardly as debilitating as FDR's polio. Above all, FDR—for all his genuine dislike of British imperialism—was a Whig in the sense I have used it in this chapter. He believed in the mission and destiny of America. He believed in the ideal of service. He was a liberal, committed to the idea that it was the function of government to improve the life of ordinary people. But he was also an aristocrat, a stylist in life as well as with language, and absolutely at ease with the idea of his own superiority. John F. Kennedy, great-grandchild of Irish immigrants, was just as much a Whig as Franklin Delano Roosevelt, scion of Dutch patroons from the Hudson Valley and direct descendant of the Dutch Huguenot Philippe de Lannoy, later Anglicized to Delano.[47] Kennedy's vision of America, like Franklin Roosevelt's, was one glorified by the aristocratic virtues of courage, style, generosity, family, and national pride. Only slowly, even reluctantly, did he acknowledge that the greatest challenge of his time was not foreign but domestic, the demand of African Americans for decency and justice. Kennedy's instinct was to give priority to the cold war, to standing up to the Soviet Union and punishing Fidel Castro. Lyndon Johnson—to his eventual cost—shared Kennedy's sense of America's historic destiny. But he was shaped by very different historical influences.

There is an old story that at his first cabinet meeting, LBJ greeted his colleagues by saying that present around the table were three men from Harvard, two from Yale, and one from Princeton, but only one from the Southwest Texas State Teachers College at San Marcos, Texas. The implication was that he was not intimidated by the educational and social credentials of the colleagues he had inherited from JFK. The story is apocryphal nonsense. There is no evidence for it, and it is intrinsically implausible: at that first cabinet meeting, LBJ was intent on persuading Kennedy's men to stay on.

Still, as the Italians say, if it is not true, it is well invented. There is plenty of evidence that Lyndon Johnson, like Richard Nixon after him, did resent those whom he called "high falutin' Harvards." (Although he was not so hostile to Harvard that he denied himself the services of its talented alumni on his staff, and not only those he had inherited from Kennedy: his domestic policy staff under Joseph Califano from 1965 to 1969 consisted of five graduates of Harvard Law School and one dean from Princeton.)[48] He once said he felt that the holdovers on his staff from the Kennedy administration—he mentioned McGeorge Bundy—were "looking at him through a monocle."[49] One of his most accomplished private comic turns was his imitation of Adlai Stevenson, complete with his British pronunciation of the word *tomato* as one of its finer points.[50] George Reedy, a loyal but undeceived aide, wrote that "the fundamental Johnsonian view of the universe was that of the rural 'po' boy' born to poverty and determined to exact vengeance from the aristocrats he regarded as holding him in contempt." There are certainly anecdotes to support that view. LBJ loved to humiliate anyone he suspected of patronizing him. He even went to the length of issuing orders to the fastidious patrician Mac Bundy while defecating.[51]

Yet another of his aides, Horace "Buzz" Busby, who was as close to him as anyone and had the advantage of coming from Texas himself, insists that while LBJ "had awfully strong class feelings," Reedy's view misunderstood those feelings. "People didn't understand," Busby said, "he was from the upper class in Johnson City. It was aristocrat against aristocrat. . . . In the social structure of Johnson City they were so far above everybody else that his problem was just that. He was never poor. Not rich but not poor."[52] Certainly his mother, Rebekah, had as high an estimation of her own worth as of her son's deserts. LBJ told Texas journalist Ronnie Dugger that "my ancestors were teachers and lawyers and college presidents and governors when the Kennedys in this country were still tending bar."[53] His resentment of the "Harvards," in this interpretation, came more from his feeling that they did not recognize a fellow *hidalgo,* a "son of something" (which is what the Spanish word means). It is also, of course, entirely possible that LBJ exaggerated feelings of class resentment according to the company he was in: instinctively manipulative, he was quite capable of taking on the "po' boy" pose when he thought he was in company that would like him for it, less likely to do so when he was with Richard Russell, Dean Acheson, or the queen of England.

The truth is that Lyndon Johnson was an extraordinarily complicated human being. His feelings about social class are only one example of the intricate patterns of contradictory feeling and conduct that made him—as George Reedy put it—"the most interesting man that ever occupied the White House."[54]

Like many, many families in the South, a defeated society whose financial capital had been shrunk by the abolition of slavery and whose agrarian character had denied it the Gilded Age of the industrial North, the Johnsons and Buntons and Baineses who were LBJ's forebears had known reverses, disappointments, and poverty.[55] But they were also proud people who had known prosperity as well as penury and had been chosen by their peers for public service.

Four times Sam Ealy Johnson Sr., LBJ's grandfather, took thousands of head of cattle from the Hill Country up the Chisholm Trail to Abilene. In 1871 he and his brother came back with $100,000 in Mexican double eagles and other gold coins, a substantial fortune at the time. They bought thousands of acres of land before they were wiped out by the coincidence of a drought, one of the last Comanche raids, and the

Panic of 1873. This Sam married a Bunton, from a patrician family proud of an ancestor who was a hero in the Revolutionary War and another who was governor of Kentucky and a member of Congress. Sam Johnson Sr. lived to be the Populist candidate for the Texas state legislature in 1892: he was defeated by his son-in-law. His son, Sam Jr., Lyndon Johnson's father, sat in the Texas legislature. Joseph Wilson Baines, his mother's father, was a lawyer, an active member of the Baptist Church, and the editor of a local newspaper who had served in the Texas legislature.

Compared to Joseph P. Kennedy, Harvard-educated multimillionaire and New Deal politician, or to JFK's namesake and maternal grandfather, "Honey Fitz" Fitzgerald, mayor of Boston, LBJ's forefathers and their serious-minded, book-reading womenfolk were obscure and provincial. But they did not take themselves for nobodies, nor, in the sparse communities where they lived, did their neighbors.

Young Lyndon did not go to Harvard or even to the University of Texas because his father had fallen on hard times. He went off to San Marcos,[56] and his first job was as a schoolteacher in Cotulla, a forlorn, largely Mexican settlement on the Nueces River in southwest Texas.[57] He taught, however, for only a single school year. Opportunities opened up, in part through family connections. Through an uncle he got a job in Houston teaching debating at a major high school. Then, thanks to lobbying by his father and his father's friends, he was hired as secretary to Richard Kleberg, a Texas congressman whose wife was the heiress to the King ranch, possibly the grandest single agricultural property in the United States.[58]

From his childhood on, young Lyndon was used to following public and even foreign affairs in the newspapers. It might have surprised some of his northern critics that he was very early aware of Nazi persecution of the Jews and personally active in trying to rescue Jews from eastern Europe. A Jewish friend in Austin, Jim Novy, got him involved in rescuing at least forty-two Jews from Poland even before the Nazi invasion there. He gave Lady Bird, as an engagement present, a book warning of the dangers of Nazism. And as a young congressman he was able to arrange a visa to enable the great Austrian Jewish conductor Erich Leinsdorf to live in America.[59]

In Washington, he skimped and saved like any other Depression youngster, but he also mingled on equal terms with a generation of future leaders: Robert Jackson, the future Supreme Court justice and Nuremberg prosecutor, was one of his early friends. Soon he was hanging out with members of Roosevelt's inner circle like Tommy "the Cork" Corcoran.[60] Before he was twenty-seven he had expectations of advancement that would be amply fulfilled. Like the nation, he was given a New Deal: in his case as a National Youth Administration coordinator, one of an army of idealistic and ambitious young men (including future senator and vice president Hubert Humphrey) who responded to Franklin Roosevelt's call. When he was newly elected to Congress, he met FDR in person, who remarked that the young man from Texas "came on like a freight train."[61]

As a young congressman admired by President Roosevelt, Lyndon Johnson soon became very close to young New Dealers such as Tommy Corcoran, Benjamin V. Cohen, William O. Douglas, Abe Fortas (later his personal lawyer), Jerome Frank, Thurman Arnold, and Eliot Janeway. Through these friends, he came in contact with a man who was to give him entry to the world of Wall Street, Ed Weisl Sr., a partner in one of Wall Street's elite "white shoe" law firms, Simpson, Thacher and Bartlett, one of whose clients was the investment bank Lehman Brothers.[62] These ties gave Johnson an emotional commitment to the ideals of the New Deal and also an impressive network of contacts in many areas of American life, especially among members of the New York and Washington bars. It has been argued that they reinforced his gifts as a "fixer" and backstage operator and perhaps encouraged his impatience with conventional restraints.[63]

Many of these men were Jews, and they also introduced him to influential Jewish circles. Weisl in particular opened the doors to a Jewish community that both helped him generously with fund-raising and also influenced his policy, especially in the Middle East. It was through Weisl that he met a man who was to be a close and loyal friend, Arthur Krim, who gave him access to Hollywood.[64] "He hasn't got a more loyal, abler, in the wider sense more disinterested friend than Arthur Krim," McGeorge Bundy recalled. "But if you think Arthur Krim is disinterested on Israel, Arthur Krim doesn't think so."[65] Not only had Johnson helped rescue Jews from Europe as early as the 1930s, he was strong in his support for Israel in the 1950s. George Reedy pointed out that "LBJ had a very important pro-Israel constituency: not large, but very important people. LBJ had more Jewish following than JFK: people like Stanley Marcus." He added that Johnson had a "better reputation among Jews than JFK because of Old Joe."[66]

Perhaps even more than John F. Kennedy, Lyndon Baines Johnson was indeed a complicated man. Those who have profiled his character have often been reduced to listing pairs of opposites. For *New York Times* columnist Russell Baker, for example, he was "sinner and saint, buffoon and statesman, cynic and sentimentalist, a man torn between hungers for immortality and self-destruction."[67] He might have added that LBJ was at once physically coarse—belching and farting and taking an adolescent pleasure in urinating and defecating in front of his staff, and even displaying his penis to female employees[68]—and at the same time, as his biographer Robert Dallek put it, "a visceral New Deal liberal with a practical talent for accommodating diverse interests as no politician had since FDR."[69] For Randall Woods, his personality was "rife with opposites and the tension between them. Ambition versus public interest. One versus many. Faith versus doubt."[70] For Robert Caro, his least sympathetic biographer, who approached his subject initially through the prism of Vietnam, there were twin threads, "bright and dark," running side by side through Johnson's life, though Caro gave the dark thread significantly more prominence.[71]

Paul Douglas, economics professor and liberal senator from Illinois, grasped the essential contradiction in LBJ's political personality as well as anyone. LBJ was a "liberal," that is, a man of the center Left, a populist, a radical, a man determined to be remembered for his commitment to eliminating injustice and to improving life for all of his fellow citizens; at the same time he was restlessly ambitious and profoundly realistic about the way the political system worked and the part played in it by interests and accumulations of power. "Johnson was an intensely ambitious man," Douglas wrote, "anxious to get power and hold on to it. He had a progressive background and I think this had entered into his spirit and was a fundamental feature of his character. . . . But Texas after Roosevelt was a very different place than it had been. . . . Johnson, therefore, had this struggle within himself of his native tendencies, his Roosevelt idealism, faced with the hard facts of power politics and economic power."[72] One might add that a similar conflict had raged within the breast of Franklin Roosevelt and, though arguably much less so, in that of John Kennedy.

The contradictions in Lyndon Johnson were ideological and also ethical. Many of those who criticized and in some cases hated him claimed to be shocked by what they saw as his unscrupulousness. Robert Caro went so far as to write that "the pattern of pragmatism, cynicism and ruthlessness that pervaded Lyndon Johnson's entire early political career was marked by a lack of any discernible limits."[73] (Caro was scarcely less censorious about Johnson's later career.)

The supreme example, for Caro and many others, was the story of Johnson's election to the U.S. Senate in 1948 by tainted means, the famous affair of "Landslide Lyndon"—his own sardonic name for himself in reference to the narrowness of his win—and the legendary box 13 of questionable votes in Jim Wells County. Most commentators now, including those unapologetically friendly toward him, admit that he and his camp did cheat by "stealing" votes from boss-run, Mexican-inhabited "Valley" counties along the Rio Grande. Specifically, it seems incontrovertible that some 203 votes never cast by Mexican voters in Jim Wells County were added to the Johnson count at the orders of George Parr, the so-called Duke of Duval and sheriff of Jim Wells County, at the behest of the candidate.

Some simply take the view, or take the simple view, that this was barefaced fraud, proven and scarcely denied, and that it must stand as an indelible black mark against LBJ's reputation forever. Others point out mitigating factors. Johnson had almost certainly been robbed of election in the special election of 1941 after the death of Morris Sheppard. When LBJ ran for the U.S. Senate in that year against W. Lee "Pass the Biscuits Pappy" O'Daniel, the singing flour man, he was cheated of victory by virtually identical methods. Such practices were time honored in certain parts of Texas. Indeed, Johnson shrugged off his defeat in 1941. "We'd better just admit that we're defeated," he told his team, "and be a good loser."[74]

He was nothing of the kind, of course. But, as he told his brother, he had no wish to be investigated himself. He knew that his campaign too was guilty of technical infringements as well as of the elementary mistake of releasing his vote, revealing how many votes he had won, thus giving the other side a precise idea of the target it had to reach.[75] When he went to Hyde Park to receive FDR's commiseration, the president teased him. Even in New York, he said, we know enough to sit on our ballot boxes.[76]

LBJ did not like to lose, and a contributory factor in the determined use of fraud in 1948 was no doubt the knowledge that Coke Stevenson, his conservative opponent in 1948, the subject of generous, if surprising, admiration in Caro's account, was one of the conspiracy that had robbed him of victory in 1941.

Many observers, both during his life and after his death, were also puzzled by the apparent ideological contradictions in LBJ. He was a populist, certainly, and an ardent New Dealer, yes. But he was also the intimate friend of Richard Russell, doyen of the southern conservatives in the Senate; he was close to and often supported, politically and financially, by Texas oil and gas millionaires, most of all by George Brown, a partner of the civil engineering firm Brown & Root,[77] with his brother Herman Brown. These men prospered along with Johnson.

As a young congressman, his twin passions were rural electrification and water, especially flood control and power generation. Lady Bird once pointed out that LBJ, the Brown brothers, and Alvin Wirtz "shared a vision of a new Texas and they were going to be part of it. By gosh, they were going to make things happen—bring Texas whatever industry and whatever had made the eastern part of the United States, the so-called elite and rich part."[78] They meant, as the phrase goes, to do well by doing good. They were going to save Hill Country housewives from the drudgery of washing day, and in the process they were going to make their political and financial fortunes. They were idealistic, and they were ambitious.

Some of Johnson's contradictions are only apparent. Texas populists, in a state where many owners of mineral rights found themselves suddenly wealthy, were not hostile to individual self-made entrepreneurs.[79] Their resentment focused on established corporate wealth, such as that of the railroads. As a consummate politician, LBJ knew how to

trim. Just as any politician on Capitol Hill will sometimes "make a record" by voting against a bill in committee, then voting for it on final
passage, so Johnson refused to join the southern caucus or to sign the
Southern Manifesto against desegregation, yet managed by a thousand
hints and private confidences to give his southern colleagues the idea
that he understood and respected them.[80] Again, he supported the oil
industry's precious 27.5 percent depletion allowance. When in 1949 Leland Olds, an opponent of the depletion allowance and a former critic
of the capitalist system, came up for reconfirmation as a member of
the Federal Power Commission, LBJ did not just vote again him. He
attacked him viciously, saying on the Senate floor that the question was
"whether we shall have a commissioner or a commissar."[81]

Johnson, one could certainly say, was a realist. As his aide Harry
McPherson said, "One could simply not oppose the 27.5% depletion allowance in Texas and stay alive as a political figure."[82] The political reality was that, as George Reedy pointed out, in Texas it was not only
the fat cats who loved the oil and gas industry and wanted to protect its
precious depletion allowance.[83] Oil revenues paid for the Texas school
system: teachers, parents, liberals, and labor all had an interest in defending them.

LBJ was a "liberal," certainly. But he was not an antibusiness liberal. Like other contemporary politicians in the South he welcomed
economic development and in particular defense expenditure. It was
no accident that the biggest defense plums—air force bases, aerospace
plants, NASA facilities, army camps and military production facilities of every kind—went to the states whose congressional delegations
manned the command posts of the Senate and House committee systems. LBJ and men like Sam Rayburn, Carl Vinson, Richard Russell, and
Walter George were well aware of the connections between congressional influence, defense contracts and flood-control investment, and the
emergence of the New South from its traditional role as a semicolonial
appendage of the financial and industrial power of the Northeast and
Midwest. In this sense, Lyndon Johnson was a figure not of the traditional reactionary South but of the New South, an industrialized, urban-
ized South, that would soon become the Sunbelt.

That deep surge of change, as young African Americans headed for the Greyhound and Trailways buses and the Illinois Central trains that would take them to a new life in Detroit or Chicago, often leaving their parents and their young children behind them, while northern businessmen built plants in the South, was the context for the most acute and most consequential ideological conflict on which Lyndon Johnson must take his stand.

In the 1950s the great question of racial justice came to the center of national politics for the first time in many decades. World War II, whether on the battlefields of Europe and the Pacific or in the munitions plants of the home front, had transformed many African Americans. As LBJ himself put it to Horace Busby as early as 1948, "And then there are the Negroes. . . . They fought the war; they filled up the war plants, they built the bombers. . . . And now they're back and they're . . . just not going to take this shit we give them."[84]

The civil rights issue erupted after the Supreme Court's 1954 decision in *Brown v. Board of Education* that "separate but equal" schools were unconstitutional, a decision reaffirmed in 1955. LBJ suffered a severe heart attack in April 1955 and came back to his work as the Senate majority leader in the winter of the year to confront a whole series of civil rights issues. First there was the question who should succeed Senator Harley Kilgore of West Virginia as chair of the Senate Judiciary Committee. Next in seniority was Senator James Eastland of Mississippi, a diehard supporter of segregation who did not trouble to hide his contempt for blacks, Jews, Italians, and eastern Europeans.

The issue revealed the gap between the mainstream of northern liberal opinion and the culture of the Senate. To the *New York Times*, for example, here was a conflict between wisdom, constitutional priority, and the seniority system, and "if something has to give way, it had better be seniority."[85] To the elders of the U.S. Senate, seniority was the law and the prophets. To Lyndon Johnson, to block the succession of a senior senator to the committee chairmanship he had been expecting would be to lose control of the Senate and so to give up his own hopes of aspiring to the presidency. On March 2, 1956, Eastland duly became chair of the Judiciary Committee. Lyndon Johnson moved the resolution, and for good measure he used a parliamentary maneuver that freed senators from being on the record on the question.

Another and severer test awaited the majority leader. On March 12, ten days after Eastland took the chair of the Judiciary Committee, the southern caucus, that is, all twenty-two senators from the former Confederate states, minus the two Tennesseans and Lyndon Johnson, met in the office of Richard Russell of Georgia and approved a document they called the "Declaration of Constitutional Principles," which immediately became known as the Southern Manifesto. Johnson's refusal to sign has been interpreted in very different ways. To his biographer Robert Caro, for example, it was a calculated move prearranged with Russell, intended to keep Johnson available as the South's first plausible candidate for the presidency since Reconstruction.[86] To Randall Woods, in contrast, LBJ's nonsigning "would be a source of pride for years to come," and Woods quoted Senator Richard Neuberger of Oregon's opinion that this was "one of the most courageous acts of political valor I have ever seen."[87] He also suggested multicausal motives for Johnson's decision, among them the desire to protect his own presidential ambitions, but also concern for the danger of a split in the Democratic Party over race in a presidential election year.

Even more difficult, and even more dramatic evidence of LBJ's exceptional subtlety and skill as a politician, was the story of the 1957 civil rights bill. After the *Brown* decision there were growing signs that the political system could no longer ignore the issue of race. There had been the shocking case of Emmett Till, a black teenager from Chicago visiting his hometown in Mississippi who was brutally murdered for daring to talk to a white woman; the disturbances after the attempt of an African American woman, Autherine Lucy, to attend the University of Alabama; and above all the bus boycott in Montgomery and the emergence as a leader of the young Dr. Martin Luther King, Jr. In that context, there were a number of legislative proposals to improve the situation of southern blacks before the Eighty-Fifth Congress when it organized in January 1957.

Most were more or less radical pro–civil rights bills proposed by Democrats. Attorney General Herbert Brownell and Vice President Richard Nixon, however, had persuaded the newly reelected President Eisenhower that this was the moment for a bold thrust to split the northern and southern wings of the Democratic Party. They proposed a bill,

HR 6127, which in due course passed the House. Lyndon Johnson was delighted to have to deal with a Republican, as opposed to a Democrat, bill precisely because he—unlike Brownell and Nixon—saw this as an opportunity to avoid disruptive divisions inside his party between northern and southern Democrats.

The bill duly went to Eastland's committee, which largely rewrote it. Title III, the most offensive to the South because it would have given the federal government power to enforce civil rights, was abandoned. The bill became essentially a measure to enforce voting rights. But a sticking point remained. The bill allowed civil rights questions to be determined without a jury trial. The civil rights forces would not allow white offenders to be routinely acquitted by white juries. The southerners would not allow passage of a bill that denied jury trials in civil rights cases.

Johnson's dilemma, simply put, was that if he pushed for a civil rights bill that did not solve this conundrum, he would be treated by the southerners as a traitor and would lose his control over the Senate; if he did solve it, he might be seen as a merely southern leader and so forfeit any hope of national credibility and a presidential career. The dilemma, moreover, was not merely personal: so intense was feeling about the issue that Johnson could see the Democratic Party splitting, perhaps permanently, over civil rights.

Harry McPherson summed up how LBJ saw the situation. "My guess is that at that time he felt that there were certain historical necessities for the Democratic Party that required the passage of legislation. That is, this was Eisenhower's bill; it had passed the House; here it was in the Senate; no [civil rights] legislation had passed in eighty-five years. Secondly, the very fact that no legislation of this kind had passed in eighty-five years was an inducement to try to pass it, to bring off a great coup of this kind." McPherson added that LBJ "was one of those men early on who disbelieved in the Southern racial system and who thought that the salvation for the South lay through economic progress for everybody."[88]

LBJ threw himself into a search for a legal solution that involved long phone calls with the most brilliant lawyers he could find, from Dean Acheson to Abe Fortas. The solution, when it came, was found in a law journal article by a professor from Minnesota, Carl A. Auerbach. Reaching back centuries into English common law, Auerbach found a distinction between criminal and civil contempt. That enabled LBJ and his allies, aided by the legal craftsmanship of no less a Democratic hero than Dean Acheson, to reassure the South that only in criminal cases would civil rights issues be tried by juries. Southerners could say to their constituents that none of them could be branded a criminal without a southern jury to protect them; northerners could argue that the bill contained ample powers of enforcement: it fell short of the hopes only of those who wanted to punish southerners for their wicked ways.

This compromise, and these arguments, were enough for LBJ to assemble a Senate majority of northern moderates, Westerners, who were relatively indifferent to southern sensitivities, and some more or less liberal Republicans. LBJ's speechwriter, George Reedy, said later that this was his old boss's highest achievement: in his voluminous oral history for the LBJ library, he came back again and again to this as a supreme example of LBJ's legislative mastery.[89]

There are many other examples from LBJ's years in the Senate of the contradiction between his subtle and incisive intellectual powers, his grasp of infinite complexities, his insight into the real wishes and fears of the men and women he had to coax or bully into agreement, and the darker threads of his personality.

Journalists at the time used to emphasize the intensity and ruthlessness of what they called "the Johnson Treatment." Long after LBJ's death, Tom Wicker described how LBJ received him when he first went to interview him, shortly after he became president, as the *New York Times*'s White House correspondent. He found LBJ in the White House barber's chair. "He just stared at me, from under heavy lowered brows, across the sheet littered with his hair clippings. I shuffled from one foot to another; still he said nothing, nor did he even move, as the seconds came to seem minutes, then hours." Wicker was not an obvious candidate for intimidation: he was no Yankee wimp but a burly country boy from North Carolina. He knew LBJ already from the Senate and had imagined they were on easy terms. "I was quickly intimidated, unnerved, reduced to a sort of nothingness by those unblinking eyes, that jowly familiar face turned implacable, that motionless form under the barber sheet, the brooding silence in which I was being regarded, or perhaps measured."[90]

There is extant a series of 1957 photographs of LBJ towering over the diminutive, elderly Senator Theodore Francis Green of Rhode Island. It begins with the tall Texan relaxed and debonair; by the end, he is leaning over the older man, finger jabbing, face jutting, and Green looks physically terrified.[91] LBJ's arsenal, the blogger Anthony Bergen has recorded, "included gentle prodding, begging, ass-kissing, logical arguments, stern warnings, threats, bullying, apologetic needling, and outright intimidation. . . . LBJ grabbed people by their lapels, squeezed their arms and legs, stamped on feet, kicked shins, and leaned on them, penetrating their personal space and becoming a part of them while hoping that they decide to just agree with him so he'll go away."[92]

McPherson, again, has a more nuanced view. He acknowledged the power of the treatment, which he compared to a bolo punch from the Cuban champion, Kid Gavilán. LBJ, he pointed out while his former boss was still alive, "could argue on any kind of level: the highest policy, the narrowest self-interest, political interest. He keeps probing until he begins to score." There was something physical about his persuasiveness, "about the tremendous drive of his confrontation; something about his physical height, which he uses very effectively. His very massiveness and bigness. That has an almost irresistible force to it." But then he added a mitigation that had escaped many who knew him less well: "There is also something, when someone really cries out 'I can't do that,' there's something that snaps him back up. I've seen him become almost tender with people who just said they couldn't do it, and he's let them alone, and that has been it. And he hasn't gone out to try to ruin them later whatever. He has a considerable respect for such men."[93]

There were psychological as well as political "dark threads" in LBJ's personality. He was a very heavy drinker, a serial adulterer, and a bully, especially to those near to him and those who worked for him. Many of these traits seemed to those who knew him best to spring from an inner loneliness and fear.

The official line on his drinking was that he cut it out after his serious heart attack in 1955. This is simply untrue. I personally witnessed an amusing instance of this. In 1964 I was in the habit of going to the

rather sparsely attended press briefings at the White House on Saturday mornings, for the simple reason that I was the correspondent of a
Sunday newspaper, the *Observer,* in London. Given the five-hour time
difference, I could be almost sure of a hard news story to file for the
front page. One Saturday, with no more than a dozen reporters present, George Reedy, then LBJ's press secretary, lumbered in to say he had
something for us. The president had been taken to the Bethesda naval
hospital. There was nothing to worry about: he was undergoing "light
salicylation."

"George," I said, as an inveterate reader of medicine bottle labels,
"That's aspirin!"

Reedy promised to find out why the president of the United States
needed to be taken to the hospital in the middle of the night for an
aspirin.

A few minutes later, Reedy reappeared with the president himself,
in unusually sunny and relaxed mood. His wife was in Austin on TV
station business, he said. "What does a fellow do when his wife's away?
He sticks his head in a jug!" And off he went with us all for a breathless
fast walk round the White House gardens, pulling suspiciously favorable
poll results out of pockets in his suit and reading them out to us.

It turned out that the jug LBJ had stuck his head in was of his
favorite Cutty Sark scotch, whereupon he slipped and fell on the floor
of his private quarters. His daughter Luci and her boyfriend found the
Leader of the Free World stretched out on the floor and sensibly decided
to make sure all was well by packing him off to the hospital.

That was a comparatively harmless incident. Often the effects were
more serious. At several stages in his life, his drinking, and his behavior
when drunk, came close to causing major problems. Quite soon after
the heart surgery he was back aboard the Cutty Sark. The drinking was
especially reckless during his years as vice president, a time when, as
he subsequently admitted, he was miserable. Even before that trial had
begun, and after the heart attack that was supposed to have put him on
the wagon, there were many alcoholic episodes. On a campaign trip in
early 1960 LBJ got very drunk in El Paso and bawled out JFK's advance
man. On campaign there was some "very, very heavy drinking." Later
that year, "on a train trip to [the] South the drinking problem became

incredible. Getting absolutely plastered every night, making passes at women he should not have been making passes at, abasing his staff."[94]

When JFK banished him to world travel as vice president, misery and boredom drove him to the bottle again. There was an episode in 1962 when he "bawled hell out of" the US ambassador to Thailand with a "wild, insane, drunken stream of words."[95] Johnson's loyal friend Arthur Krim describes an extraordinary evening at Camp David in August 1965, when the frustrating news from Vietnam set him on edge. Lady Bird went off to bed about 9:00 P.M., but LBJ sat up all night with the Krims and half a dozen friends, including the reporters William S. White, Marianne Means, and John Chancellor. Someone made a mocking reference to Jack Valenti's recent statement that he slept better knowing that Lyndon Johnson was president. The president, who had downed ten or twelve scotches, ranted uncontrollably at his guests for the rest of the evening.[96] George Reedy, no teetotaler himself, theorized that "LBJ could not bear to be alone unless he was blind drunk. . . . That was one of the reasons for all the women."[97]

There were not all that many women, at least by the standards of JFK, who confided to a bemused Harold Macmillan that if he went three days without "having a woman" he got headaches. But there were quite enough, in all conscience. LBJ's three major relationships seem to have been with Alice Glass, the tall, radiantly beautiful wife of LBJ's friend and patron Charles Marsh; Helen Gahagan Douglas, wife of Melvyn Douglas, the Hollywood star turned Democratic liberal politician (the woman demonized by Richard Nixon in a vicious political campaign as "the pink lady"); and Mary Margaret Wiley, his vivacious personal secretary, who later married his aide Jack Valenti. There were of course many other rumors, some of them no doubt true.

Lady Bird Johnson was stoical. Her attachment to Lyndon was too deep, it seemed, for her to be put off by his infidelities, even though his indiscretion must often have been humiliating for her. I can remember being taken by LBJ with a handful of other reporters on a lightning tour of the White House private quarters. He flung open a door to reveal Lady Bird resting on a bed, fully clothed but visibly annoyed at having her privacy thus rudely disturbed. He was, however, devoted to Lady Bird, and his almost childlike emotional dependence on her gave her an underlying security about their relationship that could survive even his parading his sexual conquests.

In some respects the way he treated his staff was even worse than his treatment of his wife, though there too he could make amendments with a generosity and a need for friendship—and love—that made even his most brutal behavior forgivable. Almost everyone who worked for him experienced vicious put-downs of one kind or another. Craftily and relentlessly he would probe their weaknesses. Moreover, he exacted an appalling level of work from them. Staffers were made to feel ashamed of having lunch with friends, even of seeing their families over the weekend.

When Harry McPherson was first made a member of the White House staff, he invited me to lunch at a then fashionable restaurant, Sans Souci, close by. As we entered the restaurant, the maitre d' advanced with a phone on a long cord for McPherson. I could hear the familiar voice through the wire. "Isn't the White House canteen good enough for you and your foreign friend?" It was a joke, but a pointed one.

A secretary would be mocked for accepting a drink at a party, then recompensed with a spiffy new handbag; an aide would be bawled out one day, invited to some event as a mark of favor the next. The weapons of control varied from coarse mockery to subtle insinuation. Staff, male and female, would be invited to skinny-dip in the White House pool and mocked if they showed reluctance to strip off. George Reedy, from an Irish family and a labor economist by training, was taunted by references to "labor goons and Irish thugs."[98]

The staff LBJ had assembled and in the main kept for years included some exceptionally able and strong characters, and the very fact that they put up with his bullying and occasional cruelty argues that, however unpleasant working for him could be at times, it was bearable, especially in consideration of the rich rewards it brought, both in career terms and in the sheer interest and importance of the work involved. Arthur Krim made this case: "McPherson or Califano would tell you that no matter how bitter the tongue lashing, the graciousness that followed to heal the wound was always there."[99]

Yet Harry McPherson never quite forgot one gratuitous instance of LBJ's undermining. He had accompanied the president to Australia for the funeral of the Australian prime minister, Harry Holt, presumed drowned while out swimming. LBJ instructed his aide to prepare an important speech, then in secrecy flew to Vietnam. (This was the occasion of the famous "Son, they're all my helicopters!" rejoinder to a junior officer who rashly presumed to show the president to "his" helicopter.) When LBJ returned he repeatedly and pointedly asked McPherson why he had not come to Vietnam. The reasons were plain: he had been ordered to write the speech, and in any event he did not even know that LBJ was going to Vietnam. But the implication, cruel, stupid, and hurtful, was that the former air force captain, who had been working loyally for LBJ for twenty years, was scared of visiting a war zone.[100]

Biographers and oral historians have noted several other unflattering characteristics. LBJ was something of a hypochondriac. Certainly for a man of such physical power and preternatural energy he was rather frequently ill. Several have hinted at a psychosomatic origin, associating these episodes (appendicitis in 1937, kidney stone in early 1955, the heart attack later in the same year) with stress or crisis. Doris Kearns notes that "he was . . . seriously ill shortly before an astonishing proportion of his elections."[101] It is very plausible that, like many men whose fathers died of heart attacks, he was afraid that he was destined to die young: that could explain some of the impatience, the urgency of the way he set about his work. It was LBJ's misfortune to live in the age of psychoanalysis. Many writers (Caro and Kearns among them) have trawled through anecdotes of his childhood and accounts of his dreams, looking for the origins of psychological traits.

More than most very successful men, LBJ could accept easily the role of disciple to powerful older men: Cecil Evans, the president of San Marcos; Charles Marsh; the Austin lawyer Alvin Wirtz; Franklin Roosevelt himself. Johnson was willing to listen and to accept their patronage and support. Sam Rayburn, a lonely older man whom LBJ used physically to kiss on his bald head, and Richard Russell, equally lonely and a man of immense pride and dignity, were both clearly father figures to the middle-aged Lyndon.

Such theorizing, for this writer, is interesting but inconsequential. Johnson could be a bully. He did seem to move in and out of a deep vein of pessimism. He was afraid of being alone. Like a very high proportion of American men of his generation (the Prohibition generation) he drank heavily, and like many men everywhere since the world began he sought distraction, comfort, pleasure in sexual escapades. It is tempting, especially for those of us who lived through the age of Freud, to speculate that his character was the product of manic depression or bipolar disease.

But his life cannot be reduced to a diagnosis. It was much more individual and more interesting. Intriguing as all these aspects of his personality are, they are less important than three master traits: his intelligence, his energy, and his commitment to the improvement of the life of all Americans. More interesting still, to this writer, is the way both the strengths and the flaws of his character reflected the titanic changes that occurred in the United States in the lifetime of a man who was born the year after the Panic of 1907 and died sixteen days before the Senate established a select committee to investigate the Watergate scandal.

When he first emerged as a national figure and especially after he became president, there was a rather ridiculous tendency among northern liberals and in the national media to portray LBJ as a cowboy, a hayseed, and a rural buffoon. Nothing could be farther from the truth than this caricature. One of the lawyers on his staff, Larry Levinson, a brilliant graduate of Harvard Law School, judged that "unknown to most people, the President happens to have an excellent ear, an excellent eye for prose . . . a very fine editor . . . the most phenomenal grasp of numbers. I think the President would probably have made one of the country's best lawyers in the terms of being able to present positions with great clarity and as a skilled advocate would."[102] McGeorge Bundy, who as the former dean of the faculty of arts and sciences at Harvard University had an almost unrivalled experience of mature intellectuals of exceptional ability, put it more simply: Johnson was, he said, "the most intelligent man I have ever met."[103]

There is universal testimony, from every stage of his life, to the demonic quality of his energy, his stamina, his determination. Many feared or ridiculed his manic quality. From an early age, he had learned that you had to "do it all," never to rely on luck or other people, but to make sure that you got the result you wanted. (This was a long mile from the life experience of Jack Kennedy growing up with his father's advice, money, staff, and influence always at his disposal.)

What was less appreciated was the depth of LBJ's commitment to the populist creed. He understood poverty because he had experienced it: his family was known and respected, and had been wealthy. But when Lyndon was growing up, money was short. There was nothing he was prouder of than the part he played in bringing electricity to the remoter corners of the Hill Country, and right at the beginning of his career he was prepared to take on directly the interests of the utility companies in order to do so. His commitment to the domestic programs of the Great Society was total. To be sure, he became rich, mainly through the success of his wife's radio and TV station, and that owed much to the monopoly status he protected for it. (For a long time, Austin was the biggest television market in the United States with only one TV station—the Johnsons'.)

In his lifetime, Texas and the United States became rich, and he shared the predominant view of his countrymen and contemporaries that there was nothing wrong in that. To be sure, he could be ruthless in legislative tactic or executive decision. But his dedication to a just society was sincere. His energy and his ability simply made him more effective than any of his contemporaries.

Lyndon Johnson came out of an agrarian and populist Texas, where politics were about the struggle between the capitalists and the railroads on the one hand and the farmers "at the forks of the creeks" on the other. Seven years before he was born, the gusher at Spindle-top blew. Oil and gas transformed Texas forever, as they transformed California, Oklahoma, and other states. Over LBJ's lifetime, Texas, once agrarian, developed four large cities: Houston, San Antonio, Dallas, and Fort Worth.

For decades, since the days of Henry Grady, prophets had preached the coming of a New South. Lyndon Johnson happened to be a member of the committee Franklin Roosevelt set up to look at the economy of the South.[104] At that time, it was in many ways a colonial economy, controlled by metropolitan capitalists in New York and Boston. When LBJ was in high school, a southern banker was a man who borrowed money in New York and lent it at a percentage point or more over the interest he paid. The economy of Texas and the South was dominated by railroads, mostly owned in the East, which kept southern businesses in subjection by the differential freight rates they charged.

World War II saw the coming of the first large-scale industrial plants in Texas, led by Consolidated Vultee, later Convair, which started building B-36 bombers in Fort Worth in 1943. Firms that had brought electronics to the discovery of oil and gas adapted easily to the wartime demands of the military. The company that became Texas Instruments, Geophysical Service (GSI), moved from Newark, New Jersey, to Dallas, Texas, in 1934 and won its first major defense contract in 1942. In that same year the biggest army base in the United States was founded at Fort Hood, two-thirds of the way south from Dallas to Austin. Before the war, New Dealer Lyndon Johnson was one of the Texas politicians who brought electric power to rural Texas homes and embarked on massive water-control projects like the Lower Colorado River Authority, and they in turn made the fortune of construction entrepreneurs like Johnson's close personal friends the brothers George and Herman Brown. After the war, LBJ and his influential Texas peers on Capitol Hill brought in federal money in huge quantities to build defense plants, army and navy and air forces bases, not to mention the manned flight aerospace center near Houston.

That was the Texas, that the South, that LBJ grew up with. It was not really either old-fashioned or backward or provincial, as the New Yorkers imagined. Johnson grew up at the apex of one of the most dynamic and fast-changing sections of the country—one, moreover, that had confronted before the North what was to be the greatest challenge of the century for all of the nation, the question of race.

T · W · O

One Brief Shining Moment

Only reapers, reaping early

In among the bearded barley

Hear a song that echoes cheerly

From the river winding clearly

Down to tower'd Camelot.

—*Alfred, Lord Tennyson,* The Lady of Shalott

That was my Camelot before I got to Washington in 1962: the half-remembered stanzas, learned at school, of a ripely romantic Victorian poem, *The Lady of Shalott,* by Alfred, Lord Tennyson. That Camelot was the mysterious castle of the mythical King Arthur and his court. The Kennedy Camelot was a more recent fiction, the much-loved Broadway musical, music by Frederick Loewe and book by Alan Jay Lerner, which passed into legend as a result of one of the boldest and most successful public relations campaigns in history.

On November 29, 1963, just one week after her husband's assassination, Jacqueline Kennedy summoned Theodore H. White to the family compound at Hyannis Port and gave him the interview of his life,[1] and he had landed many a scoop in his two careers as a correspondent in revolutionary China and as the chronicler of John Kennedy's presidential campaign in 1960.

It is tempting to dismiss Teddy White as the Kennedy's court journalist, and it is true that his admiration of Jack Kennedy was unbounded to the point of embarrassment.[2] As a student at Harvard, he had known, probably slightly, Joe Jr. when the latter was one of the biggest men on campus. White clearly enjoyed the experience of sharing something of the Kennedy glamour. To be fair, though, even the most sturdily independent reporter would have jumped at an exclusive with the world's most famous widow just one week after her husband's assassination.

White jumped, all right. He took a hired car in the driving rain to the Cape, arriving at the Kennedy compound at half past 8:00 on that Friday evening. He found the widow accompanied by a respectable turnout of the praetorian guard, including JFK's friend Chuck Spalding, his loyal crony Dave Powers, and Frank Roosevelt Jr.

Jackie was in voluble mood. She talked for four hours, describing the horror of the assassination in intimate detail. She recounted her experiences since the return from Dallas. She did not want to be "the Widder Kennedy," she confided. She wanted Cape Canaveral to be called after her husband; the eternal flame at Arlington; "and I wanted his name on that booster, the one that would put us ahead of the Russians." She talked about the gold ring with a single emerald that Jack had given her when their son Patrick died. She didn't want to go and live in Europe, she said, though within five years she had married Aristotle Onassis and did bring herself to spend some of her time at his private Ionian island, Skorpios, and his opulent apartment in the Avenue Foch, just off the Champs Elysées in Paris. And she told White, and the world, that Jack liked to put on the record of *Camelot,* the musical, just before they went to bed. At the end of the interview, White allowed her to scribble an afterthought in pencil on his copy: "And it will never be that way again."

White disappeared into a scullery and typed furiously for forty-five minutes. He called the story in to his editors, who suggested he had overplayed the Camelot angle. But Jackie made her last contribution: she shook her head, disagreeing. White had his scoop.

I was never a citizen of Camelot, not a knight of the Round Table, not a squire, not even a varlet. I was just a young foreign journalist. At most I inhabited one of the suburbs of Camelot, perhaps an area reserved for what Teddy White would have called "service personnel."

I arrived in Washington as the correspondent—we didn't have anything so grand as bureau chiefs in those days—of the independent

British Sunday newspaper the *Observer*, whose staff I had joined on the first day of the 1960s. (In those days several Sunday titles in London were independent organizations.) The *Observer* was edited by David Astor, an old-fashioned liberal: a man of the anti-Communist Left, passionately committed to the struggle against colonialism and racism, especially in Africa, where he had started or taken over several liberal newspapers. He was exceedingly generous, financially supporting causes from conservation to psychoanalysis as well as African liberation.

David had transformed the paper, once true-blue Tory, by packing the staff with youngish men and women who shared his attitudes. Many of them were Jewish or antifascist refugees from central Europe: Isaac Deutscher from Poland, biographer of Trotsky; Raimund Pretzel, a brilliant student of German politics, not Jewish, who wrote as Sebastian Haffner, a byline compounded from the name of a character in Evelyn Waugh's *Brideshead Revisited* and his favorite Mozart symphony; Willi Gutmann from Breslau, now Vroclaw; Lajos Lederer from Hungary; and many others. The paper's obsession was Africa; it passionately advocated decolonization and the antiapartheid movement in South Africa.

Anthony Sampson, author of the best-selling *Anatomy of Britain*,[3] who was then one of David Astor's key lieutenants, persuaded me to move from *The Times*, where I was bored, to the *Observer*, where at first I wrote a business column, *Observer*-ishly bylined Mammon. Early in 1962 off I went to Washington to replace eminent colleagues who included Alastair Buchan, son of novelist and governor-general of Canada John Buchan and a pillar of Atlanticism, and Nora Beloff, sister of the distinguished Oxford historian Sir Max Beloff.

The date of my departure for Washington was significant. I arrived a good year after the New Frontier had arrived in town. Many of the reporters who had the best access to the Kennedys and their people had covered Jack Kennedy in the 1960 election campaign. They had longer and far better credentials with the Kennedys than I could hope to have. It was something of a tradition in the Washington press corps that the reward for covering the victorious candidate was to be appointed as the paper's White House correspondent. Of those, Teddy White, who had turned his reporting into the hugely successful *The Making of the President, 1960*, was one of the closest and the . . . least critical.

I started out working in Georgetown, where the *Observer* had its office in a bijou townhouse. This was already one of the most interesting urban neighborhoods in the world. Georgetown now has the reputation, at least among spiteful conservative journalists, of being the very stronghold of the limousine liberals—or, if you prefer, Bollinger Bolsheviks. Actually, more than most American settlements, the area was a palimpsest on which a dozen generations had left their imprint since the days when Georgetown, like its sister quay Alexandria across the broad Potomac, shipped tobacco from the wealthy plantations of northern Virginia. By the early twentieth century, it was the home of modestly prosperous African American families who supported several American Methodist Episcopal or Baptist churches.

It was the New Deal that brought the first modern influx of professors, social workers, and lawyers to work for the "alphabet soup" of institutions set up by Franklin Roosevelt. (It was in Georgetown that Whittaker Chambers is said to have coaxed Alger Hiss into spying for the Soviet Union.) The election of John F. Kennedy in 1960 brought a new wave of idealists to Washington, but few could afford Georgetown. In the Camelot years Georgetown was appropriated more by New York money than by the New Frontier.

Georgetown, a mile or so west of the White House, stretches from the mild eroticism of the P street "beach," where in the humid Washington summer young female office workers used to tan themselves on the slope above the tide of traffic on Rock Creek parkway, to the austere Gothic towers of the Jesuits at Georgetown University in the west. It descends, leafy and full of blossom, from the Victorian opulence of Dumbarton Oaks, scene (along with Bretton Woods in distant New Hampshire) of one of the two postwar conferences that sketched FDR's vision for a world elevated by America ideals, to the genteel commerce of Wisconsin Avenue and Thirty-first Street. Next to Dumbarton Oaks there is a charming small park where I used to play tennis before going to work, and where Jackie Kennedy was rumored to take her little children to escape from the White House.

The new reign brought new developments to Georgetown. Stewart Davidson, a National Cash Register Company heir with a penchant for alcohol and swordplay (married for a time to a London friend of Alice's and mine) started Clyde's, the prototype of a string of bars in a mock-1900 style that brought in thirsty herds of off-duty bureaucrats and tourists. A lady who scoured Mexico for folk art was one of the pioneers of the cute retail establishments that spread up Wisconsin Avenue from the golden dome of Riggs Bank, later to be revealed as up to its genteel armpits in money laundering on behalf of some of the world's most unsavory dictators. Half a block uphill from Riggs was my own favorite place of refreshment, Martin's, a formerly Irish tavern that served draft beer and oyster stew to a mixed clientele of Georgetown graduate students and retired ambassadors. So attached did I become to Martin's that for the several decades I divided my life between Washington and England I would pay a ritual visit there for seafood the night before leaving town.

For the purposes of this study the crucial blocks of Georgetown were the blocks of N, O, and R streets between Wisconsin and Rock Creek park. There lived Phil and Kay Graham, coproprietors of the *Washington Post*. Chester Bowles, who had made his money in a New York advertising agency before being elected governor of Connecticut and a high official in the Kennedy State Department, owned a garden that ran the whole length of a Georgetown bloc, a few minutes' walk from the Kennedys'. JFK found Bowles's internationalist liberalism annoying. A near neighbor was Averell Harriman, who boasted a Van Gogh and a Matisse in his drawing room. Joe Alsop, columnist, closet homosexual (he was entrapped by the KGB as a result of a gay honey trap in Moscow), and classical scholar, a cousin of Theodore Roosevelt, lived nearby. It was to his house that Jack Kennedy went (after the inevitable love sacrifice with a friendly she-Democrat) to fête his inauguration. Joe and Susan Mary Alsop's house was the site of a regular Sunday-night dinner where a core of upper-class warriors from the CIA argued policy over some of the best French wine in Washington.[4] There were many in the neighborhood, the "cave dwellers," who found this infusion of celebrities a titillating but, on balance, annoying intrusion.

Fortunately for us, some of this discreet tribe were kind enough to invite my wife Alice and me to dinner. This was a rite conducted according to rituals which, as Anglophiles, they assumed we were used to, but which had actually gone out of usage in London since 1939, possibly earlier. There were silver candlesticks and port on the table, and after dinner the ladies went upstairs to "powder their noses" while the men discussed politics, the stock market, and the ladies.

One house to which Alice and I were invited was to be the scene, in 1976, of a robust social comedy with political overtones. Dinner was coming to a stately close when there was what my informant, Meg Greenfield of the *Washington Post,* reported as a "god-awful noise." A very large gold-colored Lincoln Continental had impertinently smashed its way through the colonial brickwork into the very dining room, its wheels spinning to a halt inches above the parquet. A tall, elegantly dressed black woman extricated herself from the driver's seat and made herself scarce. The passenger was revealed as none other than the Speaker of the House of Representatives, third senior in the Republic's official hierarchy, the distinguished and diminutive Carl Albert of Oklahoma.

My friend Greenfield did not allow her entrée into Georgetown society to make her forget her journalistic responsibilities. She called the Speaker's office, which professed to be unaware of any such incident. Weeks later, pressing her inquiries, Greenfield was told that the Speaker would be retiring because of health problems. Thus rudely could the gentle rhythm of Georgetown life be interrupted by the congress of Demos and Eros.

Most interesting of all the Georgetown real estate in the 1960s, however, was a tall redbrick nineteenth-century house reached by a steep flight of steps from the sidewalk on N Street, a few yards from Wisconsin Avenue: the home of Senator and Mrs. John F. Kennedy.

Homes in Georgetown were then unthinkably too expensive for a family of five on a British salary, so my family lived in the suburbs of Camelot. Alice and I, with our two small sons, Pierre and Francis, and their French nanny, Marie-Jeanne, settled in leafy Cleveland Park, the second most socially acceptable neighborhood after Georgetown. We had several homes over the years because Washington houses tended to be let with "diplomatic clauses," which meant that when our landlords in the nicest house, on Macomb Street, with a stream in the garden and a big magnolia, were kicked out of Cyprus (they were CIA), they correspondingly kicked us out of their home. (You could tell CIA folks in those days because when you asked them what they did, they would say, not "State" or "Treasury" or any other specific department, but "I work for the government.") Rental homes in Washington also had another clause: no Jews were welcome. I was the only one of the four Hodgsons who was not a Jew, but the realtor seemed not to care about that.

I set to work to catch up as best as I could on the reporters who had been in Washington for years or who had swept in as fellow pilgrims with the Kennedy people. I interviewed as many people in government as I could, three and four a day. It was amazing how many people in the most senior jobs were prepared to give time to a gauche twenty-eight-year-old from Britain. Part of the explanation, I guessed, was that in 1962, the Anglo-American World War II alliance was not so far in the past. Many of the most dazzling stars of the New Frontier—among them the Bundy brothers, Mac in the White House and Bill, then at the Pentagon, Bob McNamara, George Ball, Nick Katzenbach, Fred Dutton, and many more—had been young officers in Europe during the war, had served with British colleagues in joint headquarters, and knew my home country quite well and had for the most part liked it, even if wartime service had involved no central heating and a good deal of austerity. Quite a few of them, indeed—Arthur Schlesinger, Ken Galbraith, Walt Rostow, and others—had studied in Britain as Rhodes Scholars at Oxford, at Cambridge, or at the London School of Economics, where the president himself had theoretically registered as a student but not physically put in an appearance. As a result, many even of the most senior officials, up to but not including the president himself, were kind enough to agree to see me at least once. With some, that was to develop into something like the professional relationship "beat" reporters with U.S. papers had, where they would get to know personally the chief players on their assigned turf.

My introduction into the upper slopes of the New Frontier came from David Astor himself. David was characteristically modest about his almost regal American connections, but they were there all right. Once, after I had been in Washington for a while, David told me I was doing okay on the politics, but I needed to expand my contacts in the business world. Was I perhaps aware, he asked, fanning the air with an embarrassed hand, that his family had some stocks and bonds and that sort of thing? I was vaguely aware of that, I admitted. "Well, there is this man who looks after that side of life for us in New York." (David didn't actually say "this *little* man," but it came out a bit like that.) "His name is Wriston, Walter Wriston, I'm sure he'd be glad to help you." Walter B. Wriston was, at the time, the executive vice president of what was then the First National City Bank of New York, and arguably the most influential figure of the day on Wall Street.

One day when David was in town to interview his old friend the president, he invited me to the Metropolitan Club, a gloomy brownstone palace in the beaux arts style fashionable in the 1920s, for lunch to meet McGeorge Bundy, another old pal of Astor's since wartime London. Mac was a genuine American patrician: head prefect at Groton, a member of Skull & Bones at Yale, dean of the faculty of arts and sciences at Harvard, and now President Kennedy's national security adviser. His father, a corporate lawyer from a leading firm in Boston, had worked for Henry Stimson when that pillar of the establishment was secretary of war in World War II; his older brother, Bill, was married to Dean Acheson's daughter. Mac, who was famous for being frosty if he wanted to be, unbent, and the lunch passed pleasantly. As we said good-bye on the dignified brownstone steps of the Metropolitan Club, Mac graciously invited me to call him if I needed help.

Some weeks later, I was under pressure from the news desk in London to settle whether or not General de Gaulle, as was rumored, actually meant to visit Washington. I could not get a convincing reply from the French embassy or from the Department of State. I called Mac, and the legendary frost descended. Did I not realize, he said icily, that he was rather a busy man?

That was only the beginning, however, of a salutary lesson in how Washington, and perhaps the world, works. About that same time I decided to ask for an interview with a man who had previously been an economics don at Oxford, Charles Hitch, who was, as comptroller, the third most powerful official at the Pentagon after McNamara and Roswell Gilpatric. In the interview, I asked Mr. Hitch how he saw the defense budget developing over the next few years. Well, he replied, that depends a bit on these antiballistic missile sites the Russians have. Of course, I murmured, and allowed him to explain what was at the time a closely held secret: that U.S. reconnaissance (I suppose from U2 overflights) had revealed that the Soviet Union was building two antiballistic missile (ABM) sites. If the United States felt obliged to respond, that would add many billions of dollars to the defense budget. I made such checks as I could, and filed my story.

It was, I still think, the biggest hard news scoop of my entire journalistic life. This was 1962, years before anyone outside the defense bureaucracy had even heard of ABMs.[5] Later they would become one of the most controversial elements of the entire cold war strategic tangle. The *Observer* was not impressed. Someone on the news desk called the press office at the American embassy in London, whose representative said, no doubt with perfect truth, that he had never heard of any such thing as antiballistic missiles. The paper ran the story but, as they say, below the fold—well below the fold, on page 94 or thereabouts. But Mac Bundy had noticed. I had a visit from two athletic-looking men in black raincoats who said they were from the FBI. Would I like to tell them where I had got this story? Feeling like some hero of press freedom, I said I could not reveal my sources, and they accepted that.

Some weeks later, President Kennedy was in Canada for a meeting with the crusty Tory prime minister, John Diefenbaker. The president, in an unguarded moment, referred to Mr. Diefenbaker as a son of a bitch. Well, "SOB" was what he said. Canadian officials were not used to such relaxed junior officer language. The White House suavely insisted there had been a mistake: the president had merely remarked, "How do we push him into the OAS, the Organization of American States?"

My next-door neighbor on Macomb, Peter Trueman, was the correspondent for the *Montreal Star.* When the Reuter machine in my basement began to go crazy, three bells for a major story, I asked Trueman, literally over the garden fence, what the hell this excitement was all about. He told me. I reported the correct trigram while all the U.S. papers were accepting the OAS cover story. Once again, there was a visit from the black raincoats.

Gradually, I found myself being taken more seriously, even to the point of tennis at St. Alban's with the national security adviser and his brother the assistant secretary. I took the precaution of bringing along the correspondent of the *Financial Times,* Geoff Owen, who had played at Wimbledon.

Slowly other contacts were opening up. When I was a graduate student at the University of Pennsylvania, I made friends with Avery and Emily Andrews and spent many happy weekends at their house on the Main Line. Emily's family, the Woods, were "Old Philadelphia," and when I told her I was going to Washington she gave me an introduction to Ben Read, then administrative assistant to Senator Joe Clark of Pennsylvania. Through Ben, I met a circle of young, very able senatorial aides, such as Frank Sieverts, a Rhodes scholar who worked for Senator Gaylord Nelson of Wisconsin.

Through them, I met Harry McPherson, who was then working for the Senate Democratic Policy Committee, as he describes on the opening pages of his classic *A Political Education,* first published in 1972. His immediate boss was Jerry Siegel, but Harry was a Texan, a Johnson man, albeit one with more of a hinterland in his life than many of them. Through Harry, who remained one of my closest friends until his death in 2012, I met other people in the Johnson circle, such as Doug Cater, Horace "Buzz" Busby, and Bill Moyers. Above all I got to know Harry's then close friend Pat Moynihan.

The Moynihans, Pat, his wife, Liz, and their three small children, John, Timothy, and Maura, lived in Cleveland Park, like us. In fact they lived across Macomb Street NW from us, in the former stables of Tregaron, the vast mansion once inhabited by Marjorie Merriweather Post, heiress of the unforgettable Post Toasties, and her husband, Joseph W. Davies, who had been sent by FDR as America's first ambassador to the Soviet Union. By 1963, Tregaron had become the embassy of Nationalist China, but Liz, with her unfailing eye, had turned the stables into a cozy house, where she worked as a sculptor: she executed a charming head of my son Francis, then three. Liz, a high school graduate and former secretary, later a historian of Mughal India, managed for her husband the two most successful Senate campaigns in American history—while working out of her kitchen with a budget that would hardly get you elected to Congress from the smallest state these days. She was also in every way the intellectual equal of her brilliant and academically crowned husband.

As a practical matter I was spending too much time in taxis to and from downtown and Capitol Hill: in those days the streetcar tracks had not been pulled up and I can still feel the jolting as the cabs skidded on the steel rails in Georgetown. So I did what turned out to be one of the smartest things I have done in my life. I asked the editor of the *Washington Post* if I could have a desk in the newsroom. The editor at that time (predecessor to Ben Bradlee, then still at *Newsweek*) was a gentleman of the old school called J. Russell Wiggins.[6] He said yes, gruffly but kindly, so long as I didn't make a nuisance of myself by asking his reporters for too much help. So I found myself in the corner of the old newsroom, lovingly replicated in Hollywood for the Watergate movie *All the President's Men*. My desk, in the corner next to the morgue, was the one Tom Wolfe had occupied before he moved to the old *Herald Tribune* and began his glittering career as one of the founders of the New Journalism. It was not long before I had made many friends in the *Post's* newsroom. In spite of Mr. Wiggins's warning, they were generous in sharing their knowledge and contacts.

Two *Post* journalists in particular became very close friends and my tutors in the ways of Washington. Larry Stern was the national editor. He was also the *Post's* most respected exponent of investigative journalism—something that, until then, the *Post* had not practiced very much.[7] Stern almost certainly missed out on becoming even better known than he was. When the Watergate break-in happened in 1972, he was abroad, writing a book about, of all things, the Greek-Turkish conflict over Cyprus. Had he been in town, there can be little doubt that the two rookies from the metro desk, Bob Woodward and Carl Bernstein, would have been taken off the story or at best have been asked to act as legmen for Larry. As it was, they went on to imperishable glory, and Larry remained just the best reporter his friends had ever seen operating.

My other special friend at the *Post* was and still is Karl Meyer. He too was the son of a journalist, but from a rather different school, the German socialist and progressive tradition in Wisconsin. His grandfather founded a German–language newspaper in Milwaukee. Karl studied history at Madison and then did a Ph.D. at Princeton. Later he was an authoritative bureau chief of the *Washington Post* in London. For many years he was a member of the editorial board at the *New York Times*.

Karl and his first wife, Sara, were tremendous party givers at their modest row house in Cleveland Park, and it was there that I first began to meet some of the knights of the Camelot Round Table, among them Arthur Schlesinger and John Kenneth Galbraith. I also met there some of the much younger "whiz kids" from Bob McNamara's Pentagon, economists and systems analysts such as Harry Rowen (future president of RAND Corporation), and Alain Enthoven, later a very influential figure in health policy. Both were Oxford graduates a few years older than me.

I have charted my own growing network of connections both because they show how an outsider could get a distant view of the charms and glories of Camelot and they make a point about Camelot itself. It was, after all, Jackie Kennedy's term for the years she spent in the White House, not her husband's, and it referred not to political battles and victories but to a social milieu. To be sure, it was Jack who liked to listen to show tunes at bedtime. (He was famously bored by the concerts in the East Room of the White House, to which his wife brought some of the authentic titans of classical music at midcentury, among them the cellist Pablo Casals and the violinist Isaac Stern; his own taste ran to New York dance bands like Lester Lanin and Peter Duchin.)

The point is that Camelot was only the innermost ring of Kennedy Washington. Many people came to the capital in 1961 to work for the Kennedy administration. Most of them, often with a touch of embarrassment, called what they were doing not Camelot—a young, romantic widow's memory of her life with her husband—but the New Frontier. That was Jack Kennedy's own name for the political enterprise. It was a reference to his ambitions in space: he had used the phrase in this sense in his acceptance speech at the 1960 Los Angeles Democratic convention.

Not only did many hundreds come to Washington to till the New Frontier: those who came were many different kinds of people. The faces Jackie would have had in mind as she recalled Camelot would have been a mixture of Jack's personal cronies, like Paul B. "Red" Fay, Kirk LeMoyne "Lem" Billings, and "Chuck" Spalding; the more socially acceptable of high officials (many of them, incidentally, Republicans), like the Douglas Dillons, the McGeorge Bundys, and the Averell Harrimans; a sprinkling of the better-connected diplomats (the Ormsby-Gores, friends from prewar London, and the Hervé Alphands from the French embassy; and a handful of well-known "public intellectuals" (read best-sellers) like Ken and Kitty Galbraith and Arthur and Marian Schlesinger. Add to that golden circle a few journalists—Ben Bradlee, then married to Tony Pinchot, sister of the president's most emotionally significant mistress, Mary Pinchot Meyer—and a handful more.

The Kennedys might have been snobbish, but they were not exclusive, and they were happy to invite outsiders beyond this charmed circle to their bigger parties. Still, there were highly able officials at State, in the Treasury, and in the Pentagon, let alone in less glamorous corners of the bureaucracy, assistant secretaries and the like, who were no more likely to be invited to intimate events at the White House than Alice and I were. Behind them came a phalanx of young lawyers and their wives, political operatives, labor stiffs, and assorted loyalists who had come to Washington to change the world. They (and especially their wives) were fascinated by the glamour of Camelot, but they were not part of it.

The Kennedy White House was, as has often been said, a court, and so it was full of courtiers. Many sought to give the impression that they were socially close to the Kennedys, like the journalist who liked to say, "It can be said on the highest authority," so as to suggest that he had interviewed the president before writing his weekly essay in thumb sucking and guesswork, or the other who used to take a tennis racket to press conferences on a Friday so as to imply that he was off to Hyannis Port for the weekend.

The Kennedy brothers, after all, came from what their father had made an immensely wealthy family. Kennedy, as president, gave his entire salary away to charity, to the annoyance of his wife. Like royalty, he never carried a wallet, apparently because he was afraid it would spoil the hang of his beautifully cut suits. Their lifestyle was that of the other very rich who were their neighbors on Cape Cod, at Palm Beach, or on the Upper East Side of Manhattan. Those were the people they felt most comfortable with. Their social milieu was that of my boss's older brother Bill Astor, the third Viscount Astor. When he came to dinner he asked me whom his younger brother David listened to. I replied cautiously that I thought he took a good deal of notice of what John Pringle said:

John was his deputy and the *Observer*'s chief editorial writer. "Oh!" said Bill, horrified. "I didn't mean the *staff*!"

The Astor brothers had in fact been good friends of the Kennedys in London before World War II. One reason I never did interview Jack Kennedy was that my boss, his friend David Astor, kept his access to the president for himself and for select friends. Sometimes I would be asked, to my secret irritation, to arrange for others to go to the Oval Office: not just David, not even just for David's close friend Roy Jenkins, a major British politician who was also to write an excellent biography of FDR and was working on a biography of JFK when he died, but for various (white) South African liberals and antiapartheid campaigners. David Astor was sure that his friend Jack Kennedy would want to meet them. He was under the impression that Kennedy shared his own visceral passion for racial justice. This, as we shall see, was something of an exaggeration.

What Kennedy did share with the Astor family was that both were to be impacted by what came to be known as the Profumo affair. London newspapers discovered that Bill Astor, the same who assumed that his brother did not take too much notice of the staff, owned the stately Thames-side palace of Cliveden, where I had attended the *Observer*'s summer staff parties. There, specifically in the pool, a good-time girl called Christine Keeler picked up the British war minister, Jack Profumo. The trouble was that Keeler was seeing a Soviet diplomat at the time. The excitement, fanned by Fleet Street's finest, eventually brought down the Conservative government of Kennedy's mentor, Harold Macmillan. Kennedy, whose secret life also focused on the White House pool, learned that several of the available beauties who sported in the Cliveden pool had also shared his own intimacy. Something close to panic followed. In August 1963 a certain Ellen Rometsch, an East German lady married to a sergeant from the West German embassy, was hurried onto a USAF plane back behind the iron curtain. Kennedy, unlike Uncle Harold Macmillan, survived.

Doctor Fell

I do not love thee, Doctor Fell

The reason why, I cannot tell

But this I know, and know full well,

I do not love thee, Doctor Fell.

—*traditional English rhyme*

A s I watched Lyndon Johnson descend the stairs from Air Force One at Andrews Air Force Base and make his brief dignified statement to television cameras—"I ask for your help, and God's"—I was scarcely aware that Robert Kennedy had just dashed up those same stairs, still less that the plane on the flight from Dallas had been the scene of grim bitterness and hostility between the political families of the dead president and his successor.

There was "smoldering animosity"[1] between the Kennedy people, huddled round the dead president's coffin in the rear of the plane, and the Johnsons and their aides forward. "It was undeniably very, very sick," remembered Clint Hill, Johnson's favorite secret service agent, "with a great deal of tension between the Kennedy people and the Johnson people."[2]

Jack Kennedy and Lyndon Johnson were brought together by the demands of practical politics: they needed one another if the Democrats were to win the 1960 election. As practical politicians, they did not expect to be bosom friends, but both men recognized the need to maintain civil relations. Their private feelings hardly came into it. Jackie Kennedy, a woman who had little experience of politics before she married Jack and even less taste for it afterward, once expressed to her husband her puzzlement. She had been hating someone for three weeks, she said, because she thought her husband hated him. Now she found she was expected to be friendly with him. In politics, JFK explained, "you rarely had friends or foes, only colleagues, and . . . you should never get so deep in a quarrel as to lose all chance of conciliation; you might need to work with the other fellow later."[3]

Jack Kennedy, indeed, having chosen Lyndon Johnson as his vice presidential partner for political reasons, among them to make sure of carrying Texas and to give him some chance of picking up other electoral college votes in the South, took care not to offend his vice president. Johnson nevertheless was painfully frustrated. He was bored, even miserable. His aide Douglass Cater reminisced later on PBS, "You've got to believe that those vice-presidential years were agony for him."[4] JFK worried that he would turn hostile. According to LBJ's aide Bobby Baker, not perhaps the most reliable of witnesses but nevertheless a shrewd observer with access to both men, President Kennedy himself was aware of it. "I really feel sorry for Lyndon," Baker quoted him as saying. "I know he's unhappy in the vice-presidency. It's a horseshit job, the worst fucking job I can imagine. . . . Lyndon's an activist if ever one was born, and he's simply a miserable son-of-a-bitch in that office."[5]

It was Jack Kennedy's double-dating partner George Smathers, Democrat of Florida, who suggested sending LBJ abroad as a roving ambassador.[6] "A damn good idea," said Kennedy, and Johnson set off on the first of eleven trips to thirty-three countries, culminating in his encounter with Bashir, the Pakistani camel driver, whom he invited to visit the United States.[7] This fed the impression in the Kennedy camp that Johnson was a buffoon, unsophisticated in the ways of the world, and indeed there was something naïve about the way LBJ cultivated Bashir as if he were a Texas voter. On and in between these travels he was frustrated, feeling his great political career slipping away in triviality and even ridicule. He responded by becoming moody, drinking too much (sometimes spectacularly too much), putting on weight, and on occasion acting deliberately, defiantly gross.

Privately Jack Kennedy, his wife, and his political family did despise LBJ. The normally correct Jackie Kennedy referred to the vice president and his elegant, forbearing wife as "Senator Cornpone and Mrs. Pork Chop."[8] Publicly, however, JFK insisted on the proprieties being observed. He took care that LBJ be invited to all important White House meetings and once sharply criticized his aide Kenneth O'Donnell for not doing so. According to Larry O'Brien, who maintained good relations with both the two presidents, JFK used the "strongest terms." "Don't let that ever happen again," he said when he saw that LBJ was not at a meeting. "You know what my rules are and we will not conduct meetings without the Vice President being present."[9]

In fact, while the two principals maintained a veneer of correctness over their deep differences and personal rivalry, their staffs, and particularly the Kennedy staff, could not repress their contempt and bitterness. Both the "Irish mafia" of Massachusetts politicians (Kenny O'Donnell, Ralph Dungan, and Dave Powers, among others, but not Larry O'Brien) and the Kennedy intellectuals (Arthur Schlesinger, J. K. Galbraith, Dick Goodwin, and many more) assumed that Johnson was a deep-dyed rustic southern reactionary. Later, Schlesinger came to have considerable respect for Johnson,[10] as did O'Brien. But when they first met in LBJ's Senate office in March 1957, Schlesinger's diary entry is unmistakably patronizing: "While plainly intelligent he seemed little concerned with the merits of issues."[11]

In spite of cultural differences, Kennedy stuck by his vice president for hard political reasons, perhaps more loyally than LBJ expected. Kenny O'Donnell, JFK's appointments secretary and chief domestic aide, treated LBJ so rudely that JFK chewed out his loyal henchman sharply, but in terms that both warned O'Donnell and revealed a certain sympathy with O'Donnell's attitude. "I want you to know one thing," he said, "[LBJ] thinks he's ten times more important than I am . . . but he thinks you're nothing but a clerk . . . you have never been elected to anything by anybody and you are dealing with a very insecure, sensitive man with a huge ego. I want you literally to kiss his fanny from one end of Washington to the other."[12]

The contempt of the Kennedy intimates was fully reciprocated by some of Johnson's circle. Liz Carpenter, Texas journalist and close friend of the Johnsons, expressed an ethnic hostility to the Irish mafia in general and Kenny O'Donnell in particular. The Massachusetts people, she believed, recycling a Protestant canard about those polyphilopro-genitive Catholics, wanted to "keep women barefooted & have them . . . preferably pregnant on election day."[13]

Rumors that LBJ would be dropped from the ticket circulated end-lessly, though O'Brien emphatically denied that JFK was party to them. It is more likely that the Irish mafia, annoyed by LBJ's insistence on dragging their hero into the quarrels of Texas politics, took advantage of speculation about LBJ's future to give him a sly kicking. "Whatever happened to Lyndon Johnson?" the newspapers were beginning to ask.[14] I wrote a column to the same effect myself shortly before the fatal trip to Texas. But Kennedy knew that he and his vice president were bound together. On October 31 1963, little more than three weeks before his death, JFK was asked at his press conference "Would you want LBJ on the ticket and do you expect that he will be on the ticket?" He replied crisply, "Yes to both those questions."[15]

If JFK stood by his vice president, his brother the attorney general had an altogether harder hostility to him. "It was just like two dogs com-ing into a room," said George Reedy, who worked for LBJ in the Senate and in the White House. "All of a sudden you hear a low growl."[16] It was generally believed that the feud started when JFK ignored his younger brother Robert's strong opposition and chose LBJ as his vice president at the Democratic National Convention in Los Angeles in 1960. "It was before that," Reedy told an interviewer. "They just didn't like each other. There was a real Dr Fell syndrome."[17]

It is hard to say exactly why Robert Kennedy felt this way about Johnson. The fierce Kennedy family feeling would have made the younger brother see LBJ as a rival for the presidency the Kennedy fam-ily had long coveted. Boston all too easily despised Austin. Massachu-setts snobbery, Harvard snobbery, too often saw Texans as uncouth, and Massachusetts abolitionism too often stereotyped southerners as rac-ist. Yet Bob Kennedy, as I had reason to know myself, could be warm and generous.[18] His undeniable antipathy to LBJ was an exception to his usual personality, or at least an exaggeration of it.

There is a story that on a visit to the Johnson ranch in November 1959 Robert Kennedy was taken out deer hunting. LBJ gave him, instead of a rifle, a heavy caliber shotgun that recoiled hard and cut his face, also denting his pride. LBJ is reported to have said: "Son, you've got to learn to handle a gun like a man."[19] Lady Bird Johnson may have been thinking of that incident when she recalled diplomatically that Robert Kennedy's visit to the LBJ ranch was "not the most successful, warm event of our life." "Bobby did not take to hunting," she said. The relationship, she admitted, was not simpatico—indeed, it was bristly.[20]

Whatever the reason for that early lack of rapport, the schism came out in public, and might have affected the course of history, at the 1960 Los Angeles Democratic National Convention. JFK and LBJ were the principal rivals for the presidential nomination and on July 13 Kennedy defeated Johnson by a much larger margin than the Johnson forces had expected: JFK 806, LBJ 409. (Stuart Symington of Missouri got 86 votes and Adlai Stevenson, candidate in 1952 and 1956 and darling of the liberals, in spite of a moving demonstration from the floor, got 79½ votes.) Lyndon Johnson resisted advice from Speaker Sam Rayburn and many others and refused to declare himself an announced candidate until a few days before the convention, which virtually guaranteed failure.

In the course of the campaign a number of Kennedy aides had seen the logic of a Kennedy/Johnson ticket. It would win Texas for the Democratic candidate, they calculated, and with any luck add a few other electoral college votes from the Deep South that would have been off-limits to Kennedy with any of the other leading candidates for vice president, such as senators Stuart Symington of Missouri, "Scoop" Jackson of Washington, or Governor Orville Freeman of Minnesota, all strongly supported by labor and without LBJ's contacts and reputation among southern politicians. Such thoughts faded in the course of the campaign, however, because of the desperate ferocity with which LBJ and the Johnson people attacked Jack Kennedy's father, his health, and his family's closeness to the disgraced Senator Joe McCarthy.

On July 4 LBJ's campaign manager, John Connally, and India Edwards, former head of the Democratic National Committee's women's section, called a press conference in which they took the gloves off. Edwards charged that JFK suffered from Addison's disease, a life-threatening dysfunction of the adrenal gland. Loud was the outrage from the Kennedy camp, which claimed that the candidate's problem was the result of shock and malaria incurred in war service, though Edwards's claim was perfectly true. LBJ himself went further. He attacked the founding father of the Kennedy clan himself. Joseph P. Kennedy, ambassador to London before World War II, had been distinctly sympathetic to those British conservatives led by Neville Chamberlain, the prime minister always portrayed by the cartoonists with an umbrella, who sought to appease Hitler. "I wasn't any Chamberlain-umbrella policy man," LBJ assured the Washington state delegation. "I never thought Hitler was right."[21] Robert Kennedy, for one, never forgot or forgave this slur on his father, though once again there was truth in the Johnson attack. Old Joe might not have thought Hitler was right, but he was certainly sympathetic to those who wanted to appease rather than fight him.

It was, it would seem, out of emotion rather than political calculation that Robert Kennedy did what he could to prevent LBJ becoming his brother's running mate in 1960. Bobby Baker has given a characteristically vulgar and graphic account of events early on the morning of the day after JFK's victory. Baker admits that his therapy for defeat was to get "independently and calculatedly drunk." At 7:00 a.m. he was woken by Bill Moyers pounding on the door of his hotel room at the Biltmore, insisting that he get dressed and hurry across the corridor to the Johnson suite. Jack Kennedy was on his way over and the Johnson flotilla was standing to battle stations. There was the candidate, looking glum. There was Lady Bird, a robe over her nightgown. Soon John Connally arrived, dapper as ever. The two senators disappeared into an inner room.[22]

What precisely was said has been a matter of dispute for half a century. LBJ recollected that JFK had said that he had consulted his father, the columnist Joe Alsop, and Phil Graham, publisher of the *Washington Post,* who was to commit suicide not long afterward. (It says something about the role of the media in politics at that date that JFK consulted a couple of journalists and no elected politician about so momentous a decision.) Actually, JFK was subjected to an impassioned plea for LBJ from Graham and Alsop on July 12, the Wednesday; it was late on the night of July 13 that his father urged him to take Johnson. All three argued, according to LBJ's version of what JFK told him, that no one could bring more to the ticket than he.[23]

Later that evening JFK was trapped in an elevator by that veteran

Democratic operator Tommy Corcoran, known by his old patron, FDR, as Tommy the Cork. "We've got to patch up this split between you and Lyndon," he said. "I don't blame you for hating him tonight but I'm talking politics." JFK said, "Stop kidding, Tommy, Johnson will turn me down."[24]

LBJ's staffers urged him to accept. He himself warned that his friends from Texas would not be pleased. In this he was correct: "Mr. Sam" Rayburn cited the much-quoted trope of Franklin Roosevelt's vice president, "Cactus Jack" Garner, that the office "was not worth a pitcher of warm piss," usually quoted in the bowdlerized form of a "pitcher of warm spit." Senator Kerr was even more forceful. He delivered a powerful open-handed slap to Bobby Baker and then, crying, "Get me my .38!" threatened to kill everyone in the suite, though it is not clear why the intended victims would supply the enraged senator with the murder weapon.[25]

Half an hour before Moyers woke Baker from his intoxicated sleep, another intimate scene was taking place, this one in Robert Kennedy's suite. He was in the bathtub: two Kennedy aides, Pierre Salinger, the San Francisco reporter who had become JFK's press officer on the campaign, and the Massachusetts loyalist Kenny O'Donnell, were counseling the candidate's brother through the bathroom door. "How many electoral votes are we going to get," Bob Kennedy mused from the steam, "if we capture the East, North East and the Solid South?"

"Are you talking about nominating Lyndon Johnson?" asked Salinger. "You're not going to do that?"

"Yes, we are," said Bobby in a matter-of-fact tone. O'Donnell, always the most inveterate Johnson hater in the whole Kennedy entourage, protested violently.

It was about 10:00 a.m. when JFK arrived back at his suite from the meeting with Johnson. "You just won't believe it," he told his brother. "He wants it."

"Oh my God," Bobby exclaimed. "Now what do we do?"[26]

This version, cited by Jeff Shesol, assumes that JFK's approach to LBJ that morning was in the nature of a feeler, and that is exactly the word Larry O'Brien used in an oral interview many years later to describe it. If that is what it was, one is reminded of Robert Kennedy's much later use of what was called "the Trollope ploy" when, during the Cuban missile crisis, he ignored an earlier rough letter from Khrushchev and replied to a more amenable later one. That device, the myth has it, the Kennedy brothers had learned from their reading of a Trollope novel in which a young woman accepts an earlier proposal, ignoring an earlier rejection.

This may, however, be a Robert Kennedy version of what his brother meant when he seemingly offered the vice presidency to Lyndon Johnson that morning. It was Bobby who told Arthur Schlesinger that LBJ wanted to be offered the nomination and JFK "never dreamed that there was a chance in the world that he would accept it."[27]

Still, there are other indications that Jack Kennedy—guided, as he was so often, by his father's counsel—really did want LBJ on the ticket. For one thing, outside Chasen's restaurant on the night of July 12 after a labor event (twenty-four hours before Joe Kennedy dispensed his paternal advice) in front of TV cameras and under klieg lights, Kennedy said as much. Massachusetts congressman and future Speaker of the House Thomas "Tip" O'Neill passed along a crucial signal: if Kennedy wanted Johnson, Tip said, Johnson would not turn him down. "Of course I want Lyndon Johnson," Kennedy said, apparently delighted. "The only thing is I would never want to offer it to him and have him turn me down. I would be terrifically embarrassed. He's the natural. If I can ever get him on the ticket, no way can we lose."[28]

Whatever JFK really intended, his brother Bob had no intention of letting Lyndon Johnson take the second place on the ticket if he could help it. Three times that day he went to the LBJ suite to see if he could in effect withdraw the offer that LBJ thought (or was determined to insist he thought) JFK had made him, or at least to persuade Johnson to withdraw of his own accord. His first argument was to suggest that his brother was in danger of losing control of the convention to a revolt on the part of organized labor and the liberals. To avoid that, would LBJ accept instead the chairmanship of the Democratic National Committee? Speaker Sam Rayburn and John Connally had been deployed as a screen to see what Bobby wanted to say to LBJ, who was closeted with his wife and Phil Graham in an inner room. Rayburn disposed of that suggestion summarily: "Shit," said the old gentleman. (I like to imagine him, a Texan, pronouncing the word with at least two syllables.) Phil

Graham was deputed to call JFK. When he got through he found the newly crowned candidate hesitant. JFK asked for a few minutes. When Graham called back, however, Jack Kennedy's mind seemed made up. "Tell Lyndon Johnson I want him," he said.[29]

In the meantime, Bob Kennedy was back in the LBJ suite, but he was not allowed to see Johnson. He tried to persuade John Connally that Walter Reuther and the other labor leaders had never forgiven Johnson for voting for the antilabor Taft-Hartley bill in 1947. So what about the DNC chair? If JFK had changed his mind, Connally said, he would have to call himself and ask LBJ to withdraw.

Kennedy did call, but it was to read a press release confirming the vice presidential offer.

LBJ asked only: "Do you really want me?"

"Yes," said Kennedy.

"Well," said Johnson, "if you really want me, I'll do it."

Bob Kennedy came to the LBJ suite a third time, at 4:00 p.m. Once again he tried to sell the DNC chairmanship as a position from which Johnson could prepare his own campaign for the presidency. Johnson declined and said (with tears in his eyes, according in Bob Kennedy's account of the meeting) that if JFK would have him, "I'll join him in making a fight for it."[30]

"Well then," Bob Kennedy said, in his own later account, "that's fine. He wants you as Vice President if you want to be Vice President."

At this point the Johnson entourage was looking for Robert Kennedy to iron out who would make the speeches seconding LBJ. Phil Graham called Jack Kennedy and said that Bobby was in the suite, trying to persuade LBJ to withdraw. "Oh, that's all right," said the candidate. "Bobby's been out of touch and doesn't know what's been happening."[31]

The other question, of course, is: Why did Lyndon Johnson want to be vice president? He knew what John Nance Garner and others had thought about it. He was to find the office frustrating, even humiliating. The answer is, of course, that he didn't want to be vice president. He wanted to be president, and he realized that his only realistic chance at the office would be to succeed on the death of an incumbent president. Once or twice he dropped his usual discretion to allow this calculation to be seen. On a bus on the way to JFK's inauguration he was open about it to Clare Boothe Luce, an old friend. "Clare," he said when she asked him directly why he wanted the office, "I looked it up: one out of every four presidents has died in office. I'm a gambling man, darling, and this is the only chance I got."[32]

When LBJ duly did become vice president, he imagined at first, as he explained excitedly to Bobby Baker, that he could keep his Senate office, known as the Taj Mahal for its size and splendor, and from there help President Kennedy pass his program.[33] He soon found that his idea of continuing to run the Senate from the executive branch was a non-starter. Even such a Johnson supporter as Senator Clinton Anderson of New Mexico knew that the vice president continuing to lead the Senate from an office on Capitol Hill would be an unconscionable breach of the constitutional separation of powers. The new leader, Mike Mansfield, might be a friend of LBJ's, but he had no intention of playing second fid-dle. Johnson's proposal was turned down by forty-six votes to seventeen. The vice president is said to have commented, vulgarly but not without wit, that he had learned the difference between a caucus and a cactus: on a cactus, all the pricks are on the outside.[34]

One of his motives for accepting second place on JFK's ticket may have been that, with his sensitivity to the mood of the Senate, he un-derstood better than his rivals that his glory days as majority leader, when the Senate Democrats did his will and no bill could go forward to passage without his approval, were already numbered. He understood that the Senate majority leader with a young and exciting president in the White House would be in a far weaker position than he had been when the congressional Democrats were confronted by an iconic but senescent Republican in Dwight Eisenhower.

Ensconced in an opulent Washington mansion formerly the home of the celebrated hostess Perle Mesta (the name of which the Johnsons changed from les Ormes to its English equivalent, the Elms), the John-sons could entertain on the grand scale. But politically Lyndon pined. JFK gave his vice president no power, recalled George Reedy, but merely "tossed him a few bones, one of which was outer space."[35]

It was a depressing time for LBJ. Not only was his role in the Ken-nedy administration undistinguished to the point of humiliation, his reputation was damaged by two scandals. One embarrassing connection, tenuous as it was, involved a good ol' Texas hustler called Billie Sol Estes. Estes was a West Texas businessman who had made millions from federal farm programs, accumulating acreage, mortgaging empty grain silos, and selling nonexistent fertilizer tanks to farmers. LBJ had lobbied the federal government on Estes's account, as he had done as senator for similar sagebrush entrepreneurs. Rumors circulated that Estes had given the Johnsons an airplane and that they were even partners in business ventures. There was no truth in that. Even more sinister, and even more farfetched, was the suggestion that LBJ and his aide Clifford Carter had hired a convicted murderer to kill an Agriculture Department official investigating the scandal.[36]

In truth, LBJ had little connection with Billie Sol Estes and his tangled affairs. But he could not deny a close relationship with Bobby Gene Baker, the self-styled wheeler-dealer on the Senate staff. He was so close to LBJ that he was known as "Little Lyndon," and he had children named Lyndon and Lynda. Baker, whose autobiography was accurately entitled *Wheeling and Dealing,* flattered LBJ by calling him "Leader," and the two exchanged gossip, political and sexual. Baker claimed, for example, that his Leader would summon him and ask with intense interest, "Is ol' Jack gettin' much pussy?"[37] (To which the truthful answer would have had to be: "He is.") There were even those who thought that LBJ saw Baker as the son he'd never had, though that role was far more plausibly claimed for less disreputable aides such as Bill Moyers and Harry McPherson.

It was not, however, LBJ who helped Baker to make his fortune but one of Johnson's Senate "whales," the Oklahoma oilman Senator Bob Kerr. Baker invested his ill-gotten gains in a motel at Ocean City, on the eastern shore of Maryland, and held court after hours at various Capitol Hill watering holes, notably the Quorum Club in the Carroll Arms hotel. After Baker was indicted for fraud and tax evasion, reporters made much of the club's nude painting and scarlet rugs. "I'm not saying," Baker admitted in his colorful memoirs, "that nobody ever left the Quorum Club to share a bed with a temporary partner," but all in all he maintained it was about as sinister as a People's Drugstore.[38] Baker, whose salary was never more than $20,000, made a couple of million dollars on paper thanks to Kerr's loans and patronage. He also acquired something of a reputation as a senatorial pimp. He seems to have introduced both Jack Kennedy and Lyndon Johnson to Ellen Rometsch, the attractive German wife of a Bundeswehr sergeant assigned to the Washington embassy, who slept with both men and had also shared her favors with an attaché at the Soviet embassy.[39] President Kennedy was acutely aware of the contemporary "Profumo affair" in London, which as noted earlier centered on an affair between British defense minister John Profumo and one Christine Keeler, who had likewise had an affair with a Soviet diplomat. Poor Ellen Rometsch was frog-marched out of the country on the express orders of Robert Kennedy.[40]

By the summer of 1963, in short, Jack Kennedy might still calculate that he needed LBJ on the ticket in 1964, but Johnson's image and political reputation were visibly tarnished. Johnson, for his part, with his almost pathologically sensitive political antennae, could sense that his star was declining. He feared, and admitted to intimates that he feared, that Kennedy was planning to drop him from the ticket, even though the evidence suggests that this was not the case. A case in point is a memorandum dated October 2, 1962, that survives in the Kennedy Library. Dean Rusk had passed on to the White House aide Irish mafioso Ralph Dungan that the vice president wanted to make six defensive points about the recent Ole Miss crisis. (LBJ had initially asked not to be consulted about Mississippi, but when both the president and his brother the attorney general conferred with him nevertheless, he had appreciated it.) The situation in Mississippi had been handled better than he could have dealt with it. He had been better treated than any vice president in history, and he knew it. Neither he nor his staff had discussed the Ole Miss riot with newsmen, and he was distressed at reports that indicated he was dissatisfied with how the riot had been handled. Even as early as 1962, that is, LBJ was keen to scotch any rumors of disloyalty.[41]

Matters came to a head, at least in LBJ's mind, over rumors that he was losing control over his own home state of Texas. After all, his ability to deliver that state's twenty-five electoral votes,[42] taken together with the possibility that he would attract further electoral votes elsewhere in the South, was the principal reason he had been put on the ticket in the first place. The reason people were muttering that LBJ was losing control of Texas had to do with the feud between two of the most influential politicians in the state, the incumbent governor, John Connally, and liberal progressive politician Ralph Yarborough. Connally, a former close aide and protégé of LBJ, was the favorite of wealthy Texans, especially of the oil and gas interests, who judged political leaders to a remarkable extent by their willingness to fight tooth and nail for the oil industry's 27.5 percent depletion allowance. Connally was not only reliable on this issue, he went on to become a Republican and indeed secretary of the treasury in the Nixon administration. Yarborough, on the contrary, the darling of organized labor in Texas, was anathema to conservatives in the Lone Star State and—if truth be told—to LBJ too.

In the summer of 1963, therefore, LBJ hit upon a plan to bolster his waning reputation in the state and in the process shore up his value to JFK. The idea was that the president should make a trip to Texas, visiting all four of its major urban centers: Fort Worth, Dallas, San Antonio, and Houston. That would demonstrate to both Texas and the national media the love in which the vice president was held in his native state and Texas's loyalty to the Democratic cause.

Texas was in a strange mood in those years. The rising din of the civil rights struggle annoyed many Texans, and the state's conservatives, especially businessmen, were beginning to shake off the hereditary bonds of their Democratic loyalty. Within a few years, indeed, few of them would remain Democrats. A number of incidents had convinced the northern and national news media and their readers, listeners, and viewers that Texas was a wild and woolly place, full of violent extremists. A Mink Coat Mob, as one Dallas paper called it, led by the conservative congressman Bruce Alger, even attacked LBJ and Lady Bird during the 1960 campaign with placards reading "LBJ Sold Out to Yankee Socialists" and "Beat Judas." In October 1963, Adlai Stevenson was attacked and spat upon by conservatives when he went to Dallas to give a speech on behalf of the United Nations.

The president was irritated by the prospect of a trip to Texas, but it was finally decided in early June. John Connally was keen to avoid being too closely identified with the Kennedy administration, in which he had served as secretary of the navy before running for governor, because he knew how unpopular it was with his powerful backers in the oil and gas industry and among newspaper publishers like Edward Dealey of the *Dallas Morning News.* But he was trapped by JFK and LBJ into agreeing.

LBJ really was losing influence in Texas. He was at odds both with

Yarborough, whose labor backers and liberal coloration were a bit too vivid for Johnson's more conservative friends, and also with John Connally, who was already drifting toward the Republican Party. Kennedy himself was at best lukewarm about a Texas trip, and some of his staff, notably Kenneth O'Donnell, were infuriated by LBJ's importunity in demanding it. LBJ, on the other hand, needed to get the president into Texas. He also saw an opportunity to embarrass Yarborough into showing a minimum of loyalty. It is even reported that Johnson was so scared that he would be dumped from the ticket that he was seriously considering standing down and taking a job as the president of his alma mater, the Southwest Texas State Teachers College at San Marcos.[43] To a man of Johnson's pride, far better to end your own political career than to have anyone else end it. Fate, however, was to deal him a different hand before the time came when he would finally obey that rule of conduct.

Robert Kennedy learned of his brother's death while lunching by the pool of his house, Hickory Hill, on the Virginia side of the Potomac, upriver from the capital. The pool was famous for the high-spirited horseplay of the inner circle of the New Frontier. Not a few men of political eminence had been pitched into its waters. Now Robert Kennedy was having lunch there with his wife, Ethel, the U.S. attorney for the Southern District of New York, Robert Morgenthau, and an assistant; they were lunch-hour refugees from a big conference at the Justice Department on the fight against organized crime.[44] At 1:45 p.m. the party was finishing clam chowder and tuna sandwiches and the attorney general and his colleagues were about to leave to go back into town when the white phone by the pool rang. It was a White House phone, extension 163 of the White House number RE7-1414. (There were four White House extensions at Hickory Hill alone.) Ethel Kennedy answered. "This is urgent," said the White House operator. The caller was the legendary director of the FBI, J. Edgar Hoover. She handed the phone to her husband.

"I have news for you," said the director. "The president's been shot."

Kennedy asked if it was serious.

"I think it's serious," said Hoover. "I am endeavoring to get details." He promised to call back when he knew more.

Robert Kennedy started back toward his wife and his guests. For the first and last time in the day, he allowed his horror to show. "Jack's been shot," he said.

Soon phones were ringing and the attorney general was answering them, bringing the government together to face this unimaginable catastrophe. John McCone, the director of Central Intelligence whose Langley headquarters was just down the road from the attorney general's house, came over. Kennedy called his brother-in-law, Sargent Shriver, former manager of the family's vast Chicago company, Merchandise Mart, and his close friend Robert McNamara, the secretary of defense, several times, asking for information and also for helicopters. At one time he was heard to mutter, "There's been so much hate!" The implication was that his brother had been killed by ideological enemies, presumably on the Right, and he was by no means alone in jumping to that conclusion that day.

Kennedy drove back into town with his press secretary, Ed Guthman. They went to the Pentagon and on the way up to the E Ring, where the secretary's office was, he said to Guthman, "People don't realize how conservative Lyndon really is."[45] It was his first reference to the man who, only hours earlier, had become president of the United States. The remark might seem to contradict the implications of his remark about "hate." It also revealed how little Robert Kennedy understood a man whom he already disliked intensely.

Air Force One was due at Andrews at 6:05 in the evening. At 4:30 Shriver warned his brother-in-law that "everybody"—White House staff, family friends, congressional leaders, cabinet officers—was going out to Andrews. Kennedy's instinct was that they should be prevented. Only he and his two closest friends in the upper reaches of the government, Defense Secretary McNamara and General Maxwell D. Taylor, should meet the plane carrying his brother's body. Arthur Goldberg, the former secretary of labor appointed Supreme Court justice by JFK, dissuaded him. The diplomatic corps would be there, he pointed out. "How will it look if only foreigners are there—no Americans." That argument, according to William Manchester's narrative, was decisive.

Robert Kennedy and his two friends McNamara and Taylor went out to Andrews by helicopter. Kennedy was determined to be the first to comfort his sister-in-law. Not wanting to be filmed by the prowling television cameramen, he vaulted into the back of an air force truck and hid there until Air Force One taxied to a halt. While the attention of the gathering crowd was focused on the huge yellow lift that was lowering the coffin from the back door of the plane, mobile steps were being wheeled into place at the front door.

Almost before the steps had stopped moving, Robert Kennedy dashed up them and into the plane. He arrived so suddenly that some of those who had flown from Dallas were surprised, thinking he must have been with them all the time, unnoticed. The big figure of the new president blocked his way. Kennedy brushed passed him, ignoring his outstretched hand. There were fifteen people in the narrow corridor, and it seemed to some observers, including the new president himself, that he was the least among them. "Where's Jackie?" was all Kennedy said. "I want to see Jackie."

In normal circumstances, Lyndon Johnson would have been the last person in the world to allow himself to be shunted aside in such a way and at such a moment. A day later, after his first cabinet meeting, he complained to one of its members that he had "real problems with the [Kennedy] family." But, "What can I do?" he said. "I don't want to get into a fight with the family and the aura of Kennedy is important to all of us."[46]

The tension between the Kennedy loyalists and the Johnsons and their staff that day did not end on Air Force One. On the contrary, as Jeff Shesol, the historian of the feud between LBJ and Robert Kennedy, has carefully shown, from the moment of the assassination, a whole series of incidents had racked up the tension. "There were four or five matters," Bob Kennedy admitted later, "that made me bitter, unhappy at least, with Lyndon Johnson."[47]

In fact, there were at least six "matters," according to a formal memorandum drawn up by one of the new president's aides, probably Bill Moyers, the one with the best relations with the Kennedy people.

3.30 p.m. Wednesday, November 27
Memorandum of Conversation.
There are several points of misunderstanding that should be

cleared up between the Attorney General and the President. Everyone's interest is involved—the President's and Bobby's, the Party's, the country's.

Here are the points about which there is misunderstanding, rumor, gossip, all of which has reached Bobby and the family. (1) The question of the plane's departure. Is it true that LBJ said the plane could not take off until he was sworn in? Did Johnson hold up the departure? Why?

(2) What was the cause of the argument with [air force aide] Godfrey McHugh? Did the President curse him?

(3) There is supposed to be something the President said about wanting to move into the White House office right away. Is it true that the President or someone on his staff had [JFK's] furniture moved?

(4) The Attorney General has heard the rumor that the President has said he is going to move into the White House right away.

(5) The question of the National Cultural Center. Steve Smith called Bobby and said the President would not send up a bill which also asked for money. The family feels that it is kind of an empty gesture to change the name [to the Kennedy Center] without asking the money to make it tangible. . . .

(6) The Attorney General has the feeling that the President does not deal directly. The only way to deal with Bobby is directly. The arts of the Hill are not his arts. You have to be straight forward, matter-of-fact, tough, determined, open.[48]

As this remarkable document is headed "Memorandum of Conversation," it reads like a report by Moyers or whoever wrote it of a conversation with Bob Kennedy himself or conceivably with another member of the family or a close, unreconciled aide such as Kenny O'Donnell.

Some of the matters raised have more substance than others. The question of why Air Force One did not leave Love Field in Dallas until LBJ had been sworn in as president caused much anger. General McHugh, JFK's air force aide, was an excitable man who felt an intense loyalty to the Kennedys in general and especially to Jackie Kennedy,

whom he had dated before she married JFK. He ordered the captain of
Air Force One, Colonel James Swindal, to take off. Swindal hesitated.
McHugh said, "Mrs Kennedy and Kenny O'Donnell want it." "General,"
said Malcolm Kilduff, the acting press secretary in the absence of Pierre
Salinger, who was with five cabinet secretaries on the plane to Tokyo,
"they're not in charge any more."[49]

O'Donnell, in his passionate conviction that LBJ was a usurper,
seems to have thought that the Johnsons had no business on Air Force
One; they should have flown to Washington on Air Force Two, the vice
presidential plane that had flown them to Texas. "There was a feeling,"
said the columnist Stewart Alsop of the Kennedy aide, whom he knew
well, "that LBJ was the usurper, that he was a Macbeth."[50]

The reason Johnson held up the plane was precisely that he was
afraid that other people besides O'Donnell might think of him as
a usurper. He wanted to be sworn in as president before he left Dallas, and he sent for a federal judge who was a supporter of his, Judge
Sarah Hughes, to perform the brief ceremony. Unfortunately, he gave
O'Donnell and the other irreconcilables the impression that he had
asked Bobby Kennedy's permission, which he had not. (He *had* contacted Bobby's deputy, Nick Katzenbach, who had checked with a constitutional expert at the Justice Department and prescribed the forms
for the oath.)

There was an unfortunate incident when Jackie Kennedy went to
her stateroom on Air Force One to tidy her hair and found LBJ sitting
on the bed, dictating to a pretty secretary, Marie Fehmer.[51]

Great offense was caused by a series of misunderstandings about
the Oval Office. Robert Kennedy arrived there at 9:00 a.m. on November 24 to find President Kennedy's devoted secretary, Evelyn Lincoln,
in tears. She said that LBJ had told her that he had a meeting at 9:30
and "would like you to clear your things out of your office so that my
own girls can come in." McGeorge Bundy was able to clear that up. LBJ
gave Mrs. Lincoln until noon, and she was out well before that. Further
offense was taken because JFK's famous and much-celebrated rocking
chair was upside down in a hallway: the reason was not a studied in-
sult from the boorish Texans, as Robert Kennedy and Kenny O'Donnell seem to have assumed, but the fact that the whole office had been

redecorated during the ill-fated Texas trip. And so on. The impression was given that the Johnsons wanted to move immediately into the White House residence, as opposed to the West Wing offices, when in fact they discreetly planned to stay at the Elms for some time.

Deliberately or not, Robert Kennedy arrived at LBJ's first cabinet meeting five minutes after the meeting had started. Mac Bundy had to "virtually drag" him into the meeting.[52] There was another pointless argument about when LBJ should make his address to the two houses of Congress.

No doubt much of the resentment and bad temper on the part of JFK's loyalists sprang from ancient, unexamined prejudices against Texas and the South. In the case of O'Donnell and O'Brien, this was understandably exacerbated by the absurd intervention of Dr. Earl Rose, the Dallas County medical examiner, who took it upon himself to insist that under Texas statutes the dead president's body could not be removed from the state until an autopsy had been performed. There was a hideously painful standoff at a funeral home until the Kennedy aides, in a flying wedge, removed the presidential coffin.[53] To the bereaved Irishmen, this official seemed to be turning a tragedy into a reprise of a century of states' rights issues. Understandably, O'Donnell and the others, who had lost a leader and a friend, were outraged, and strong language was used.

Other Kennedy partisans, left behind in Washington, instantly and instinctively blamed Texas and Texans for the assassination. When the news reached Washington, a number of "New Frontiersmen" gathered in the offices of Ralph Dungan, near the Oval Office. Hubert Humphrey, liberal senator from Minnesota, burst into the room in tears. "What have they done to us?" he cried, and those who heard him took it for granted that "they" were the Texans, as Daniel Patrick Moynihan, one of those present, reported.[54]

Another revealing episode was what became known as "the Harvard lunch." The day after the assassination, Arthur Schlesinger and his wife, Marian, J. K. Galbraith and his wife, Kitty, JFK's friend the artist William Walton and his son, Professor and Mrs. Samuel Beer of Harvard, Richard Goodwin, Paul Samuelson of MIT, and the Minnesotan Walter Heller had lunch in a private room at the Occidental Grill, a

block from the White House.[55] The meeting was more about mourn-
ing than conspiracy, but Ken Galbraith recorded later in his diary that
Schlesinger "was dwelling on the possibility of a ticket in 1964 headed by
Bob Kennedy and Hubert Humphrey."[56]

This was one of a number of incidents that brought out in LBJ a
paranoia that at least matched the troubled spirits of Robert Kennedy
and the Irish mafia. The new president was not merely nettled by what
he imagined was the contempt of "the high-falutin' Harvards," he was
for a time seriously afraid that there might be a move, led by Robert
Kennedy, to deny the legitimacy of his succession. "During all that period," he told an interviewer years later, "I think [Bobby] seriously considered whether he would let me be president."[57]

In the summer of 1964, when LBJ's personal feud with Bob Kennedy came to a head over the question of who would be his vice presidential running mate, Johnson's suspicion and resentment were scarcely
concealed. At a famous interview, he virtually taunted the younger Kennedy, having invented a principle that no member of his cabinet should
be on the ticket—a transparent device for excluding Kennedy.[58]

In the immediate aftermath of the assassination, however, whatever his private doubts and resentments, LBJ exhibited admirable restraint. He knew that many of the men and women he would have to
work with did not like him and did not trust him. He understood very
clearly that for a year he must present himself as the successor whose
duty was to fulfill John Kennedy's legacy: once he was elected in his own
right, he also understood, he would be free to choose his own path and
build his own reputation.

With that goal clear in his mind, he ignored, or pretended to ignore,
the suspicion and the snubs. He invited each one of Kennedy's team of
cabinet officers and White House staff advisers to stay on and work with
him to safeguard the Kennedy program.[59] To the amusement of some,
he used the same formula with almost everyone: "I need you," he would
say, his eyes boring into theirs, "more than he did."[60] For some, it was too
much to ask. O'Donnell stayed on until 1965. Arthur Schlesinger handed
in his resignation on the day of JFK's funeral. LBJ refused to accept it,
but Schlesinger resigned again on January 27, 1964, and this time it was

accepted by noon the following day. LBJ went out of his way to be gentle and thoughtful, even in a gauche way flirtatious, with Jackie Kennedy.

For others, even some of those who in their different ways had been closest to Jack Kennedy—Larry O'Brien, Ted Sorensen, Bob McNamara, and Mac Bundy, for example—there was a more or less grudging admiration of Lyndon Johnson's sheer energy, expertise, and strength.

Continuity was the keynote of his address to the joint session of Congress. He began by saying, "All I have I would have given gladly not to be standing here today," and he stressed his commitment to one after another of JFK's programs and achievements. In his 1961 inaugural address, he recalled, John Kennedy had said "Let us begin": "Today in this moment of new resolve, I would say to all my fellow Americans, let us continue." He ended in a powerful sentimental flourish with the hope that Americans would be "one people in our hour of sorrow," and on this eve of Thanksgiving he quoted "familiar and cherished words":

America, America,
God shed His grace on thee,
And crown thy good
With brotherhood
From sea to shining sea.[61]

It might have been corny, even "cornpone," to use the Kennedy people's favorite term for what they thought of as the Texas style. But at the time, as I felt when I watched it, it worked. I noticed, too, as did the political nation in Washington and many across the country, not least African American viewers, that before his sentimental peroration he was more specific, and more political, than that. No memorial or eulogy, he pointedly said, could more eloquently honor President Kennedy's memory than the earliest possible passage of the civil rights bill for which he had fought so long, and to which—LBJ might truthfully have reminded a more private audience—President Kennedy had assigned a much lower priority than he, Lyndon Johnson, did.

Second, he insisted to the professional watchers on Capitol Hill and on Wall Street, no act could more fittingly continue Kennedy's work than early passage of his tax bill. With crisp, specific commitment he touched other personal bases: education, youth unemployment, foreign aid.[62] Neither the professional audience in Washington nor the millions gathered at home to mourn their dead president and to celebrate Thanksgiving could be in any doubt. Lyndon Johnson meant to be a strong and vigorous president, one who would not abandon his predecessor's legacy, and one who was determined to go beyond it if he could.

Part Two
The Actions

F · O · U · R

Rumors of War, Rumors of Peace

We're eyeball to eyeball, and I think the other fellow just blinked.

—*Dean Rusk, whispered aside during the Cuban missile crisis*

W
hile Lyndon Johnson languished unhappily in the vice presidency, his victorious rival "ascended unto the heaven of brightness."[1]

Jack Kennedy was a foreign policy president. He had perhaps been more interested, as a senator, in foreign policy than in domestic affairs. While he devoted the requisite amount of time to the home front in his 1960 campaign, it always seemed to be for him merely a necessary chore. The business of getting elected was so much more exciting than the humdrum stuff of domestic politics. His brilliant inaugural address was almost exclusively developed to the role of the United States in a world divided by cold war, and it was on the world stage that he dreamed of placarding a great reputation.

It has to be said that the venture did not start well.

On November 18, 1960, less than two weeks after his electoral success, the victorious candidate took time out from the pleasures of triumph and the organization of the transition to power to be briefed at the poolside of his father's house in Palm Beach by Allen Dulles and Richard Bissell of the CIA. The plans they presented to get rid of Fidel Castro before he could contaminate the Caribbean with Communism were already more than six months old. Other anti-Castro plots verged on fantasy: Jack and Jackie had heard whispers at a dinner party at their own home (one, appropriately, where Ian Fleming, the creator of James

Bond, was present)[2] of plans to make Fidel's beard fall out by putting thallium in his boots. In machismo-conscious Cuba, the theory was, the dictator would lose his charisma along with his whiskers. There were other equally adolescent ideas floating around: to shoot down Fidel's plane, to hire the Mafia to set up a hit.

Jack Kennedy had moved a long way from his father's politics. But in one respect he had not moved as far as his liberal admirers assumed. He remained an instinctive and committed anti-Communist in the simple sense that he expressed in a talk to the New York Young Democrats when he was first running for Congress. He had been asked, he recounted, how he felt about Soviet Russia. It was, he replied, "a slave state of the worst sort. I told them that Soviet Russia is embarked upon a program of world aggression. I told them that the freedom-loving countries of the world must stop Soviet aggression now, or be destroyed."[3] This, and more to the same purpose, came from the heart. Later, he was to display subtlety and restraint in his policies toward the Soviet Union. But his attitude to that country as such changed perhaps much less than his admirers have assumed.

Liberals, in the United States and elsewhere, came to assume that he was one of theirs. He did have an intelligent and generous empathy even toward those with whom he had no agreement. He also understood how dangerous was confrontation with the Soviet Union and grasped that nuclear war was unthinkable. None of this shook the conviction he had formed for himself as a young man touring Europe on the brink of World War II: the Soviet Union was an implacable enemy, controlled by unscrupulous rulers, a terrible place where life was incomparably worse than in the United States.

By March 11, less than two months after his inauguration, JFK was briefed again by Bissell at a formal White House meeting on the latest plans: to land 750 Cuban exiles on the south coast of Cuba. The *New York Times* had already reported they were being trained, supposedly in darkest secrecy, in Guatemala, The idea was to trigger an uprising against Castro. The very day after the White House meeting, the colonel the CIA had put in charge of the plans moved the landing beach to a site so far from the Escambray Mountains (where Fidel had launched his own successful coup) that an uprising was impossible. The president commented on the agency's plans that they "sounded like D-day," only he wanted "less noise."[4]

On April 17, when the landing went ahead, everything went very wrong. One of their four landing ships was sunk by a Cuban fighter-bomber. There was no air cover until it was too late. The exiles of "Brigade 2506" fought bravely and overwhelmed the first wave of militia defenders, killing more than one hundred of them. But they had no hope once the Cuban regulars arrived with Soviet weapons, commanded by Fidel in person. About twelve hundred of them were captured. More than thirty were executed out of hand, the rest sentenced to thirty years in prison.

President Kennedy was humiliated, ashamed, and furious. The night the news came through that the invasion had been a disaster, the president and his wife had scheduled a grand reception for members of Congress and their wives. When the Kennedys appeared, the Marine Band struck up "Mr. Wonderful." The host was at his gracious best, putting the bravest of faces on his sorrow and shame. He felt anything but wonderful. At 4:00 in the morning, in white tie and tails, he broke off a conversation and walked out into the White House rose garden, unable to conceal his emotions.[5] His response, so far as it can be pieced together, was complex. He, who had been brought up to win, was humiliated by defeat. He was ashamed of having allowed hundreds of brave young men to be lured into a trap where many were killed, others made prisoners, in part because he had deprived them of air cover out of a dishonest wish to have the prize of their victory without taking the political risk of supporting them. He and his brother Robert were determined to rescue as many as possible of the Cuban prisoners, and they did rescue hundreds of them. He was furious with the CIA, with the military, and above all with himself.

His confidence both in the CIA and in the military, "the brass," as he called his commanders, was more or less permanently shaken. In public, he insisted that in a presidential system of government the responsibility was his alone. In private, however, he shouted about his generals and admirals: "Those sons-of-bitches with all the fruit salad [medal ribbons] just sat there nodding. . . . I've got to do something about those CIA bastards."[6] And he insisted that after an interval Allen W. Dulles, director of Central Intelligence, and Richard Bissell must go. He is credibly reported to have said that he wanted to "splinter the CIA in a thousand pieces and scatter it to the winds."[7]

He and Robert, who took the Bay of Pigs disaster very personally indeed, did negotiate the release of most of the captured Cuban exiles through the good offices of a New York lawyer, James B. Donovan. The attorney general, who had no official role in this fiasco, nonetheless took a lively interest in Operation Mongoose, including renewed plans to murder Castro. The shadow of Cuba hung over the Kennedy enterprise to the end. Perhaps it even led to his death. Although both the Warren Commission in 1964 and the House Select Committee on Assassinations in 1979 rejected them, among the myriad conspiracy theories that claim to explain Kennedy's assassination, most involve Cuba. Some argue that Fidel Castro, aware of the U.S. government's secret plans to assassinate him, organized Kennedy's death. Some blame not the Cuban government but émigré Cuban groups, either pro- or anti-Castro. Others are impressed by the numerous links between the assassination and the Mafia, especially the "family" led by Carlos Marcelo, the New Orleans Mafia don. Others again emphasize Lee Harvey Oswald's connections with Cuba.

In any case, the Kennedy brothers never gave up their dream of avenging their defeat at Castro's hands. Like the ancient Roman who ended every speech with the demand that Carthage must be destroyed,[8] Jack and Bob Kennedy's secret motto was: Castro must go.[9] For many years, more or less chimerical schemes for killing him were pursued within the U.S. government.

Like the Bay of Pigs, the second stage in JFK's career as a world statesman could also have begun better. He was eager to get involved in what he saw as the most important task of his presidency: the central confrontation with the Soviet Union and its tough leader. He must engage personally with his opponent, the general secretary of the Communist Party of the Soviet Union. Nikita Khrushchev was a former metalworker. He won his spurs as a political commissar linking the generals with Stalin in the epic battles with the Wehrmacht, including the siege of Stalingrad and the great tank battle of Kursk.

Kennedy was afraid that Khrushchev would think him naïve and weak, and that is in fact exactly what the Soviet leader and his advisers did think. No doubt they fell for the Left's illusion that aristocrats cannot be tough. So Kennedy set in motion plans for a summit meeting with Khrushchev, and at the same time put himself into training with intensive briefings from Charles "Chip" Bohlen and other senior American experts on the Soviet Union. Meanwhile, Khrushchev got ready to bounce him.

The meeting was set for June 3 and 4 in Vienna. Kennedy traveled by way of Paris, where General de Gaulle was said, by the Kennedy claque, to have been impressed by Jacqueline Kennedy's French, an unlikely thought. Jack himself got off one of his self-deprecating quips, saying he was the man who had accompanied Jacqueline Kennedy to Paris.

Vienna was a sterner test. On the second day, Khrushchev went for the young American president's metaphorical jugular. He threatened to sign a German peace treaty that would formalize the division of Germany and end American rights in Berlin. He mocked American pretensions to world leadership, contemptuously contrasting the 350,000 U.S. casualties in World War II with 20 million Soviet dead. He stopped only just short of threatening nuclear war.

Kennedy, too, had intended to take a hard line on the issue of nuclear tests. He was taken aback not only by the Soviet leader's aggressiveness but also by his grasp of world affairs and the ruthless confidence with which he marshaled his arguments. Shaken, Kennedy could only end the meeting by quipping darkly that it would be a cold winter.

On the way home, the Kennedys were scheduled to stop over in London. There was to be a party to christen Jackie's newborn niece, daughter of Princess Lee Radziwill, and the Kennedys were to be guests at the prime minister's residence, Number 10 Downing Street. Prime minister Harold Macmillan had almost literally avuncular relations with JFK: his wife, Dorothy, was the aunt of Billy Hartington,[10] husband of the president's late sister Kick. Jack Kennedy was so visibly shattered by the bruising from Khrushchev that Uncle Harold took one look at the younger man, canceled a formal dinner, and sent him upstairs with a stiff scotch. Later, and revealingly, Jack passed off the experience of negotiating with Khrushchev to his brother Bob with a family reference: "It was like dealing with Dad—all take and no give!"[11]

Vienna was not just an isolated shock. It was the beginning of one of the two or three most acute crises of the cold war, a prolonged and in some respects obscure wrestling match from which Jack Kennedy emerged in the end not only with restored credibility but with success of a kind.[12]

Within a few days Khrushchev published a truculent aide-mémoire demanding a settlement of the Berlin situation within six months. He followed that by threatening to test a fifty-megaton bomb and by saying at a Kremlin meeting celebrating the defeat of Nazi Germany that while the peace treaty was needed for peaceful reasons, the "correlation of forces" in the world had changed. It was a bluff. Khrushchev knew that the United States was decisively stronger than the Soviet Union, militarily and economically.[13]

Yet to call that bluff would take nerve and skill. There were places where Khrushchev held the stronger hand, and one such place was Berlin. Kennedy began by responding with a press conference in which he said it was "of the greatest importance that the American people understand the basic issues involved and the threats to peace and security of Europe and of ourselves posed by the Soviet announcement that they intend to change unilaterally the existing arrangements for Berlin."[14]

By early July the cold winter seemed to have arrived early. Khrushchev announced that he was increasing the Soviet defense budget by one-third. He pointedly reminded the British ambassador that it would only take six atomic bombs to wipe out the United Kingdom.[15]

On July 25, after weeks of confabulations with his advisers, Kennedy countered with a firm speech in which he said that the United States could not and would not allow the Communists to "drive us out of Berlin."[16] Already Kennedy, wary of the "brass," both military and civilian, had decided to make use of a form of collegial leadership that would be highly praised for its handling of the Cuban missile crisis, less admired for its performance in Southeast Asia.

The urbane New York lawyer John McCloy, Kennedy's special adviser on disarmament[17] (often nicknamed "the chairman of the foreign policy establishment"), spent four days with Khrushchev in the last days of July at the Black Sea resort Sochi (forty-four years later home to the Winter Olympics), where the Caucasus Mountains run down to the sea. Although there was a minor explosion from the Soviet leader when he read Kennedy's speech, diplomatic historians believe this was the moment when Khrushchev realized that Kennedy had raised the stakes to a level he could not match. That argument was rammed down his throat in October by McNamara's deputy at the Pentagon, Roswell Gilpatric, who coolly enumerated the strength of U.S. nuclear forces, revealing their overwhelming superiority, especially in strategic weapons.[18] So much for the imaginary "missile gap" that JFK had used to get elected.

Second, Khrushchev realized that the German Democratic Republic was hemorrhaging educated and skilled workers through West Berlin at a rate neither Moscow's puppet East German state nor the Soviet Union itself could afford. That was the immediate motive behind the East German government's sudden decision to raise the stakes by building the Berlin Wall: to keep its own people in.[19]

Five days after the Wall went up, Lyndon Johnson played a walk-on part in Kennedy's campaign to meet Khrushchev's threats of force with demonstrations of America strength. He traveled to West Berlin to hand its determined mayor, Willy Brandt, a letter in which Kennedy said he was convinced that the best answer to Soviet pressure was to send another sixteen hundred American soldiers up the autobahn to the beleaguered city.

Behind the scenes that autumn, largely unnoticed by Western publics, another power game was being played, this one between Khrushchev and China. The Chinese leaders suspected Khrushchev, not altogether wrongly, of seeking an accommodation with the United States. The dispute played out in part through proxies in Eastern Europe. The Chinese upheld Albania's Enver Hoxha as the exemplar of Communist orthodoxy. They accused the Soviet Union of tolerating the Yugoslav leader Tito's more liberal version of Marxist ideology. A meeting of the Soviet presidium was scheduled for October, followed by the Soviet party's XXII Congress. So while Soviet diplomacy alternated between a front of aggressive intransigence and the search for some accommodation with the United States, the Chinese attacked Khrushchev as a traitor to Communist dogma. Chinese number two Chou En-lai, now emerging as Mao's effective successor, actually appeared in Moscow for the Party Congress and bitterly denounced Khrushchev.

At first Khrushchev seemed to be upping the ante. On August 30 he announced that the Soviet Union would begin immediate nuclear tests, and the very next day he proclaimed the testing of an enormous fifty-megaton bomb: he also put it about that the Soviet Union possessed an even more monstrous hundred-megaton weapon.

Yet in the first week of September a complex series of events took place that substantially changed the whole pattern of the cold war. On the one hand, Khrushchev responded to Chinese accusations that he was betraying socialist solidarity by seeking an accommodation with the United States. On the other, in relatively subtle ways for such a blunt-seeming man, he did just what he was accused of. For the fact is that Khrushchev, at Vienna and in his subsequent efforts to force a diplomatic victory over Berlin, was bluffing. And Jack Kennedy, refusing to accept that there was no alternative between humiliating defeat or nuclear cataclysm, coolly and astutely called his bluff.

Events moved fast. On September 3 Kennedy and Macmillan called on Khrushchev to stop all atmospheric tests.[20] The next day Khrushchev won a victory in the presidium, which accepted both Cuba and Yugoslavia as members of the "socialist camp." By the end of the week, Khrushchev had been authorized to meet Kennedy again and to step back from his implied threat to test the hundred-megaton bomb.

There was a brief confrontation between American and Soviet troops on the autobahn, but the Berlin crisis was over. Khrushchev summoned C. L. Sulzberger, a member of the family that owns the *New York Times*, and they met on September 5. In spite of the journalist's efforts to be sure he had grasped the Soviet leader's meaning, Khrushchev called him back a couple of days later to transmit some reservations or corrections. Sulzberger filed a number of columns. The gist was summed up in the phrase that Khrushchev "would not be loath to establishing some form of contact . . . to reach a settlement." Or, as a Soviet official involved in the talks put it later to Kennedy's press secretary, Pierre Salinger, "The storm in Berlin is over."[21]

Not quite over, however. There was a second intensification of the crisis. Khrushchev was in difficulties not only with the West, but also with the "antiparty group" of old-timers, including Vyacheslav Molotov, Georgi Malenkov, and Lazar Kaganovich, who had tried to overthrow him in 1957, and with the Chinese. These three pressures came together at the Twenty-third Congress of the Soviet Communist Party, a formal event to which not only hundreds of Soviet officials but also representatives of other Communist parties from around the world had been invited.

On the opening day of the Party Congress, Khrushchev made a six-hour speech in which he lifted his ultimatum on a German peace treaty but insulted the Chinese by attacking the Albanian party, an unmistakable proxy for China. Chou En-lai was so furious he refused to shake Khrushchev's hand. He proclaimed that the United States was "the common enemy of the peoples of the world." He personally reproved Khrushchev for "openly exposing disputes between fraternal parties," and in case anyone had missed his point he laid a wreath on Stalin's grave and left early for Beijing. The breach was not total: in spite of the bitterness, minimum courtesies were observed. But attacks on the "antiparty group" by Khrushchev himself and his chief ideologue, Frol Kozlov, had infuriated Chou and seriously damaged Sino-Soviet relations.[22]

The arm wrestling between Communist hawks and doves continued in Moscow in the curiously stilted style in which all Communist factions liked to clothe their murderous disputes. The outwardly urbane Chinese prime minister, Chou En-lai, led the faction calling for strict Marxist interpretation. Some diplomatic historians believe that Chou had lost his case by early September. But because of the Congress, it was not until late October that the victory of Khrushchev's "line" became clear.

Halfway through the Congress, on October 21, Robert McNamara's deputy at the Pentagon, Roswell Gilpatric, who was close to the Kennedys socially, finally disposed of the "missile gap" by opening the cupboard and revealing to the world just how superior the United States was, both in its stockpile of nuclear weapons and in the means for delivering them.

Kennedy had called Khrushchev's bluff, all right. But he had planted two poisonous seeds. Khrushchev would have to find a way of getting his own back. And his failure to press home his advantage over Berlin would lead to his overthrow and his eventual replacement by the more aggressive Brezhnev.

After his hesitant, even panicky, opening in Vienna, Jack Kennedy had proved himself no tyro at the game of war and peace. He had coolly calculated the odds and refused to be panicked by Soviet aggression or stampeded by his own military advisers into dangerously precipitate reaction.

His handling of the Berlin crisis is doubly important to our story. It is a significant justification for the high reputation Kennedy acquired in the world of international relations. It is also relevant to the claim of those of his defenders who were to argue that his instinct would be to avoid rash commitment in Vietnam, and that he would have had the skill and political and personal strength to avoid being pushed into escalating as Lyndon Johnson was in 1965. At the proper time we will have to weigh those arguments carefully.

The next cold war crisis, which Russians call the Caribbean crisis and Americans the Cuban missile crisis, was perhaps the most dangerous of all the confrontations between the United States and the Soviet Union over the nearly half a century between the end of World War II and the collapse of the Soviet Union. Those on both sides of the conflict who knew most about what was happening agree that it was the closest the world has ever come to nuclear war. It is also claimed as Kennedy's supreme achievement as an international statesman.

Kennedy certainly did handle this crisis with great skill and ultimate success. Careful study of these dramatic events, however, does call into question important elements in the widely accepted version of what occurred. As we shall see, that story, derived largely from journalistic reporting at the time and from accounts by some of Kennedy's circle, including his brother Bob's best-selling narrative, *Thirteen Days*,[23] does in important respects give a misleading account of events and of President

Kennedy's part in them.[24] Specifically, the world has generally accepted a picture of President Kennedy facing down the Soviet threat and refusing all compromise, when in fact the solution was critically helped by a deal he and his brother Robert were at pains to deny they had done.

When I arrived in the newsroom of the *Washington Post* on the morning of Monday, October 22, a cluster of some of the most experienced foreign policy reporters in Washington was gathered literally round the water cooler, among them Murrey Marder, Chalmers Roberts, and Karl E Meyer. The previous day, Sunday, the *Post* had run a story about troop movements in the United States under a five-column splash headline, "Marine Moves in South Linked to Cuban Crisis."[25] Yet the next morning, the *Post*'s pundits, for all their contacts, were still not sure what was going on. They had noticed that important members of the administration had departed from their usual weekend behavior, crying off dinner invitations, canceling tennis games, and the like. But they were still not sure what was the reason. Cuba, said some. Berlin, said others. What none of us realized is that for a whole week the highest echelons of the American government had been fixated by the gravest confrontation of the entire cold war.

The administration's press officers, from the White House's Pierre Salinger on down, had been astonishingly successful in concealing the anguished debate that had absorbed more than thirty of the Kennedy paladins, who had been meeting all day, sometimes in the cabinet office at the White House but more often in Undersecretary of State for Economic Affairs George Ball's less press-scrutinized office on the top floor of the State Department building in Foggy Bottom, a mile to the west. By the end of the week, nevertheless, some Washington reporters, including James "Scotty" Reston of the *New York Times,* had worked out a pretty good idea of what was going on.[26] For the insiders of ExCom, the crisis had broken a whole week earlier. For weeks there had been reports by Republican senators, especially Senator Kenneth Keating of New York, who had presumably been briefed by sources in the CIA unhappy about the administration's ostensible lack of interest in Cuba, about Soviet missiles being installed in Castro's island. These early reports probably referred to surface-to-air (SAM) antiaircraft missiles, not to the strategically crucial medium- and intermediate-range missiles, offensive weapons that could reach much of the United States as well as targets in the Caribbean and the northern tier of South America.[27]

It was on Sunday, October 14, 1962, that a high-altitude U-2 reconnaissance aircraft had flown over Cuba, the result of President Kennedy's yielding to the pleading of his CIA director, John McCone, for confirmation or refutation of growing rumors of a Soviet arms buildup on the island. The next day, Monday, October 15, CIA analysts in a nondescript building in downtown Washington found pictures of long missiles, longer than SAM antiaircraft weapons. They were able to match them against images of Soviet SS-4 missiles that had been passed to British intelligence and thence to the CIA by Oleg Penkovsky, perhaps the most important spy the West ever had in Moscow in the whole cold war. That night McGeorge Bundy was called out of a dinner party at his own house to hear a cryptic confirmation on the phone from Ray Cline, the CIA's deputy director for intelligence. "Those things we've been worrying about," said Cline, "it looks as though we've really got something." Bundy thought about calling his boss right away, then reflected that he would be in need of sleep after campaigning late in New York State. At 8:45 the next morning, October 16, with the first reconnaissance pictures under his arm, Bundy knocked on the president's door. Kennedy was sitting on the edge of his bed, wearing a bathrobe and slippers, surrounded by newspapers. "Mr. President," Bundy said, "there is now hard photographic evidence that the Russians have offensive missiles in Cuba."[28]

By ten minutes to noon that day, the president met his advisers in the cabinet room, whence his five-year-old daughter Caroline had just been shooed. The advisers were later given a kind of official status as the executive committee of the National Security Council, or ExCom, but in typical Kennedy fashion he called those advisers whose opinion he wanted, not by virtue of their office.

That first morning all of Kennedy's men were agreed that Khrushchev's action in sending to Cuba delivery systems would, once these were topped with nuclear warheads, change the strategic nuclear balance in the whole cold war. It was outrageous, and something must be done.[29] The Kennedy brothers took personally the realization that the Soviet leaders had compounded aggression by deceit. They were shocked that the Soviet foreign minister, Andrei Gromyko, had sat in the Oval Office and tried to deceive them, three days after the Americans knew there were offensive missiles in Cuba.[30]

JFK's first reaction, within minutes of learning of the missiles' presence, was that they must be taken out by an air strike. That was also the first reaction of most of the advisers he had summoned. Formally, this was an executive committee of the National Security Council. This had been set up under President Truman, who did not, however, use it much. It expanded under President Eisenhower, and a Senate sub-committee under Senator Henry "Scoop" Jackson of Washington in 1961 criticized it for excessive bureaucracy. President Kennedy reduced its size, and under him the role of the National Security adviser expanded because of Kennedy's confidence in Bundy's intellect and competence. The statutory members of the NSC were the vice president, secretary of state, secretary of defense, and chairman of the Joint Chiefs of Staff. In practice, Kennedy called in not only the highest officials but others he wanted to hear from. The most influential of them, who sometimes acted like a deputy chairman, was his brother Bob, who as attorney general was not even formally a member of the NSC.[31]

Kennedy's advisers thought the United States should immediately launch a "surgical" strike on the missile bases. The air force, led at this time by General Curtis LeMay, the ultimate believer in strategic bombing, made it plain that the airmen's idea of a strike resembled not so much a scalpel as a bludgeon. General Maxwell Taylor, the only senior military commander who enjoyed much of the president's trust, explained that even a surgical strike would involve hundreds of sorties over several days. Robert McNamara, as secretary of defense, said a strike would have to be carried out before the missiles became "operational" or not at all. When the Joint Chiefs of Staff had their day in court, it turned out that they could not take out the missile launchers without suppressing all enemy air capability, that this would take at least eight hundred sorties a day for five days,[32] and that even so the generals could not guarantee to destroy more than 90 percent, perhaps as little as two-thirds, of the targets. Moreover, bombing on such a scale must mean many casualties, Cuban and Russian.[33]

In the heat of those early days after the U2 reconnaissance uncovered the missile sites, there was talk, too, of an invasion of Cuba, and impressive forces were actually assembled to give the president that option. (It was their movement that the *Washington Post* had picked up.) It was not long, however, before that was seen as something that could be done only after air strikes, and even then perhaps not for many days.

In the context of each of their options, moreover, the president and his advisers had to decide whether to announce publicly what they were going to do. The advantages of secrecy were obvious: to announce in advance air strikes or an invasion might take the world straight to the brink of nuclear war. Yet from the beginning several of the advisers brought up the precedent of Pearl Harbor: the argument was perhaps decisive in ruling out an air strike. It would have to be secret, but the advisers did not want the United States to appear before the world in a disgraceful light. Robert Kennedy passed his brother a note saying ruefully that he knew how General Tojo felt when he was planning Pearl Harbor.[34] George Ball, in many ways the dovish devil's advocate at a table of hawks, had already reminded his peers that "we tried Japanese as war criminals because of the sneak attack on Pearl Harbor."[35]

Gradually an alternative began to emerge as the best first move. This was the idea of a naval blockade to stop the Soviet Union sending any more matériel to Cuba, an option that made all the more sense since the Americans never did know for sure whether any nuclear warheads had actually reached Cuba. A blockade in international law is an act of war, so the State Department's lawyers suggested calling it a naval quarantine.

So on Monday, October 22, the day that had begun with the *Washington Post* newsroom wondering whether the crisis was in Berlin or in Cuba—and of course in a sense it was in both places—the world learned the answer. At 7:00 p.m. the president himself went on every TV network and told the country both what the Soviet Union had done and what he proposed to do about it. "This secret, swift and extraordinary buildup of Communist missiles" in an area that had a special relationship with the United States, in violation of Soviet assurances, he said, was "a deliberately provocative and unjustified change in the status quo which cannot be accepted by this country if our courage and our commitments are ever to be trusted again by either friend or foe."[36]

JFK went on to list the initial steps he had directed to be taken immediately, stressing the word *initial*. First, a strict quarantine on all ships bound for Cuba. Second, close surveillance of Cuba: should offensive military preparations continue, further action would be justified. Third, any nuclear weapon launched from Cuba on any nation in the Americas would be seen as an attack on the United States and would result in a "full retaliatory response upon the Soviet Union." That threat alone was enough to show how deadly serious the U.S. government was about the threat the missiles posed. Fourth, the base at Guantánamo Bay (which few younger Americans had then heard of) would be reinforced. Fifth and sixth, the United States would call for emergency meetings of the Organization of American States and of the United Nations Security Council. Lastly, the president called on Chairman Khrushchev "to abandon this course of world domination and join in an historic effort to end the perilous arms race."

At home, Americans recognized the speech for what it was: a warning that the cold war had heated up to the highest temperature it had ever registered. Officially, the military was on the third-highest state of readiness, known as DEFCON-3: General Curtis LeMay's Strategic Air Command declared DEFCON-2 for its own forces; the remaining military branches remained DEFCON-3. DEFCON-1 would have been war itself.

The next day, October 23, we White House correspondents were invited to a press conference at the State Department—I was there—at which we were shown, blown up on easels, the pictures Major Rudolf Anderson's U-2 had taken. They were explained by men from the CIA and introduced by Secretary of Defense McNamara himself. Although the pictures were fuzzy enough to need some explanation, no one could seriously doubt what they showed: that the Soviet Union, in spite of denials, had indeed shipped to Cuba and started installing missiles there with the range to reach most cities in North America and many in Latin America besides.[37]

There was a run on the Giant supermarket on Wisconsin Avenue. Alice and I imagined our neighbors stocking up on bottled water and canned food before heading for the relative security of their weekend homes in the Blue Ridge. Certainly there was a palpable feeling that week that nuclear war was a real possibility, and that we lived close to ground zero.

Already, the mood of ExCom had moved: from outrage that the Soviet Union should have dared to bring to the United States what World War II had not brought—the end of a sense of inviolability—to a cooler calculation of the realities of the situation. The president shared that initial outrage, but he was quicker than some to recover his cool. After the crisis, McGeorge Bundy pointed out that his boss had always chosen the more moderate of the choices open to him. "It is true that he chose to begin by a public military action [that is, the naval "quarantine"] because he found no hope in unaided diplomacy and no net gain in a diplomatic first round. In every choice after that he took the most moderate course he could find: naval action and not the air strike; a selective quarantine instead of a full John Paul Jones blockade; individual presidential selection of ships to be challenged; moderation and not anger in every message to Khrushchev."[38]

The quarantine was no simple matter. The line was moved closer to Cuba to give Khrushchev more time to decide what he would do. There were Soviet ships that had already passed the line and were close to Cuba. There was a Soviet submarine in the area, which had to be forced to the surface with a depth charge, a moment of special danger. Finally, on the morning of October 24, less than two days after Kennedy had announced the quarantine and only twenty minutes after it took effect, John McCone, director of Central Intelligence, one of the first to guess that the Soviet Union might be putting missiles into Cuba, left the cabinet room to check the situation with the Office of Naval Intelligence. He came back with good news. Six named Soviet ships, not tankers but freighters, the ones the Americans suspected of carrying missiles, had either turned around or stopped.

It was at this point that Dean Rusk murmured something in his soft southern drawl to Mac Bundy, who laughed quietly. It was a recollection of Rusk's childhood in rural Georgia, where kids competed to see who could stare into another's eyes longer without blinking. "We're eyeball to eyeball," he muttered, "and I think the other fellow just blinked."[39]

The success of the quarantine had not ended the crisis. It remained to be seen what Khrushchev's response would be. On Friday, October 26 the signs looked brighter. A letter arrived from Khrushchev in the form of four sections of cable, some apparently with the chairman's hand-written notes on them. It was a long, rambling communication in which he could not stop himself from making some ideological points, but the overall impression was one of humanity, of one human being charged with terrifying responsibility reaching out to another. "I got the feel-ing," it began (referring to Kennedy's message of the previous day) "that you have some understanding of the situation which has developed and [some] sense of responsibility. I value this." War, he continued, "is a ca-lamity for all of the peoples." On he went, sometimes chiding the quar-antine as a "piratical measure," sometimes appealing to Kennedy as a fellow "military man." Then, on the fifth page, he came to the point. "Let us therefore show statesmanlike wisdom. I propose we for our part will declare that our ships, bound for Cuba, will not carry any kind of armaments. You would declare that the United States would not invade Cuba with its forces and will not support any kind of forces which might intend to carry out an invasion of Cuba. Then the necessity for the pres-ence of our military specialists in Cuba would disappear."[40]

Finally, employing one of those earthy proverbial figures of speech he liked, Khrushchev added, "Mr. President, we and you ought not now to pull on the ends of the rope in which you have tied the knots of war, because the more the two of us pull, the tighter the knot will be tied. And a moment may come when that knot will be tied so tight that even he who tied it will not have the strength to untie it, and then it will be necessary to cut that knot. And what that would mean is not for me to explain to you, because you yourself understand perfectly of what terri-ble forces our countries dispose."[41]

This message, and the deal it seemed to be proposing, strangely echoed a communication conveyed through a back channel, one that probably did not come from Moscow but from the imagination of a So-viet actor in Washington. "Aleksandr Fomin's" cover was as a Soviet jour-nalist in Washington: his real name was A. Feklisov, and he was a KGB agent. (It was generally assumed in Washington that Soviet journalists and diplomats worked either for the KGB or for the military GRU: they were not unpopular figures. We had our own KGB agent, a jolly man who liked to play the current Russian pop hit "Moscow Nights" with brio and thick chords on the unreliable piano in our rented house.)

"Fomin" contacted an acquaintance who was a real journalist, John Scali, a dapper ABC television reporter, and suggested that the worst could be averted by a deal: the Soviet Union would dismantle the missiles under UN supervision; Castro would promise not to accept any offensive weapons; and the United States would promise not to invade. This was probably a freelance feeler, not a message from Moscow, but it gave the advisers tensely gathered in the White House and at the State Department encouragement.

Those hopes were dashed at midmorning on Sunday, October 28. This was the tensest day of the whole crisis. I spent the day, like the other reporters, in the lobby outside Pierre Salinger's office, waiting for news, our dozens of coats thrown over the big round table in the middle. At one point, my friend Fred Holborn, a junior but respected member of Kennedy's staff, came out and took me to one side. He was white and shaken. An American reconnaissance plane (the official line was that it was doing routine air monitoring to check if there had been nuclear tests in the Soviet Union) had flown through Soviet air space in the Chukotsk peninsula, the easternmost tip of Soviet territory, just across the Bering Strait from Alaska. Fighters were scrambled from an Alaskan base to escort the errant plane safely home. We would not have been reassured if we had known that those fighters were themselves armed with nuclear missiles. Fred had been instructed to tell the president about this incident and went to do so in trepidation. The president laughed and responded like the junior officer he had once been, wise in the ways of war: "There's always some son of a bitch who doesn't get the word!"[42]

The ExCom was meeting to decide how to respond to Khrushchev's letter when a second, very different Khrushchev letter arrived. This time is was not personal and private but public and aggressive: it was a broadcast message and therefore already in the hands of the media worldwide. JFK learned of it when news ticker tape was handed to him by Ted Sorensen. Khrushchev introduced a new factor—not new to the Americans but new to the context of the terms on which the crisis in the

Caribbean might be settled. Now Khrushchev chucked onto the scales of war and peace the fifteen Jupiter missiles the United States had mounted in Turkey. True, they were obsolete, solid-fuel weapons that Kennedy himself was keen to remove, but they were cherished by the Turks. In fact, they had been made ready only as the crisis over Cuba unfolded. But they put the cat among the pigeons, not least because they had been installed not officially by the United States but by NATO. They could not therefore be removed, the Americans thought, without long, painful, and above all public arguments with the Turks, who were proud of their contribution to their country's defense. Khrushchev's new bid upped the ante. "We agree to remove those weapons from Cuba which you regard as offensive weapons . . . the United States for its part, bearing in mind the anxiety and concern of the Soviet state, will evacuate its analogous weapons from Turkey."[43]

The immediate reaction was something close to horror. The hope that Khrushchev would continue in his unexpected revelation of common humanity now seemed an illusion. In retrospect, this reaction seems overwrought. Was the insertion into the negotiating equation of the missiles in Turkey so insufferable? Later, certainly, McGeorge Bundy argued that the fear felt by the president's advisers was exaggerated. Someone had called the missiles in Cuba a cobra. Well, Bundy wrote, perhaps they were a paper cobra. No one could be certain, at the time or later, whether any actual nuclear warheads reached Cuba. (Bundy recounted that he had questioned two supposed experts on the matter: one thought warheads had arrived, the other thought not.)[44]

The mood was darkened by the news that Major Anderson, the brave pilot whose overflight of Cuba had revealed the existence of the missiles in the first place, had been shot down by a Soviet SAM. The men in the ExCom, Bundy acknowledged, felt a duty to avenge him, and also wanted to protect the other pilots who would have to follow him. With the calm of hindsight, Bundy pointed out that Kennedy and his men should have known that the missiles in Cuba, armed or not, could in any case not be used, since Khrushchev had been clearly warned that any use of them would lead to a "full retaliatory response"—in other words, to a nuclear war that Khrushchev, if he were at all rational, could not risk. "A closer look," Bundy realized more than a quarter of a century after the event, "would have shown us that the Soviet government dared not escalate in Europe, must not deliberately use its missiles in Cuba, and could not break the blockade."[45]

This is not nothing. Reflecting in tranquility, one of the best-informed and most sagacious of Kennedy's advisers, and one who had taken a fairly hard line in their debates, concluded that in the overheated atmosphere, with fear of nuclear calamity in the air and suspicions of a Götterdämmerung, a convulsive twilight of the gods, over Berlin on their minds, the members of the ExCom did not realize that they had already won.

The truth is that those in the Kennedy circle themselves had an interest in promoting the drama of the crisis, a drama that lost nothing in the telling, either in Robert Kennedy's posthumous account, *Thirteen Days,* or in journalistic accounts like the famous *Saturday Evening Post* piece "In Time of Crisis," by Stewart Alsop and Charles Bartlett.[46] They had a collective interest in presenting themselves as the wise men who had saved the world from nuclear calamity.

It was Robert Kennedy who, in *Thirteen Days,* thought up what he called the "Trollope ploy." The idea, taken from a half-remembered Victorian novel in which a girl chooses to ignore a rejection and accepts what she interprets as an earlier proposal of marriage, does neatly describe the decision Kennedy's advisers, no blushing virgins they, but experienced, even hardboiled, lawyers, diplomats, and men of affairs, came to on Saturday, October 27.

The ExCom decided to see if Khrushchev would accept a deal on the lines of his first emotional letter. Ted Sorensen and Robert Kennedy went off to draft it, which was quickly done. After the full committee had broken up, the president invited a smaller inner group to meet in the Oval Office. There were eight men besides himself: his brother; Rusk; McNamara; George Ball; Roswell Gilpatric; Llewellyn "Tommy" Thompson, currently the ambassador-at-large and former ambassador to Moscow who had talked to Khrushchev at length as recently as July; Bundy; and Sorensen. They had been chosen to brief Robert Kennedy on what he should say to the Soviet ambassador, Anatoly Dobrynin, who was waiting at the Justice Department to see him.

Back in his cavernous office at the Justice Department, the attorney general spoke sternly, even with undiplomatic plainness, to the ambassador. The United States knew that work was continuing on the missile bases in Cuba. American U2s, unarmed planes, had been fired upon and a pilot had been killed. "If the Cubans were shooting at our planes," he reported he had said, "then we were going to shoot back." Dobrynin said the Americans were violating Cuban air space. If they had not been doing that, Kennedy said, "we would still be believing what Khrushchev and he had said, that there were no long-range missiles in Cuba." The ambassador had better understand the situation and he had better communicate it to Mr. Khrushchev. Those bases had to go, by tomorrow.

"What was the American offer?" Dobrynin asked. Kennedy cited the first Khrushchev message.

"What about the missiles in Turkey?" the Russian asked. It was not a naïve inquiry. The missiles in Turkey, obsolete and unnecessary from an American point of view, had already been the subject of feelers, and of discussion in ExCom. They were an obvious way out of the murderous strategic dilemma, but at the same time one the Americans were reluctant to grasp.

This was a NATO matter, Kennedy said. There could be no quid pro quo—no deal of this kind could be made. NATO could make no such agreement under threat. But if some time elapsed—he mentioned four or five months—he was sure that these matters could be satisfactorily resolved. It was Rusk, in the Oval Office meeting, who had come up with the idea that Bobby Kennedy should hint that, after the excitement had calmed down, the president would have no objection to removing the missiles from Turkey. The Turks, it was assumed, would be content with a guarantee backed by the newly deployed submarine-launched Polaris missiles.[47]

This formula—stern threats from the Kennedy brothers softened with a strong hint that Khrushchev's unwelcome trade would be acceptable, but only if it were not made public—did the trick. On Sunday, October 28, President Kennedy received a long message, civil in tone but grumpy in detail, from Chairman Khrushchev. The Soviet leader continued to complain about American violations of Soviet air space, about a pinprick raid, presumed to be by Cuban exiles backed by the United States, on the Havana seafront, and more generally about American hostility to the Castro regime. This was bluster to cover the essence of the matter: Khrushchev was acknowledging that he had been forced to back down.

Certainly the U.S. media greeted the end of the crisis not just with relief but with some triumphalism. The conventional wisdom about the crisis was that President Kennedy had very properly responded to an outrageous secret threat to the security of the United States with restraint but also with firmness.

With the benefit not only of the passage of decades but also of the opening of some Soviet archives and the cooperation of some Soviet officials and academics in more or less sincere efforts to understand what really happened, we can see that the conventional wisdom glosses over several questions that are more than details. For example, Khrushchev and other Soviet officials had a point when they contrasted the outrage the Kennedy administration felt at the arrival of the missiles in Cuba with its total failure to empathize with the Soviet sense of encirclement by American nuclear missiles in the United Kingdom, Germany, Italy, and Turkey. Further, there is something Boy Scoutish about the abhorrence expressed in Washington simply because Gromyko and Dobrynin were following their orders when they denied or equivocated about the existence of offensive missiles on the island: Khrushchev decided to send the missiles in May, in the course of a state visit to Bulgaria; it was perhaps unreasonable to expect his men to jeopardize such a major enterprise for fear of breaking the Kennedy family's (somewhat contingent) code of honor.[48]

Most interesting is the importance of secrecy in relation to the deal on the missiles in Turkey. I vividly recall the indignation with which, as I snuffled my way round official Washington trying to find out for the benefit of my paper's readers what had really happened, American officials all scoffed at the idea that any deal had been done, as if anything so pragmatic was quite unworthy of the dignity of the United States. A young foreign reporter was made to feel that he was questioning the "sacred honor" of the United States, or at least of the Kennedy brothers, if he so much as mentioned the missiles in Turkey. The fact is that throughout the ExCom discussions (and no doubt through other discussions in Washington during the "thirteen days" that did not happen to be tape-recorded), the president frankly acknowledged the possibility of trading away missiles that he had already tried to get rid of; he was even slightly irritated they were still there.

Interesting, too, that though Vice President Johnson rarely, if ever, spoke when the president was present, when Kennedy was not in the cabinet room, LBJ did speak up frequently, and with good sense. On the tense afternoon of October 27, 1962, for example, he cut into an argument of Robert McNamara's about the danger of Soviet attacks elsewhere in the world; LBJ said with practical reductionism, "Bob, if you're willing to give up your missiles in Turkey, . . . why don't you say that to him and say to him, we're cutting a trade, make the trade there, save all the invasion, lives and everything else?"[49]

To some extent, JFK's reluctance to do a deal on the Turkish missiles can be explained by a perfectly sensible desire to avoid a row in NATO. As Kennedy knew, taking away the Turks' Jupiters might cause several countries in NATO to doubt American commitment to their own defense.

I cannot, however, avoid the suspicion that the real reason for secrecy was more political. Robert Kennedy, oddly, admitted as much, to the Soviet ambassador Dobrynin of all people. "The appearance of such a document," Dobrynin said Robert Kennedy had told him, meaning the formal Soviet letter accepting the Turkey deal, "could cause irreparable harm to my political career in the future."[50]

JFK must have thought it was far better to present himself, as he did in fact get away with presenting himself, as the stern leader standing up to the wicked Communists than to be caught doing private deals with them. The Soviet story was that they had put the missiles in Cuba to defend against a capitalist threat to the independence of a socialist country. This version was disingenuous: Khrushchev's motive had far more to do with improving the strategic balance from the Soviet Union's point of view. But it was all the more plausible (as Kennedy must have realized, to his annoyance) because of the Bay of Pigs and the subsequent efforts to overthrow Castro, known as Operation Mongoose. Yet Khrushchev did admit that there were other motives for his dangerous ploy; as he put it in his memoirs, "In addition to protecting Cuba, our missiles would have equalized what the West likes to call 'the balance of power.'"[51] Both in an open society like the United States and in a closed one like the Soviet Union, leaders had political motives to conceal. Kennedy must not seem weak; Khrushchev must divert attention from his failing economy, especially its agricultural sector.

Khrushchev liked to remind Americans that they didn't know what it felt like to be threatened with nuclear weapons from the territory of their neighbors. The essence of Kennedy's policy was not, as I and others were asked to believe, that America had boldly stood up to a Soviet plot and faced the Soviet leader down. It was that Kennedy, by choosing the quarantine, had indeed called Khrushchev's bluff. But he had also gone along with the deal Khrushchev needed to save his face—but only when the president thought the fact that he had done so could be kept secret. Since Woodrow Wilson, American diplomats had liked to say that they did only "open agreements, openly agreed to." The back channels and the secret diplomacy in the Cuban missile affair showed that, with the risk of nuclear catastrophe hanging over you, it was acceptable to do deals, so long as the American public did not know that you were doing them. Not, in other words, "openly arrived at." The Cuban missile crisis, in other words, was a glorious success in the cold war. It was also another stage in the loss of that innocence in international affairs of which Woodrow Wilson made so much.

The resolution of the Cuban missile crisis was curiously untidy. For example, the United States never did formally commit itself not to invade Cuba. Nor was there any verification of the removal of the missiles. There never was any UN inspection, and substantial Soviet forces (forty-three thousand in 1962, still more than twenty thousand strong when the Soviet Union collapsed in 1991) remained in Cuba for decades.[52] The American media and the American public simply registered that the Soviet Union had backed down, congratulated themselves that this was achieved by the macho qualities of the young president, and moved on. The president and his administration were happy to have the episode seen as proof of their courage and skill, and to avoid examination of the role played by the Jupiters in Turkey.

Jack Kennedy, however, like Nikita Khrushchev, had been profoundly and personally affected by the crisis. Both men, spectacularly different as they were in age, experience, ideology, temperament, and every other way, had looked over the edge and peered into the nuclear abyss. Both had experienced the cold dread of realizing that their actions could unleash the ultimate horror. In their different ways, each drew the same conclusion: nuclear war must be made impossible.

Khrushchev stopped boasting about his ability to test ever more enormous weapons. One consequence of the crisis and its resolution was that he once again came under fire from his Chinese comrades. They had criticized him for "adventurism" in dispatching the missiles; now they criticized him for "capitulationism" in taking them out. On November 19, 1962, little more than three weeks after the crisis was resolved, he reported to the plenum of the central committee of the CPSU; but as there is no available text we do not know exactly what he said. On December 12, however, he spoke publicly and at some length to the Supreme Soviet. He began by justifying sending the missiles to Cuba as an act of solidarity with a socialist government and with the people of Cuba. But at the end of the speech he defended his decision to reach an accommodation with the United States. "If we had taken an uncompromising stand," he said, "we would only have helped the wild men's camp to utilize the situation for dealing a blow at Cuba and for unleashing a world war."[53]

"Who won?" he asked. "You might say victory belongs to reason, the cause of peace and security." Reason won, he answered himself, "the cause of peace and of the security of nations won." A week later he sent a message to Kennedy saying that "the time has come now to put an end to all nuclear tests."

As for Kennedy, he had before the crisis opposed any limitation of nuclear tests. He was no doubt powerfully influenced by the probability that Republicans and some conservative southern Democrats in the Senate would denounce any constraint on testing, knowing there was a risk that such opposition would impede his other legislative proposals. He did not immediately change his mind. It wasn't until the editor of the *Saturday Review,* Norman Cousins, visited Moscow and came back with the impression that, as a result of the missile crisis, Khrushchev might be ready for an innovative agreement on nuclear tests that JFK began to consider the idea. By May 1963 JFK let Mac Bundy know that he was

ready to make a major speech about peace, and that it would focus on
nuclear testing. Ted Sorensen was assigned to write it, as he had written
most of Kennedy's speeches, big and small, including the inaugural, the
civil rights speech, and the various speeches about the Cuban missile
crisis. This was a project close to his liberal heart. Rusk and McNamara
were briefed, but apart from them, the project was closely held for fear
that leaks might "set off alarm bells" and stir up right-wing opposition.

Sorensen was a loyal as well as a close collaborator. But the fact
that this speech was more than usually his and the president's joint work
without the input of bureaucracies, working groups, and the roiling debate that accompanied most moves the Kennedy administration made,
may well have allowed Sorensen to follow his own instincts more than
in other speeches. The plan was for Kennedy to deliver the speech at
the commencement exercises of American University in Washington on
June 10, 1963. Since the date came immediately after that of a meeting
JFK had scheduled in Honolulu, Sorensen was able to write a draft and
then work with his boss on it during the long flight back to Washington.
Whatever the respective share of the two men, the speech was one of the
most passionate and personal Kennedy ever made.[54]

It was not a narrowly technical argument for a test ban treaty but
the broadest possible plea for peace, with the test ban falling into place as
merely the first small dividend on such a new policy. Kennedy wanted,
he said, "not a Pax Americana enforced upon the world by American
weapons of war. Not the peace of the grave or the security of the slave.
I am talking about genuine peace, the kind of peace that makes life on
earth worth living. . . . We all inhabit this planet," he went on, "we all
breathe the same air. We all cherish our children's future. And we are all
mortal."[55]

He chose as his envoy to Khrushchev Averell Harriman, the former
Democratic governor of New York, a man whose diplomatic experience
went back to wartime London and Moscow and whose experience of
dealing with the Soviet *nomenklatura* went back even further to his adventures as a metals investor in the 1930s. He was—admiringly—known
in the Kennedy circle as the "crocodile" because of his shrewd toughness
and something intimidating about his half-closed eyes.

Forewarned that he would like what he heard, Khrushchev gave

JFK's peace initiative a fair wind. Soviet print media were allowed to publish the speech, and Soviet radio and television to broadcast it. In the circumstances, the result was almost unprecedentedly swift. By July 25 the Soviet Union agreed to sign a limited test ban treaty, forbidding all but underground tests of nuclear weapons. By August 5 the United States, the United Kingdom, and the USSR signed the treaty. On September 23 it was ratified by the Senate by eighty votes to nineteen, and on October 7, less than a year since he had been briefed by Mac Bundy on Major Anderson's fateful photo reconnaissance, Jack Kennedy signed it into law. It would be thirty-three years before the Soviet Union, now on the brink of extinction, would agree to the Comprehensive Nuclear-Test-Ban Treaty, forbidding even tests underground.

Kennedy's appeal, both to his followers and to a large segment of the wider public, was not based on an audit of his achievements so much as on an instinctive attraction to his personality: his wit, his style, his charm counted for more than the treaties he negotiated or the legislation he passed. His willingness to break with the stuffy conventions of diplomacy and to try new approaches, such as the Peace Corps, won him a reputation for radicalism that was in truth undeserved or at least exaggerated. Postcard portraits of the young American president were tacked up in poor farmers' shacks and slum hovels from Indonesia to Brazil. It is unlikely that these admirers realized how unswervingly anti-Communist their new hero was, let alone how comparatively indifferent to the great issues of class and race that dominated the politics of what was known as the third world.

Still, if his domestic successes were disappointing—his most important legislation was passed by LBJ after his death—his foreign record was undeniably impressive. As we have seen, he started in a hesitant manner. But not only did he grow in confidence and touch, he had a knack of turning even his frustrations into successes.

Other Americas

Forty to fifty million people are becoming increasingly invisible.

—*Michael Harrington,* The Other America

J ohn Kennedy did commit himself to an attempt to reduce poverty in the United States. His efforts in this regard in his first two years in office were modest and not wholly successful. Sadly, when he was killed he was on the brink of a more ambitious commitment.

A nucleus of individuals in his administration, especially in the Council of Economic Advisers and the Bureau of the Budget, were pushing him, perhaps farther than he had yet decided to go. His efforts were more tentative than Lyndon Johnson's. Ideologically, they were more conventional: they focused on providing greater opportunities for poor people to lift themselves out of poverty rather than on government action to reduce poverty. Politically, they were more cautious: when he died, his government's plans involved a gradual testing of programs in selected demonstration areas. Johnson immediately saw the political advantage of pressing ahead faster and on a national scale.

It is hard to avoid the judgment that Kennedy, rich and brought up almost exclusively in the company of the rich, had little real sense of the urgency of the need for government to help the poor. When, on the contrary, two days after the assassination, Johnson, now rich but raised relatively poor,[1] was briefed about plans for measures to reduce poverty, his reaction was prompt and heartfelt. "That's my kind of program," he replied. "It will help people. I want you to move full speed ahead." LBJ meant to run in 1964 not on the promise of a future war on poverty, as JFK had planned to do, but on the program itself.[2]

In the late 1950s the "Eisenhower recession" alerted economists to the fact that economic growth was slowing. That was part of what Jack Kennedy meant when he campaigned in 1960 on the need to "get America moving again." There was a new awareness that this could mean that the healthy pace at which Americans had been leaving poverty might also slow. So there was a rediscovery of poverty, something that most Americans thought had been abolished in their country by the spectacular growth of the economy during World War II and by the rise in working-class incomes associated with collective bargaining between industrial unions and major corporations. (The 1950 Treaty of Detroit, negotiated between the United Auto Workers and General Motors, granted not only high wages but also pension rights and health care benefits and was seen as a model that would ultimately bring all Americans into middle-class security.) In the later years of the Eisenhower administration, a number of developments called that optimism into question. Several writers drew attention to the truth: alongside previously unimaginable affluence, millions of Americans still lived in very real poverty.

This rediscovery had led at the end of the 1950s to a dispute among social scientists and some concerned politicians about the nature and causes of poverty. This echoed the famous exchange between Scott Fitzgerald and Ernest Hemingway. "The rich are different," Fitzgerald was supposed to have said. "Yes," Hemingway replied, "they have more money."[3] There were those who accepted the theory, persuasively argued by the anthropologist Oscar Lewis, that there was a "culture of poverty." That school suggested the poor were prevented by cultural characteristics from taking the opportunities that were available. Lewis first developed his theory as a result of his work among the poor in Mexico, then later adapted it to the psychology of poor people, especially poor black people, in the United States.[4] As a Marxist, Lewis was especially conscious of the widespread lack of any ideological interpretation or sense of class solidarity among the poor. They were, he said later, aliens in their own country. They lived in and for the present, Lewis and his followers argued, and were incapable of planning ahead, saving money, or acquiring skills. "Like the Asian peasant," wrote Michael Harrington, in this, at least, following Lewis, "the impoverished American tends to see life as fate, an endless cycle from which there is no deliverance."[5]

Nonsense, said economists like the old New Dealer Leon Keyserling, Kenneth Boulding, and the Swedish social democrat Gunnar Myrdal. "The one universal characteristic of all the poor," Keyserling wrote, "is lack of money."[6] He believed that poverty was an economic problem, not a cultural one. If the government increased its budget by 50 percent, that would work wonders. Myrdal stressed the obstacles placed in the way of poor people who sought to escape from their poverty: the key word for him was *exclusion*. The thoughtful social worker Elizabeth Wickenden (a friend of Lyndon Johnson since his days at the National Youth Administration, who had continued to lobby on poverty issues) pointed out that it was a short step from talking about a culture of poverty to suggesting that poverty was the fault of the poor.[7] Later critics of the "culture of poverty" thesis spoke of "blaming the victim."

Also coming to the fore of public consciousness was the related issue of juvenile delinquency. As early as 1955 Benjamin Fine had written a sensational account called *1,000,000 Delinquents*.[8] Social scientists Richard Cloward at Columbia, Lloyd Ohlin at Columbia and later Harvard, and Albert K. Cohen had also focused attention on juvenile delinquency and urban street gangs.

Kennedy became interested in addressing these issues when he read a paper on poverty by Leon Keyserling.[9] He also, and this may have been a clincher, read an article in the *New York Herald Tribune*,[10] the voice of traditional moderate Republicanism, hinting that the Republicans were planning to make poverty an issue in the 1964 presidential election. Such a hint would tingle the presidential synapses.[11]

In these discussions of poverty just before and shortly after Jack Kennedy became president, race did not yet play a leading part. Adam Yarmolinsky, a lawyer who was an aide to McNamara at the Pentagon and later helped draft Johnson's poverty bill, making him a likely choice to be Sargent Shriver's deputy in the War on Poverty (before being fired by LBJ, disgracefully, as a sacrifice to southern prejudices in Congress), was influential in the Kennedy circle's thinking about poverty, and he pointed out that "most poor people in America are not black, and most black people are not poor."[12]

Later it was to be suggested[13] that the Kennedy and Johnson administrations became interested in poverty because of their concern about black discontent. That ignores the actual political motives of the Kennedy administration. It is also anachronistic. Kennedy and his circle were liberals in the manner of the 1950s. They did not share LBJ's fervor for raising up the downtrodden. They were not thinking in terms of a war on poverty. Rather, they wanted to do what they could without serious political risk within the limits of political realities, at a time when Congress was essentially controlled by a conservative coalition made up of midwestern Republicans and southern conservatives. They were offended by the contrast between American affluence and its exceptions. They were ashamed of foreign criticism. And they were aware of the economic wastefulness of unemployment, underproduction, and underconsumption.

In the Johnson years, the War on Poverty acquired undertones of racial change. The Kennedy approach to poverty was rooted in essentially conservative doctrine. The brothers and their advisers had decided to defer substantial progress on civil rights to a second term. They were also rebuffed or defeated in some of their earlier attempts at reform. What survived were cautious, modest policy proposals, rooted in largely uncontroversial "American" principles.

While in the Senate, Kennedy had not been wholly uninterested in poverty and other social issues. He had, for example, supported Medicare, federal aid to education, and manpower training. In the 1960 campaign, as we have noted, he had been moved by the poverty he observed. He had even used the phrase a "war on poverty" in the context of the twenty-fifth anniversary of the Social Security Act. Although his celebrated inaugural speech was mainly devoted to foreign policy, he did allow himself three passing references to the poor.

In his first two years in office, Kennedy's domestic record was not altogether, as is sometimes suggested, that of a do-nothing president, wholly diverted from domestic issues by his obsession with foreign policy. It is true that he and his advisers, including both Kenny O'Donnell and Larry O'Brien, were very aware of the dominance in Congress of the conservative bloc. They did not want to arouse the hostility of this formidable opposition any more than could be avoided. Their instinct urged them to focus first on reelection, leaving politically dangerous innovation to a second term. Kennedy's guru during the presidential transition, Richard Neustadt of Columbia, advised him in so many words to "postpone the postponable."[14] For O'Donnell and O'Brien and for JFK himself, a bold plan for abolishing poverty in America would certainly come in the category of the postponable. One of his favorite columnists, Joseph Kraft, pointed out that "by nature he was cautious," and that "his motto might have been: 'no enemies to the right.'"[15] James Tobin, a member of his own Council of Economic Advisers and later a Nobel laureate, said "Kennedy was afraid of offending two establishments: the conservative Democrats in Congress and the wider financial establishment."[16]

JFK has been remembered around the world as the fearless champion of civil rights for African Americans. But the historical record shows that, until his sharp political intelligence told him that the danger of inaction was greater than the danger of action, he was wary of the political danger of pushing aggressively for civil rights legislation. A recent full-length study concludes that "until the Birmingham riot in 1963 . . . Kennedy abdicated his responsibility to lead the great social revolution of his age. And by then it was too late."[17]

His domestic record in his first years in office, therefore, was not that of a shining liberal. He expended some goodwill in Congress by his fight with the ultraconservative Judge Howard Smith of Virginia, the chairman of the House Rules Committee. There were twelve members of the committee, a physical representation of the alliance between Republican and Democratic conservatives. Given four safe conservative Republican votes, Judge Smith and his colleague from the Mississippi Gulf Coast, William Colmer, could block any legislation. Kennedy had assumed that Speaker Rayburn would appoint more liberal members to the committee, but Rayburn, who had been in Congress since 1913, would not do that. He told Kennedy he just didn't have the votes.

On January 30, 1961, JFK delivered his first State of the Union speech. Like his inaugural, it was largely about foreign policy and specifically about the threat of world Communism. The next day Rayburn metaphorically laid aside his Speaker's gavel and spoke on the floor as an ordinary member, albeit one who enjoyed extraordinary respect in the House, on behalf of Kennedy's plan for expanding the Rules Committee. He ended simply: "Let us move this program." The House voted with him, but for all the respect in which "Mr. Sam" was held, the vote was only 217-212. Thanks to this intervention by the old Speaker, who would be dead within the year, Kennedy won that Rules Committee fight, though there would be further problems from that direction. But his caution had been reinforced by the experience.[18]

An arguably even more significant achievement from the perspective of the future were the tax cuts Kennedy asked Congress for. They stimulated growth and provided the marginal resources to make LBJ's domestic reforms possible. Here again Kennedy's instincts were cautious. His Keynesian chairman of the Council of Economic Advisers (CEA), Walter Heller, when he was first interviewed for the job, asked if the administration would cut taxes. Kennedy at first said no: he felt he could not cut taxes when he was asking Americans to make sacrifices.[19] For the first two years of the Kennedy administration, the economy recovered, admittedly modestly, from the mild recession of 1960. Heller continued to argue that a tax cut would enable the economy to function at full capacity, while Douglas Dillon, the secretary of the treasury, argued for leaving tax rates as they were but embarking on a sweeping project of tax reform to eliminate loopholes. Wilbur Mills, Democrat of Arkansas, the powerful chairman of the House Committee on Ways and Means, was even more skeptical; only patient persuading by Heller won Mills over. The House did pass a tax-cut bill and it became law early in LBJ's administration. But Kennedy sat on the fence until August 1963. The tax cuts would not arrive until 1964. However, they did deliver the growth that enabled LBJ to move rapidly forward on domestic policies to reduce poverty.

It was not just that JFK was cautious about framing legislation in the area of poverty. His doctrinal conservatism also limited the character of the legislation he was willing to commit to. His approach respected the traditional American belief in opportunity, frequently expressed in the phrase that the poor should be offered not handouts but a hand up.[20] President Kennedy's efforts to reduce or alleviate poverty were not only more cautious and more tentative than LBJ's full-blooded War on Poverty, they were rooted in a different ideology. Jack Kennedy, like most Democratic politicians of the 1950s, and indeed like Lyndon Johnson until he had the opportunity and the motivation to take bolder initiatives, was constrained by the idea that both redistribution of wealth and direct government action to reduce poverty were somehow un-American.

So his legislative record in his first two years was cautious. But it was not negligible. He passed with relative ease measures that continued the New Deal/Fair Deal tradition: increases in the minimum wage, extension of Social Security benefits, and new money for hospital and school building. He fared less well with legislative proposals of his own. He did pass a bill improving provision for mental retardation[21]—a subject on which he had strong feelings because of the experience of his sister Rosemary. He tried to create a Department of Housing and Urban Development, but even the newly expanded Rules Committee would not allow it, mainly because of southern fears that Robert Weaver would be put at its head as the first African American cabinet secretary, as did eventually happen. Likewise, JFK failed to pass a bill giving federal aid to elementary and secondary schools because the issue got tangled up with strong feelings from both southern Protestants and northern Catholics about aid to parochial schools.[22]

It was entirely in keeping with Kennedy's Whig political instincts that measures to reduce poverty should be undertaken out of a sense of noblesse oblige. They would demonstrate to the world the generosity of the new imperial America; they would also blunt Soviet propaganda about inequality in American society. For government to spend massive resources on making poor people richer could not be justified in terms of traditional political values. To use the resources of government to open the windows of opportunity to the American Dream was quite another thing.[23]

There was interest in the Kennedy family and circle in the issue of juvenile delinquency. The president's sister Eunice, married to Sargent Shriver, the serious-minded Catholic businessman who had run the Kennedy family's Merchandise Mart in Chicago, was keen on doing something about this issue. So was his brother Robert. The result was the President's Committee on Juvenile Delinquency and Youth Crime.

This was inspired by the research of Richard Cloward and Lloyd Ohlin and separately that of Albert K. Cohen with New York street gangs. It was set up following a presidential initiative as early as May 11, 1961. The attorney general was chairman, and the executive director was Bob's close personal friend David Hackett. (It was typical of the Kennedy administration's style that, when setting up a significant domestic policy initiative, it reached out not for an experienced civil servant, a professional reformer, or even an academic, but for a banker, a gifted athlete, who had been a hero of Robert Kennedy's at their boarding school, Milton Academy. It is fair to add, however, that Hackett proved to be an energetic and thoughtful administrator and that after leaving government he devoted much of his life to the cause of helping underprivileged young people.) The Committee on Juvenile Delinquency worked closely with the Ford Foundation, where public affairs director Paul Ylvisaker had initiated a number of so-called gray areas projects in different parts of the country. The one on the Lower East Side of Manhattan, mounted with the support of New York City's mayor, Robert F. Wagner, was the largest. It was called Mobilization for Youth. Because of the perceived success of the Peace Corps, the administration also became interested in the idea of a "domestic peace corps." On February 14, 1963, JFK proposed the formation of a National Service Corps. It never really took off, or rather it survived as an underground river, surfacing from time to time, especially in Democratic administrations, with different names, different emphases, and different fortunes.[24]

Again, Kennedy had been personally shocked by the deprivation he saw during his 1960 primary campaign in the coal mining valleys of eastern Kentucky. Later he also read a series about Appalachian poverty written by the veteran *New York Times* reporter Homer Bigart.[25] And in 1963 the president was one of many who were moved by a book, *Night Comes to the Cumberlands,* by east Kentucky lawyer Harry Caudill.[26]

It is interesting that in the late 1950s and even in the early 1960s there was still little or no association of poverty with black people, either in the rural South or in urban ghettoes, though in the summer of 1961 there was an unpleasant debate about welfare caused by events in the small Hudson River valley city of Newburgh, New York. The local city manager, Joseph Mitchell, cut back on welfare payments for able-bodied men, unmarried mothers, and new applicants for aid. Mitchell was an outspoken reactionary who believed that "the mushy rabble of do-gooders and bleeding hearts ... have marched under the Freudian flag toward the omnipotent state of Karl Marx."[27] It turned out that his fears were exaggerated: in a city of thirty thousand inhabitants only ten able-bodied males were on welfare.[28]

The national concern, amounting for a time almost to panic, about African American ghettoes, poverty, welfare, and the specter of a black underclass given over to drugs and crime was still in the future. Poverty was not yet specifically associated with race, and the stereotypes of the black mugger and the black "welfare queen" had not yet taken hold. There was, however, a new awareness of poverty as a reality in a supposedly affluent America, and of specific aspects of poverty, notably juvenile delinquency and white poverty in pockets such as the Appalachians and the Ozarks. So in his very first month in office Kennedy was urging both houses of Congress to enact a bill to help "distressed areas," meaning in the first instance Appalachia, and by May 1, 1961, he was able to sign an Area Development Act.

Kennedy also plunged cautiously into the thicket of health care legislation. Several rival proposals were attempting to survive the expected buffeting from the American Medical Association's lobbyists and the well-funded hostility of the health care industry. Yet on the very day that JFK was assassinated, Larry O'Brien's top House liaison man, Henry Hall Wilson, actually agreed with Wilbur Mills on a formula for funding a Medicare bill similar to that eventually passed by LBJ.[29]

The last—but of course by no means the least—of the Kennedy administration's claims to legislative achievement was the civil rights bill. Here again Kennedy's reputation as a champion of the civil rights revolution is exaggerated. JFK's original assumption, shared by O'Brien and his other key aides, was that there should be no civil rights bill until the second term. Each successive engagement in the civil rights struggle in his first term, however, dragged a reluctant president closer to committing himself to a major civil rights measure.[30] The violent response to the Freedom Rides shocked the Kennedy brothers and their circle. Not only were African American activists and their radical white allies brutally beaten, their rented coach set on fire, and their lives openly threatened. John Seigenthaler, a white journalist on the *Nashville Tennessean* who was a friend and seconded as close aide to the attorney general, was savagely beaten with a baseball bat, requiring hospitalization. President Kennedy's first reaction was to call Harris Wofford, the most liberal of his aides, and ask, "Can't you get your goddamned friends off those buses?"[31]

The Ole Miss rioting that occurred after James Meredith was registered as the first African American student there taught the Kennedy brothers and those in the Justice Department responsible for the issue, like Burke Marshall, that a patient campaign of litigation to enforce the Supreme Court's 1954 *Brown* decision would not be enough. Kennedy did not, however, finally make up his mind until June 1963, after George Wallace had "stood in the schoolhouse door" on the campus of the University of Alabama at Tuscaloosa.

In January 1963 someone drew President Kennedy's attention to an article in the *New Yorker* magazine by the veteran radical Dwight Macdonald. The article, "Our Invisible Poor," was a lengthy review of several books on a subject that had largely disappeared from the American political consciousness.[32] The subject was poverty, and Macdonald began by taking issue with John Kenneth Galbraith, certainly one of the intellectuals with the most consistent influence on Kennedy's thinking. Galbraith's best-seller *The Affluent Society,* published in 1958, is remembered for contrasting "private affluence and public squalor."[33] Macdonald pointed out that Galbraith's title was inaccurate, though his error might be understandable and was certainly common. Some of the society was affluent, but by no means all of it. Macdonald reviewed a number of books on poverty, several of them massive statistical studies that he found tedious. The book he found both fascinating and important, and the one that caught the president's attention when he too read it, was called *The Other America.*[34] It was written by Michael Harrington, brought up by Jesuits but by the time he wrote the book a lapsed Catholic, though he had been greatly influenced by his work with Dorothy Day's Catholic worker movement and as an editor of its magazine, *Catholic Worker.*

Harrington's book was short—well under two hundred pages—

well written, and passionate. In it he argued that America was indeed not altogether an affluent society; a very large proportion of the population, perhaps as many as 40 to 50 million out of 180 million, or roughly one in four, lived in poverty and in a culture of poverty that made the condition self-sustaining through successive generations in some families. He argued that the poor were largely invisible, that they lived at the margins of society, that many of them were old or very young, that they lived in city ghettos or on farms, and that one-quarter of them were African American or Puerto Rican. These facts both explained the illusion of universal affluence and militated against effective efforts to change the situation. He also insisted, with the moral force of an Old Testament prophet, that, whatever the precise statistics of the number of the poor, "they should be read with a sense of outrage. . . . For until these facts shame us," he ended, "until they stir us to action, the other America will continue to exist, a monstrous example of needless suffering in the most advanced society in the world."[35]

It is, however, a myth that Kennedy's interest in poverty was triggered by reading either Harrington's book or Macdonald's review. For one thing, JFK had, as noted, always had a certain interest in the politics of poverty. For another, the review was not published until January 19, 1963, presumably shortly after publication of the book. Already in the previous month JFK had first broached with Walter Heller, chairman of his Council of Economic Advisers, the idea of a major initiative to diminish poverty in America. He did not commit himself to any remedial program at this stage. He simply asked Heller to assemble the facts and figures about poverty in the United States. Heller promptly hired Robert Lampman, an economist from the University of Wisconsin who had already published studies on the definition and the statistical extent of poverty. Lampman's resulting memos, written with great care, were published over the next months. In June a joint task force of officials from the Council of Economic Advisers and the Bureau of the Budget was set up to collect and evaluate proposals for a poverty program. It was not finished until the Economic Report in early 1964.

More generally, a caucus of enthusiasts for some kind of a campaign against poverty was gathering in the administration.[36] It included people from very different backgrounds. There were officials, including veteran federal civil servants like the very able Wilbur Cohen (an "in-and-outer" who had worked in Washington off and on since the New Deal), Heller, William Capron at the Council of Economic Advisers, Charles Schultze, the deputy director of the Bureau of the Budget, and William Cannon at the Bureau of the Budget. They were in contact with reform professionals at the Ford Foundation led by Paul Ylvisaker and including David Hunt, who had set up Mobilization for Youth in New York City, which helped to inspire a "gray areas" project.

One tenet of this crowd was that the existing institutions dealing with poor people, from school boards to hospitals and various charitable organizations, were ossified and generally did more harm than good to the poor. The administration officials were also in an ambiguous relationship with radical academics such as Lloyd Ohlin, Richard Cloward, and Frances Fox Piven from the New York School of Social Work at Columbia University, a group both fertile of ideas and a constant irritant. It was observed (not least by Daniel Patrick Moynihan, then a relatively junior but influential official at the Department of Labor) that all these groups came from a relatively narrow background: the study of poverty and how to alleviate it was largely a monopoly of upper-middle-class residents of New York City rather than a national political movement, let alone an uprising of the downtrodden.

On July 10, 1963, Lampman sent his first memo, "An Offensive against Poverty," to Walter Heller.[37] A second memo ("Post-war Poverty Trends") followed on August 5. Lampman's work confirmed Harrington's central point: there was indeed, in spite of postwar prosperity, a great deal of poverty in the United States. In the summer of 1963 Heller assigned William Capron, a Stanford economist on his staff, to focus on poverty issues. Meanwhile, the climate of opinion inside the administration was shifting in the direction of taking social issues more seriously. The March on Washington passed off triumphantly on August 2.

On October 29, 1963, Heller circulated a memo prepared by his staff[38] on what he called "the poverty cycle." There was no one magic point, the memo argued, where the cycle of poverty could be broken. Instead he recommended a three-pronged attack. First, the government should try to stop people becoming poor to begin with. Second, it should try to rehabilitate those caught in the cycle. And third, it should make it easier for those who could not be helped by rehabilitation to help themselves out of poverty. On November 5 Heller wrote members of the cabinet asking, by November 15, for their proposals "that might be woven into a basic attack on poverty and waste of human resources, as part of the 1964 legislative program." Their ideas should "concentrate on relatively few groups and areas" where the problems were most severe and the solutions most promising. He argued that such an attack in a few areas would be more effective than what he called a "shotgun" approach. The program should maximize self-help and minimize "handouts." He suggested it should be called "widening participation in prosperity" to avoid the word *poverty,* though he admitted that the president "was in the market for a more effective title."

The next day David Hackett from the President's Committee on Juvenile Delinquency proposed both to Heller and separately to his friend the attorney general a "process." There should be five demonstration projects—depressed areas, urban slums, Indian reservations, migratory labor, and persons in institutions.

The proposals from the departments were thought to be disappointing. "All they did," Capron said later, "was pull out old ideas which had been knocking around and put them in a package."[39] Each cabinet officer bid for the biggest share of the budget for his own department. Hackett's approach was more in line with the president's, and he was therefore asked to draft a program, which he did. He stressed experiment in a limited number of areas, followed by careful analysis. He also focused hard on the need for coordination, something that appealed to many in government who feared interdepartmental chaos and a waste of resources.

At this stage, while there was much discussion of "community action," the idea that the poor themselves should play a role in their redemption had scarcely surfaced. Later, community action was to become something of a fetish among reformers. It provoked a serious backlash from elected politicians. They hated to see government money going to often uncouth and radical "community activists" (and not passing through their hands), all the more so when these people often badmouthed official Democratic politicians in state government or at city hall. In Kennedy's lifetime the emphasis remained not on group or community action but on ways in which the government might help individuals to find opportunities to escape from poverty. Moreover, serious and reasoned opposition to the more ambitious ideas circulating in the academic social science community had already appeared in Congress, not least in the formidable shape of Congresswoman Edith Green of Oregon, a former schoolteacher with a passion for education. She took the realist but limited view that the purpose of legislation was not to reform urban society but to reduce juvenile delinquency.

Before JFK's death, therefore, the actual record of legislative success with substantial measures of domestic reform was meager. Even so, some important steps had been taken. More to the point, a body of civil servants, congressional staffers, and academic experts had begun to gather who would form the shock troops of the War on Poverty under Kennedy's successor. They were as diverse as David Hackett, Wilbur Cohen, and Daniel Patrick Moynihan; and it is also notable that many of those who would take the lead in the War on Poverty under Johnson —Richard Goodwin, Theodore Sorensen, Adam Yarmolinsky, and Lee White, for example—were appointed by Kennedy and generally thought of as "Kennedy people."

Only three days before Dallas, on November 19, 1963, Walter Heller saw JFK again. He told the president, "We are having great trouble getting a program together" because of the bureaucratic infighting that was going on among his cabinet officers. He still asked if antipoverty measures should be included in the 1964 legislative program. "Yes," said Kennedy simply, and asked Heller to come back with proposals in two weeks. Characteristically, politician to the last, he also asked for something to be done for suburbs, not then generally identified as the homes of the poor.

Once the Kennedy administration made up its mind to go for an antipoverty program, responsibility for it moved to the Bureau of the Budget. The key figure now was William Cannon, a University of Chicago graduate working closely with Charles Schultze of the CEA and with Hackett. After Walter Heller met LBJ, two days after the assassination, this was now a Johnson program, and both the timetable and the conception of an antipoverty program changed dramatically. Instead of a cautious interval of testing and analysis, the government was now going—in the new president's own words—"full tilt."[40] That meant getting the program pushed through Congress in time for the 1964 presidential election, only a year away.

"The new President," wrote the young Richard Blumenthal two years later, "believed deeply that this was, indeed, his kind of program, and he wanted to stamp it as truly his own."[41] There were to be no more careful trials in a handful of locations. The president communicated to his officials the political imperative of acting on a national scale. (They were already aware that Congress was frustrated by the time consumed by the juvenile delinquency committee in careful research and testing.) *Community action,* a phrase that slipped into discussions only at the margins before the assassination, became the official title of the entire project. In papers prepared by the Bureau of the Budget in January 1964, the words *demonstrate* and *testing* disappeared almost totally. Now, however, "the central purpose" was an "attack upon the basic causes of poverty." The federal government must "harness the full and sustained energies and resources of our local communities, our states and the Federal Government" in an "all out continuous . . . war."[42] The military metaphors were now inescapable: "weapons" were to be deployed on "fronts" until the enemy, poverty, surrendered to commander in chief Johnson.

The contrast should not be too sharply drawn. Kennedy was never wholly insensitive to the issue of poverty in America, or wholly cynical in his attitude to it. Moreover, his political antennae were sensitive enough that he adapted to new evidence of the urgency of certain aspects of urban poverty. Yet the distinction between JFK and LBJ is clear. When LBJ became president he took hold of the federal government's policy in regard to poverty with new ambition and energy. He broadened its scope and accelerated its timetable. He changed the goal—and here it is possible that he was not fully aware of what he was doing—from widening opportunities of escaping from poverty to proposing an entitlement to that escape. It was, after all, natural for LBJ to "get" poverty. His family had been poor, and he had grown up in a section of the country that was then still relatively poor. He had been poor himself. He lived and worked among poor people. His first work as a public official was occupied with alleviating poverty among young people. Many of his first concerns as a member of Congress involved "attacks" on various "fronts" of poverty.

When we come to the counterfactuals with which this book is concerned, it would be unjust to assume that Kennedy would have done little to reduce poverty in the United States. It is probable that no substantial federal initiatives to reduce poverty would have happened before the 1964 presidential election. It is certain that he would not have made them an overriding goal as Johnson did. As I have pointed out more than once, LBJ was helped in this regard by JFK's death. Yet it is not credible that JFK would have accomplished the astonishing record of domestic reform that should be seen as LBJ's enduring monument.

Surpassing Kennedy

We seek not just legal equity but human ability, not just equality as a right and a theory but equality as a fact and equality as a result.

—President Lyndon B. Johnson, Howard University speech, June 4, 1965

I n his first public statement after taking over as president, LBJ stressed his determination to carry out JFK's programs: "Let us continue." Specifically, he committed himself to the Kennedy civil rights bill. "No memorial oration or eulogy," he said, "could more eloquently honor President Kennedy's memory than the earliest possible passage of the civil rights bill for which he fought so long. We have talked long enough in this country about equal rights. We have talked for a hundred years or more. It is time now to write the next chapter, and to write it in the books of law."[1]

That was the public commitment. In private, however, Johnson repeatedly told his friends that he meant not just to carry out John Kennedy's proposals but to surpass them. The very first night after he came back from Dallas, he talked late into the night at the Elms with three of his closest aides, Bill Moyers, Cliff Carter, and Jack Valenti. They asked him what he planned to do. "Well," he replied, according to Valenti, "I'm going to tell you. I'm going to pass the civil rights bill and not change one word of it. I'm not going to cavil and I'm not going to compromise. I'm going to fix it so everyone can vote, so everyone can get the education they need. I'm going to pass Harry Truman's health care bill."[2]

Later still, at 3:00 in the morning, he said a strange thing to another aide, Horace Busby. "Buzz," he said, "do you realize that when I came back to Washington tonight as President there were on my desk the same things that were on my desk when I came to Congress in 1937?" He meant federal aid to education, health care, and civil rights.[3]

A few months later, when he summoned his aides Bill Moyers and Dick Goodwin to swim with him in the White House pool and laid out his plans for a Great Society, he said the same in different words: "Kennedy had some good programs, but they were stalled in Congress. I had to pull them out of the ditch. . . . But it's not enough to just pick up on the Kennedy program and try to do a better job. . . We've got to use the Kennedy program as a springboard to take on the Congress, summon the states to new heights, create Johnson programs, different in tone, fighting and aggressive."[4]

It was as bold a program of social reform as any president had ever set himself as a goal, and at that moment it was far from clear that he could succeed. Within two years he had done just what he promised: civil rights, health care, Medicare, federal aid for education, voting rights, and other legislation, such as immigration reform. It must be conceded that, while he succeeded in legislating an impressive spread of programs, many were conceptually and politically flawed. That was perhaps the inevitable price of ramming them through Congress without more careful development. Those flaws do not diminish the sheer impact of Johnson's success with his domestic programs.

In just over six months, he had passed a civil rights bill that it was highly unlikely Kennedy could ever have passed. He did so by using, with a master's hand, every political skill or technique available, including his long and intimate knowledge of colleagues in the House and Senate, most of whom were little more than names to Kennedy. He was able, too, to take advantage of the new mood caused by the very fact of Kennedy's death. Senator Richard Russell of Georgia, arch-strategist of the South's resistance to desegregation, acknowledged the importance of that factor. "We would have beaten President Kennedy," he told the *Washington Afro-American,* "but now I won't predict the outcome. Now it will be three times harder. President Kennedy didn't have to pass a strong bill to prove anything on civil rights. President Johnson does."[5]

LBJ's aide Harry McPherson told me an anecdote that, to him, revealed how shallow JFK's commitment to civil rights was before he was president. McPherson recalled that after a civil rights victory on the floor, liberal senators and Johnson aides gathered round their triumphant leader in back-slapping mood, congratulating one another. The senator from Massachusetts would have voted right. But two "gorgeous babes" had been sitting in the gallery. Long before Johnson's crowd had finished celebrating, the babes were gone: so too were their dates, Kennedy and his friend George Smathers of Florida, who of course had voted against the civil rights measure. Civil rights, however important they may have become later, were not high on Jack Kennedy's list of priorities before he was president.

The essential feature of the battlefield that a successful civil rights campaign would have to negotiate was the underlying conservative alliance between southern Democrats and others (both Republicans and some Democrats, especially from the West) to whom civil rights for African Americans were not a high priority. Before his death, President Kennedy had faced difficult choices as he and his men maneuvered to get the civil rights bill to the floor of the House. The bill went first to the House Judiciary Committee, whence it would have to secure the approval of the Rules Committee, where the power of the arch-reactionary Judge Smith had been checked but not broken. The Judiciary Committee, chaired by Emanuel "Manny" Celler, a veteran Brooklyn liberal responsive to civil rights organizations, voted out an alternative version that looked stronger than the president's own bill. It was, however, in the opinion of JFK's right-hand man Ted Sorensen, of doubtful constitutionality. It might, Sorensen thought, lead to (unspecified) "turmoil." Cautiously, Kennedy went for bipartisan consensus on the full Judiciary Committee. That meant reaching compromises with the ranking Republican on the committee, William McCulloch, an elderly moderate from Ohio, and with the House minority leader, Charlie Halleck of Indiana.

At breakfast on January 22, 1964, the new president told the Democratic leaders in the House that the time had come to take the bill from Smith's grasp. The next day they did a deal with Halleck and McCulloch to vote to take the bill out of Rules and give it to Judiciary. Johnson cleverly used the upcoming Lincoln's birthday holiday to embarrass the Republicans. "I thought it would be rather unbecoming," he said, "to go out and talk about Lincoln, when we still had the civil rights bill, that Lincoln would be so interested in, locked up in a committee that couldn't act on it."[6]

On January 30 the House Rules Committee gave the civil rights legislation a "rule," that is, allowed it to go to the full House, by eleven votes to four. Only Smith and three fellow southerners voted against. The very next day Speaker John McCormack called the House to order to consider the civil rights legislation that JFK had proposed and LBJ said he wanted passed "without a word or a comma changed."

That was hardly realistic. From the start the southerners pushed hard. William Colmer of Mississippi and Rules Committee member, for example, asked, "What's the rush? Is all of this done out of fear? Is the Congress of the United States to yield to threats of further demonstrations . . . blackmail, if you will ?"[7] African Americans might have replied that this was no rush for them: they had been waiting a century for equality. The implication that civil rights could be granted only out of fear of civil unrest, too, revealed just how out of touch the bourbon South was with the reality of the national mood.

On February 3 the debate reached the most controversial section of the bill, Title II. It provided that no one could be denied the use of "public accommodations" by reason of "race, color, religion or national origin." At this point the defenders of the South's segregated ways became nasty. Judge Smith argued that chiropodists, if their office was in a hotel, might be forced to cut corns whether the feet "smelled good or bad." He tried to claim that the Thirteenth Amendment, passed after the Civil War to liberate African Americans, protected the right of chiropodists to refuse to work on black feet. Colmer of Mississippi brought up the viscerally racist question of barbers having to cut black people's hair.[8]

The southerners offered more than one hundred hostile amendments, and liberal congressmen from the Democratic Study Group worked with Larry O'Brien's White House liaison staff to shepherd liberal majorities to meet and beat each one of them. On February 8 Judge Smith himself offered the most surprising and the most significant of all the amendments, and the one that has had most impact on America life. Smith added to the list of individuals to be protected against discrimination the largest group of all: women.

It has generally been assumed that Smith's motive was simply to re-cruit to the defense of racial prejudice the gender prejudices of a House where men were in an immense majority, but if so, he had miscalcu-lated the temper of the House. However, it has been pointed out that the judge, whose sister had been one of the first women members of the West Virginia legislature,[9] had long supported an Equal Rights Amendment. Whatever the motive for his gambit, it failed: his amendment, meant to sink the bill, passed resoundingly, 168 to 133. Sex discrimination, hence-forth, thanks to the most crusty reactionary in the Congress, would now, in theory at least, be against the law. In practice, Title VI, guaranteeing equal rights for women, had significant consequences. For example, it opened the way for later legislation that promoted equal facilities for sports for women in schools and colleges.

On February 10, the House of Representatives passed the 1964 Civil Rights Act by 290 to 130. A jubilant LBJ phoned Clarence Mitchell of the NAACP, sometimes called the "101st senator" for his ubiquitous and ge-nial presence, and Joe Rauh to thank them for their lobbying efforts. "All right, you fellows," he said, "get on over to the Senate and get busy!"[10]

Neither LBJ nor his lieutenants had any illusions about how tough the fight in the Senate would be. Already on December 3, 1963, he had convinced Martin Luther King Jr. that he was serious about passing a great civil rights bill. Before the end of the year he had had meetings with Roy Wilkins and other major African American champions as well. King's friend Clarence Jones had pointed out to the reverend that John-son, as a southerner, had far more in common with him than had Jack Kennedy. King emerged from his meeting with the new president to tell reporters that he was "very impressed by the president's awareness of the needs of civil rights and the depth of his concern. As a southerner, I am happy to know that a fellow southerner is in the White House who is concerned about civil rights." He added that LBJ had made it plain that he wanted the bill out of the Rules Committee before Christmas. "He means business. I think we can expect even more from him than we have had up to now."[11]

King remained wary of LBJ's motives, but at least now the president could count on support from the civil rights movement, freeing him to concentrate on the bill's opponents. He began by making it painfully

clear to two of the South's great champions in the Senate, Dick Russell of
Georgia, chairman of the Armed Services Committee, and Harry Byrd
of Virginia, chairman of Finance, that they should not deceive themselves that he could be moved by appeals to southern loyalty.

It was clear that their strategy would be to delay the tax bill that
the president needed in order to hold up the civil rights legislation that
he wanted.[12] LBJ haggled with Byrd over the size of the federal budget,
knowing how reluctant the Virginian always was to allow federal spending to balloon. If the president kept spending below $100 billion, Byrd
grudgingly agreed to allow the bill to come to the floor. With Russell, his
mentor and closest friend in the Senate, Johnson was more brutal. At a
showdown lunch in the White House, he told his friend, "I'm going to
roll over you." "It'll cost you the election," Russell replied. "If that's the
price I have to pay, I'll pay it happily."[13]

Three days before the bill's final passage in the House, the president
had sat down with Nick Katzenbach, Robert Kennedy's number two at
the Justice Department, to calculate the bill's prospects. (It was easier
to talk to the agreeable former law professor, toughened by two years
in a Nazi prisoner of war camp after he was shot down over Europe,
than with the attorney general himself; relations there were approaching
rock bottom.) Thanks to Rule 22, passed in 1919 and not amended until
1975, sixty-six votes, two-thirds of the one hundred senators, would be
needed for "cloture," that is, to overcome a filibuster and pass the bill.
Filibusters were then much rarer than they have become since 1975. LBJ
and Katzenbach reckoned they had fifty-eight safe votes and would need
at least nine more.[14] Those nine, they figured, would have to come from
seventeen uncertain senators, eight of them Republicans and nine conservative Democrats not irrevocably tied to the South.[15] The Republicans
were conservative midwesterners, many from largely agricultural states
with small populations: Roman Hruska and Carl Curtis of Nebraska;
Bourke Hickenlooper and Jack Miller of Iowa; Karl Mundt of South Dakota; Milton Young of North Dakota; Frank Carlson of Kansas; and Clifford Hansen of Wyoming. The potential Democratic votes would have
to be found from a more diverse group: Albert Gore Sr. and Herbert
Walters from border-state Tennessee; J. Howard Edmondson from
Oklahoma; LBJ's bête noire from Texas, the awkward labor-backed lib-

eral Ralph Yarborough; the crusty conservative Democrat Frank Lausche
of Ohio; and four westerners from states that then had small populations and few African Americans—Alan Bible and Howard Cannon of
Nevada; Frank Moss of Utah; and Carl Hayden of Arizona, at eighty-six
the oldest man in the Senate and its president pro tempore, who had
been in Congress ever since his state joined the Union in 1912.

Katzenbach persuaded LBJ that he himself was the key to obtain-
ing the sixty-six votes needed for cloture: "If you do anything publicly
but indicate that we're going to get cloture on this bill, we can't possibly
get cloture," Katzenbach recalled later. "And the only way we can get
it is for you with your experience to express absolute confidence publicly and privately that we're going to get cloture on this bill, which was
putting his neck right on the line. And then he did that. I think it was
basically the reason that we got it, because they all thought that he knew
the Senate."[16]

Whatever his men's fortunes might be with this motley crew of
senators, Lyndon Johnson had understood from the start that the key
to victory lay with Senator Everett Dirksen. A mellifluous man much
mocked for his earlier unsuccessful career as a Shakespearian actor (actually, he had been a playwright in a modest way), Dirksen came from
Pekin, Illinois, the marigold capital of the world, not far from Peoria.
With a wide mouth and a prominent quiff, he sported curly white hair
like a Bedlington terrier and was never at a loss for words, flowery, rhetorical, and unstoppable: his enemies called him "the Wizard of Ooze."
He did ooze rhetorical emotion, but he was not without wit, tactical
cunning, and a genuine old-fashioned Republican patriotism.

It was this strange creature that Lyndon Johnson set out to capture.
He did so with his usual combination of shameless flattery and shrewd
understanding of motive. His chief lieutenant, Hubert Humphrey, said,
"I would have kissed Dirksen's ass on the Capitol steps" to get his support for cloture, and he proceeded to do just about that metaphorically, calling him "a great American" on television and predicting that
when the bill passed the glory would be his. On April 13 Robert Kennedy reported to LBJ by phone that he believed the administration had
an agreement with Dirksen on the civil rights bill. LBJ congratulated

him warmly, their feud temporarily suspended, and immediately called Dirksen and to further lather him with flattery.[17] He promised to give Dirksen the credit, with heavy hints that the senator from Illinois was a second Lincoln.[18]

Dirksen told Humphrey privately that the bill was a good one and that he would support it. But he wanted to avoid cloture. Humphrey said no. So Dirksen was admitted to the group of Humphrey, Majority Leader Mike Mansfield, and Nick Katzenbach, who were in charge of the fight and in effect allowed Dirksen to write the bill. The substance was the same, but the language was Dirksen's, ornate and flowery. With an angler's skill, Lyndon had landed his fish.

Some senators got judicial appointments they hankered after, others presidential support for "pork barrel" projects in their states. On May 11 LBJ even landed Carl Hayden, who had never voted for cloture in more than half a century on the Hill, by offering his administration's help to fund the senator's pet project, one of the most ecologically unsound schemes ever conceived, the Central Arizona Project, to divert water to Tucson and Phoenix from the Colorado River. Once Johnson and his allies knew they had the requisite votes without Hayden, however, LBJ relented,[19] and Mike Mansfield told the old man his vote was not needed.

The vote on cloture came on June 10. It had some of the drama of great Senate occasions in the past, like the impeachment debate on President Andrew Johnson in 1868. All one hundred senators voted. Senator Clair Engle of California, who was dying of cancer, was pushed into the chamber in a wheelchair. He couldn't speak, but he voted "Aye" by pointing to his eye. Cannon and Edmondson both voted aye. LBJ had the votes he needed: seventy-one of them, in the end, to twenty-nine.

Final passage, after that, was something of an anticlimax. The Republicans said that LBJ would reveal his megalomania by signing the bill on Independence Day. Clare Booth Luce even called him (claiming the privilege of ancient, intimate friendship) to counsel against that idea. In the end he did not. The Senate voted at 2:30 on July 2, and the president signed the bill in the East Room at 6:45 in the presence of Robert Kennedy, Everett Dirksen, Hubert Humphrey, Martin Luther King Jr., and over a hundred others who had fought the good fight. There was very satisfactory television coverage into the bargain.[20]

Passage of the civil rights bill opened the gates for the rest of LBJ's legislative program, and a remarkable list it was. But it is worth pausing at this point to notice how the legislative battles took place against the backdrop of a series of strange and disturbing events. The 1960s have been profoundly and often deliberately misunderstood. They are remembered as a time of political, cultural, and sexual radicalism when everyone, from Maine to California, blinked through a fog of pharmaceutically induced gratification. That is a bit like believing that the 1920s, that time of conservative Republican administration, business dominance, Prohibition, and swollen Ku Klux Klan membership, were defined entirely by short skirts, the Charleston, and the triangular martini glass.

Demographically, the 1960s saw the baby boom generation pass from adolescence to young adulthood. They saw the economic dominance of the United States challenged by the recovering economies of Japan and Europe, while American military power was more or less seriously threatened by the Soviet Union. John Kennedy came to power on a tide of frustration with the conformism of the 1950s, but also in a world of rapid, unpredictable change that many Americans found both confusing and frightening. This context both facilitated the administration's task and gave to the national life in 1964 a lowering, thunderous feeling. This sense of tension, even of national crisis, was to intensify in 1965, but the barometric pressure, metaphorically speaking, was already rising in the year between Dallas and the presidential election.

The most obvious tension was apparent in the series of trials of strength between the civil rights movement and the essentially Democratic state and local governments of the Deep South. The Kennedy administration had already been compelled by the Freedom Rides, the Ole Miss riot, the March on Washington, and the events in Birmingham to take the black uprising seriously As a consequence JFK was forced to advance major civil rights legislation from a possible place on the calendar in a second Kennedy administration to an urgent, immediate priority. In the same way, after his death a sequence of racial clashes, some relatively minor in themselves, in Southside Virginia, the Eastern Shore of Maryland, and St. Augustine, Florida, played in counterpoint against events of national politics.

In June 1964 hundreds of (mostly white) graduate students from the most famous colleges in the land were undergoing training in nonviolent demonstration techniques at a small campus in Ohio before joining the Mississippi Freedom Summer voter-registration project when the news came through that three of their comrades had disappeared in Mississippi. They were subsequently found to have been murdered, their bodies stuffed into a newly dug earth dam, by policemen who were themselves members of the Ku Klux Klan.[21]

In July the Democratic national convention in Atlantic City turned into a crude racial clash over the seating of a mainly black Mississippi Freedom Democratic Party in place of the lily-white delegation led by former leaders of the congressional Democratic Party like Senators James Eastland and John Stennis. The national television audience was shocked by the raw account Fanny Lou Hamer gave of the way she had been humiliated and savagely beaten by the police in Winona, Mississippi, in June 1963.

In August LBJ chose Hubert Humphrey as his vice presidential running mate, thus denying Robert Kennedy the nomination he had set his heart on and bringing into the open the hidden but seething rivalry between the two camps in the Democratic Party.

These events were cracking the primal alliance between southern conservatives and northern workers and their intellectual allies that had held the Democratic Party together since the days when it was still called Republican, and Thomas Jefferson and James Madison went together to meet New York leaders on a botanizing expedition up the Hudson; certainly that alliance had been the core of the party since the days of Woodrow Wilson and Franklin Roosevelt.

Other, even stranger things were happening. When I covered the civil rights movement in 1962–63, the common assumption among my fellow reporters, most but not all of them from the North, and no doubt among most of their readers and viewers, was that it was inevitable that the South, sooner or later, would become more like the rest of the country. Later, it seemed that in many ways the rest of the country had become much more like the South.[22] One particular aspect of this process was the surprising discovery that the feisty, resentful populism of Alabama governor George Wallace was far more attractive to many in the North than anyone would have suspected. In November 1963 Wallace spoke at Harvard and other Ivy League colleges, where he was greeted with something between reluctant tolerance and grudging admiration.[23]

Many working-class northerners, however, had a simpler reaction: they understood that Wallace was expressing something they felt themselves: resentment and rage that their own political leaders were not expressing their patriotism, frustrations, and fears. In 1964 Democratic primaries in Wisconsin, Indiana, and Maryland, Wallace astonished mainstream media with his success. Wallace himself told friends he would shake the establishment if he could win 10 percent of the vote in a northern state: in Wisconsin he won 33 percent, in Indiana "only" 30 percent, and in Maryland more than 40 percent of the vote, only a few points behind the president, and he secured an actual majority of white voters.[24]

If the Wallace campaign suggested that, where the politics of race were concerned, the North was not quite so different from the South as northern politicians and journalists would have liked to think, at this very time evidence began to accumulate that, in terms of crude sociological realities, the North was also deeply and bitterly divided about race. In the summer, race riots, some small, some not so small, took place in New York City, Rochester, New York, in three New Jersey cities, in Chicago, and in Philadelphia. They were triggered, as such upheavals often are, by an incident involving a policeman: a fifteen-year-old boy, James Powell, was one of a number of students from Robert F. Wagner Junior High School in Harlem who were skylarking in the street. A building superintendent sprayed the boys with a hose, and Powell chased him back into the building. Officer Thomas Gilligan, summoned, shot Powell dead. Rioting spread all over the city and lasted for five days and nights.

Such incidents drew attention to facts that had been generally ignored: that most big American cities were residentially segregated not just by custom and happenstance but as a result of redlining and other deliberate discriminatory practices on the part of local business elites.

As a consequence, the school systems in the North were in practice almost as segregated as those in the South; by the end of the twentieth century, indeed, New York, Chicago, and Detroit were by some measures actually more segregated than Atlanta, Memphis, or New Orleans. While a few African Americans were taking advantage of opportunities to make money and succeed in the professions, most were penned in ghettos where they had to contend with poor housing, poor health, rampant crime and drug use, and far higher rates of unemployment than those found among the white majority.

In the middle 1960s, it began to dawn on many Americans that achieving de facto racial equality in the North might be as hard as, or harder than, legislating de jure equality in the South. Lyndon Johnson might be able to produce votes in Congress that would make overt discrimination illegal in the South; to change psychological assumptions and deep economic structures to abolish inequality in the rest of the nation might be quite another matter.

Wallace's success in reaching northern voters was one of the early signs of a new conservatism that would soon replace New Deal liberalism as the predominant public philosophy in the United States. In a 1995 biography, the southern historian Dan T. Carter argued unhappily that "the Alabama governor seems vindicated by history." "If he did not create the conservative groundswell that transformed American politics in the 1980s, he anticipated most of its themes. It was Wallace who sensed and gave voice to a growing white backlash in the mid-1960s; it was Wallace who warned of the danger to the American soul posed by the 'intellectual snobs who don't know the difference between smut and great literature'; it was Wallace who railed against federal bureaucrats.... If George Wallace did not create this mood of national scepticism, he anticipated and exploited the political transformation it precipitated."[25]

Professor Carter's perception of Wallace's importance and influence is persuasive; certainly it is far more true than the half-amused, half-horrified sneer that was the typical response of northern politicians, journalists, and intellectuals in Wallace's lifetime. But Wallace was far from the only harbinger of the new conservative ascendancy in the very years when Lyndon Johnson seemed all-conquering. At first, this took the form of organizing outside the electoral process and of the growing acceptance of ideas that would once have been seen as outside the American mainstream. A key moment was the foundation in 1960 by William F. Buckley Jr. of Young Americans for Freedom (YAF). By 1964 YAF, aided by William Rusher's efforts in forming the Draft Goldwater Committee, could attract eighteen thousand supporters to a rally in support of Senator Barry Goldwater's campaign for the Republican presidential nomination.

At first the Democratic administration's response to the new conservative wave was to see it merely as an opportunity to discredit Goldwater and his backers. In late 1961 President Kennedy had openly attacked the Far Right in a speech in Hollywood. In those same years, however, several books were being published and widely read that helped to remove the conservative cause from the category of easily dismissible "right-wing nuts," which the wild pronouncements of the John Birch Society and its leader, Robert Welch, had encouraged. Phyllis Schlafly's *A Choice, Not an Echo*, published in April 1964, sold 3 million copies in 1964 alone.[26] Its immediate contribution was to strengthen the "New Right" by its attack on the traditional, moderate Republican leadership symbolized by the presidential ambitions of Nelson Rockefeller.[27]

LBJ's crushing defeat of Goldwater in the 1964 presidential election greatly improved his chances of passing his legislative program. It also obscured for most of the political world the rising strength of the new conservatism. Two other events cast their shadows in the first few months of LBJ's presidency: the rise of political feminism and the approach of the Vietnam War.

Betty Friedan's *The Feminine Mystique*, published in 1963, was an immensely influential book, but to a new generation of activist women its author came to be regarded as little better than a reactionary. Younger, more radical women activists were greatly influenced by the experiences of women who had taken part in the Mississippi Freedom Summer: they had signed up as activists and faced the danger of brutal repression yet their male colleagues still expected them to type their letters, make their coffee, and sleep with them. This inequality was first cogently expressed in Casey Hayden and Mary King's "Sex and Caste: A Kind of Memo" written in 1965.[28] But it was not until 1967 that the National Organization for Women (NOW) took up the languishing Equal Rights Amendment. The tide of congressional support for the ERA did not become full until 1971–72, after which it ebbed. The issue of abortion, which was to divide politics so bitterly in later decades, had not yet surfaced: *Roe v. Wade,* first argued in 1971, was not decided until 1973.

On May 22, 1964, while the furious lobbying for the civil rights bill was still at its height, President Johnson went to the University of Michigan at Ann Arbor and set himself an even more ambitious goal. The test of America's success as a nation, he announced, would be its success in pursuing the happiness of the people. Now, he proclaimed, was the time to build a Great Society, a place where every child could "find knowledge to enrich his mind and enlarge his talents." It was not a safe harbor or a resting place but a challenge constantly renewed "in our cities, in our countryside, and in our classrooms." He ended by calling on his audience to "join in the battle to build the Great Society, to prove that our material progress is only the foundation on which we will build a richer life of mind and spirit."[29]

In this speech, and again in his speech on June 4, 1965, at Howard University, when he proclaimed that what we must seek for African Americans must be "not just equality as a right and a theory but equality as a fact and as a result," Johnson was aiming at multiple goals.[30] Each was a political statement intended to strengthen the president's position, to attract support, and to outpace competitors. At another level, those two great speeches were inspired by his deep yearning to match the eloquence and style of John Kennedy's best speeches, and in particular of his inaugural. (It is interesting that while both speeches expressed his purposes and reflected many inputs, both were "written" by a member of Kennedy's speechwriting team, Richard Goodwin, a man of whom historian Randall Woods wrote, "He would spend his nights ridiculing LBJ and his days working to shape the policies of the man who had usurped JFK.")[31] They also expressed the genuine, passionate beliefs and aspirations of this titanic public man, who could descend into crass coarseness and cynicism but could also soar into realms of vision too romantic for his predecessor, the cool Whig, whose dreams were not of social redemption but of nationalist triumph.

From the very first day of his presidency, as we have seen, LBJ had made plain to his intimates that he meant not just to carry out JFK's agenda but to surpass it. That might be a difficult task, but it was not hard for him to imagine, because it would draw on ambitions that had their roots deep in his personal experience, from Johnson City, San Marcos, and Cotulla to New Deal Washington. As soon as he became president, LBJ badgered his team for a slogan that would summarize what he wanted to achieve and at the same time serve as the banner for his campaigns, the equivalent of Wilson's New Freedom, FDR's New Deal, and Kennedy's New Frontier. He was attracted by a phrase of Walter Lippmann's: "the Good Society."

The Damascus moment, the descent of inspiration, happened in a sublimely Lyndonian moment of low comedy and high thinking. In February LBJ summoned Goodwin and Bill Moyers to the White House pool, where he was swimming, as usual, naked. He ordered his aides to strip off and join him. Goodwin captured the scene. "We entered the pool area to see the massive presidential flesh, a sun bleached atoll breaching the placid sea, passing gently, sidestroke, the deep-cleft buttocks moving past our unstartled gaze. Moby Dick, I thought. . . . 'It's like swimming with a polar bear,' Moyers whispered."[32]

At this moment, inspired like an Old Testament prophet or a father of the church, LBJ began to expound the vision he had already confided to his friends at the Elms on the very first night of his presidency. He always meant not just to fulfill JFK's aspirations but to go beyond them; he had always dreamed of an America that could be a land of plenty, but also one that aspired to excellence in all matters public, from education and culture to technological innovation and social conscience.[33] He charged his two young aides to express this vision in a speech, and for the next three months Goodwin went to work on that task. It was Goodwin who found the label for this titanic vision, in a pre–World War I book by the British socialist and educator Graham Wallas: *The Great Society*.[34]

After civil rights, LBJ's first priority was education. Here he enjoyed a peculiar advantage over John Kennedy: he was not a Roman Catholic. Since the mid-nineteenth-century time of Archbishop John Hughes, American Catholic leaders had faced a somewhat paradoxical dilemma over schools. While their flock was largely recruited from the immigrant poor, whose need for the best possible public education was paramount, the hierarchy could not happily allow federal aid to go to public schools, since that would give them an advantage over the church's own parochial schools. To his credit, JFK—the product of elite, more or less Protestant schools—proposed to override this historical taboo and allow federal aid to public schools.

In March 1961, faced with this prospect, no fewer than five cardinals, with eight bishops and archbishops, met in Washington and pronounced that "in the event that a federal aid program is enacted which excluded children in private [that is, parochial] schools those children will be the victims of discriminatory legislation. There will be no alternative but to oppose such discrimination."[35] *Roma locuta est, causa finita est:*[36] Rome had spoken, and the case was closed. The church was aided by several congressmen, many of them Irishmen from the Northeast such as Hugh Carey and James J. Delaney, with a future Speaker, John McCormack, acting, as was said, almost as floor leader for the hierarchy. Kennedy's education bill, an important measure in itself and a vital test of his claim to be able to rise above tribal politics, was—through no fault of his own—stone dead.

Lyndon Johnson cared passionately about public schools. He had not only been a student in public schools, he had taught in them. Not only was this a tailor-made opportunity to show that he could do what Kennedy could not do, it was an issue on which he had genuine, long-held convictions.

The education commissioner whom LBJ had inherited from JFK, Francis Keppel of the Harvard School of Education, came up with the tool that would open the door. In 1947, in *Everson v. Board of Education,* the Supreme Court had ruled that federal aid for parochial students was constitutional so long as the aid went to poor children, not to schools. Keppel proposed what he called "categorical aid" to children in urban slums and deprived rural areas. Johnson seized on the idea. On January 12, striking while the iron of electoral landslide was hot, he sent a message proposing an elementary and secondary education bill to Congress. He insisted that his staff dig out a quotation he remembered from Mirabeau Buonaparte Lamar, the obscure second president of the

Republic of Texas: "The cultivated mind," he had said, "is the guardian of democracy. It is the only dictator that free man acknowledges. It is the only security that free man desires."[37]

The very next day a meticulous lobbying campaign was launched. Bill Moyers and Doug Cater, the Alabamian former magazine editor who was in charge of both education and health care in the White House, took Congresswoman Edith Green to lunch; then the president invited Mrs. Green in to the White House for some political stroking. There was a brief flurry of difficulty from Harlem's Adam Clayton Powell, the unpredictable and flamboyant African American chairman of the House Committee on Education and Labor. It turned out that Powell, who had retreated to Puerto Rico with his usual accompaniment of good-looking young women, wanted to hold the education bill hostage to call off an investigation into his improper use of expenses. A six-figure sum lubricated passage through the committee. Larry O'Brien used his considerable expertise to put out other fires. One of them was lit by Republican senator Winston Prouty of Vermont, who complained that the issue was not educational but constitutional: the bill, he claimed, threatened "the future of the Senate as a co-equal partner in the legislative process." Few senators shared his fears, and the bill, having passed the House comfortably on March 26, now sailed through the Senate by seventy-three votes to eighteen on April 9.

LBJ could now mount one of the symbolic bill-signing spectaculars that were to be his trademark. He invited the press to watch him sign the bill at the one-room schoolhouse, a mile down the road from the LBJ ranch, where he had begun his own education. He even invited Miss Katie Deadrich, who had managed to teach eight grades at the same time there. "Come over here, Miss Katie, and sit by me, will you?" LBJ said to the old lady in his most honeyed tone. "I started school when I was 4 years old, and they tell me, Miss Katie, that I recited my first lesson while sitting on your lap."[38]

The Elementary and Secondary Education Act was both a virtuoso display of all aspects of the Johnson treatment—from deep planning and understanding of political history by way of flattery, threats, and genteel bribery to outrageous schmaltz—and an authentic landmark in social history. Having won that decisive battle, LBJ had no difficulty in following it with the Higher Education Act (1965), which helped hard-pressed state institutions cope with the tide of baby boomers. By 1970 one-quarter of all students in American colleges were the recipients of federal aid under the act. LBJ signed this bill in the gymnasium at San Marcos.

Reform of the health care system was an issue that had perplexed presidents as long ago as FDR and would continue to perplex them for another half century. In 1934 the University of Wisconsin economist Edwin Witte was appointed executive director of the Committee on Economic Security by President Franklin Roosevelt. The committee's task was to recommend means "to provide at once security against several of the great disturbing factors in life—especially those that relate to unemployment and old age." The committee looked at many possible solutions and came down on two recommendations: a minimum income for the elderly (Social Security) and government-promoted health insurance.

The former was passed by the Congress in the Social Security Act, signed by FDR on August 14, 1935. Health insurance, on the other hand, became "the orphan of the New Deal." So many telegrams opposed to health insurance flooded Capitol Hill—much of the opposition was promoted by the American Medical Association and the health insurance industry—that it looked as though the whole Social Security program would be in danger until the House Ways and Means Committee struck it out. FDR was personally influenced by the opposition to public health insurance by the father-in-law of his son James, Harvey Cushing, neurosurgeon and surgeon in chief at Peter Bent Brigham Hospital at Harvard.[39]

In 1945, in the new confidence and prosperity of victory, Democratic senators Robert Wagner of New York and James Murray of Montana and Democratic congressman John Dingell of Michigan proposed a government-run health care plan for all Americans. With President Harry Truman supporting the bill and polls showing up to 74 percent approval, the United States might have had a national health service before Britain did. But after the Republicans took control of Congress in 1946, and as a result of the rapid growth of private health insurance, the bill languished and in 1951 eventually died.

In 1957, Representative Aimé Forand of Rhode Island, a senior member of Ways and Means, introduced a bill providing for mandatory hospital insurance, funded by a payroll tax, for all Social Security beneficiaries. The bill could not even get out of Ways and Means. The first federal health care legislation was passed in 1960. This was the Kerr-Mills bill. It provided for some coverage for the indigent elderly, but its costs were to be shared with the states. Only the richest states could afford to take part: 90 percent of the money went to just five of the wealthiest states.

Once elected, John Kennedy picked up the issue and sent to Congress his version of the Forand bill, hospital insurance for the elderly, which he called Medicare. The bill's prospects were not good in Kennedy's lifetime. Wilbur Mills, worried because of the loss of seats in his home state of Arkansas (as a result of reapportionment and of the fall-out from the Little Rock school desegregation row), was reluctant to support the bill. The American Medical Association, near its political zenith, raised a fortune for lobbying campaigns. LBJ included Medicare in the list of Kennedy initiatives he was determined to pass. But Mills, universally admired as an exceptionally able legislator, expressed doubt in his oral history that Medicare (or indeed other Johnson social legislation) would have passed with Kennedy or without Johnson.

The second key figure in this transformation of the prospects for health care reform was the other Wilbur: Wilbur Cohen, now of the University of Michigan but a veteran of social policy fights going back to the Roosevelt administration. He was to be one of the most effective of LBJ's helpers in his legislative triumphs. Cohen was an academic. But he had also come to Washington as early as 1934 when he became the first employee of Witte's committee, and subsequently was the first permanent employee of the Social Security Administration. Wilbur Cohen, in short, was one of the first as well as the ablest of those in-and-outers who served the federal government so well between the 1930s and the 1960s, though in truth he was more in than out. He had helped to draft the Wagner-Dingell legislation, shaped the Forand plan in 1957, and saved Kerr-Mills by inventing the concept of "medical indigence" to allow those who were not currently poor but would be impoverished by hospital bills to be beneficiaries of Social Security. Cohen was not only vastly knowledgeable, experienced, and committed; his personality made him an exceptionally effective advocate of reform. He was willing to work with Republicans as well as Democrats, with the AMA as well as labor unions. Above all, he seemed not to seek credit for himself. It was inevitable that the Kennedy administration would enlist him as deputy director of the department of Health, Education, and Welfare for legislative affairs. Nevertheless, even Cohen was not able to pass the two bills that mattered most to Kennedy on the domestic front: Medicare and federal aid to elementary and secondary education.

The Kennedy Medicare legislation was defeated by what at the time was thought to be the most intense and expensive lobbying effort in history: the AMA. The doctors spent $50 million and sent twenty-three lobbyists to Capitol Hill. Here, as elsewhere, LBJ was determined to do better, and here, too, circumstances made it possible for him to succeed where JFK had failed.

LBJ's initial personal priority in health care was rooted in his family's and his own medical history. His father had died at sixty of coronary disease, his mother of cancer, and one of his grandmothers had been immobilized by a stroke. He himself had almost died of a heart attack at forty-six, and after that he did not like to sleep alone: if Lady Bird was away, he would ask a friend or an aide to sleep at the White House with the door open to hear if he cried out. His priorities, then, were that of the National Institutes of Health, funded in part by his friend Mary Lasker: heart, cancer, and stroke. Later many doctors pointed out that these were precisely the diseases that middle-aged, prosperous white men of sedentary habits, like most members of Congress, were most afraid of, and Johnson was no different from his former colleagues on the Hill in that respect.[40] In March 1964 his main interest was in creating the Commission on Heart Disease, Cancer and Stroke.

As the 1964 election approached, however, influenced by the pollster Oliver Quayle's evidence of public enthusiasm for health care, LBJ made Medicare one of his highest priorities. By July, though, when Wilbur Cohen asked the president to get a commitment on Medicare from Wilbur Mills, LBJ had to reply that he hadn't been able to do so. It was not LBJ's famous treatment but the 1964 elections that made up Mills's mind.

After LBJ's landslide defeat of Barry Goldwater, everything changed, and Mills, like the shrewd operator he was, changed too. He became the manager of LBJ's health care bill. The AMA, in desperation, came out with its own "Eldercare," a plan for means-tested health insurance. A Republican congressman came out with another scheme. Mills then put forward his own answer. He proposed a "three-layer cake" composed of hospital care, a voluntary plan for paying doctors, and a combined federal/state program for the indigent. In seconds, everything had changed. When Mills presented his plan to the whole House, he was given a standing ovation: within ten days the House had voted through the Mills plan by 313 to 115.

Two obstacles remained: the Senate and the doctors. No scheme would work unless surgeons and physicians the length and breadth of America agreed to make it work. Senate passage depended in the first place on favorable treatment of the bill in the Senate Finance Committee. The chairman was Harry Byrd, proud descendant of a colonial dynasty, proud too of his Northern Virginia apple orchards and of his power over the committee that could block any legislation held obnoxious by the Senate's southern barons.

With a wily ploy, LBJ mousetrapped this theoretically mighty legislative tyrant. He invited the congressional leadership of both houses to discuss health care. Unknown to his guests, he had arranged television coverage. With the cameras running, he asked Senator Byrd for his observations. Byrd admitted he had not yet studied the Medicare legislation but would hold hearings. "And you have nothing that you know of that would prevent that coming about in reasonable time?" asked the president. "No," Byrd was heard to say quietly, caught unprepared in front of his peers. "So," pursued LBJ relentlessly, "when the House acts and it is referred to the Senate Finance Committee, you will arrange for prompt hearings?" "Yes," said the chairman, his power to delay legislation neatly stripped from him by being put on the spot in front of the TV cameras. The hearings unfolded without incident and on July 9 the Senate approved amendments to the Social Security Act of 1935, creating Medicare and Medicaid, by sixty-eight to twenty-one.[41]

The doctors were disarmed by an even more audacious gambit. On June 29 Johnson met the leaders of the AMA, most of them inveterate opponents of government intervention in health care, which they called "socialized medicine." He stood and delivered a panegyric on the wonderful work of the doctors who had treated his own father. He stood, and they stood. He sat, and they sat, then once again he stood, and they stood. It was now, wrote a historian of the Great Society, perfectly clear who was in control.[42] LBJ then announced that he wanted physicians to volunteer to treat the civilian population in Vietnam. Would the AMA help? The AMA leaders said they would be glad to. LBJ then brought in the press. One reporter asked whether the AMA was going to boycott Medicare. The president answered, "These men are going to get doctors to go to Vietnam and they might be killed. Medicare is the law of the land. Of course they'll support the law of the land." And he turned to the head of the delegation. "We are, after all," he said, "law-abiding citizens and we have every intention of obeying the new law." A few weeks later the AMA announced that it would support Medicare.[43]

Lyndon Johnson's reforms all changed America profoundly. Within a few years, federal aid to education had reached $68.3 billion.[44] By the second decade of the twenty-first century, health care in general and Medicare in particular were among the prime topics of political conflict. But the reform that changed America more than any of them was not essentially Lyndon Johnson's policy. It was for him a second order of priority, and its chief advocates hotly denied that it would change much at all. Yet the Immigration and Naturalization Act of 1965 did change America more than any of those resounding achievements of the first session of the Eighty-ninth Congress, more even than the Voting Rights Act, and that contributed to profound changes in political parties and party politics. Immigration reform changed the national origin rules regarding immigrants and therefore the culture and character of the American people, and in a dramatic way.

Back in 1958, as a senator, Jack Kennedy put his name to a pamphlet called *A Nation of Immigrants,* later, after his death, reissued as a best-selling book. The idea was not originally his. The Harvard historian Oscar Handlin had written much about immigration, stressing the painful experience of "the uprooted" almost as much as the successes of the "golden door." Handlin worked closely with the Jewish Anti-Defamation League (ADL), and it was the ADL that proposed to Senator Kennedy that he publish under his own name a version of an outline written by Arthur Mann (later a professor of history at the University of Chicago), who had been one of Handlin's doctoral students at Harvard.[45] The pamphlet, as rewritten by the senator or his staff, differed significantly from Mann's outline. It played down Mann's (and Handlin's) stress on the painful side of migration and assimilation to present something closer to the traditional July 4 patriotic narrative.

This narrative, after all, was a considerable part of the Kennedy family myth, and immigration reform became part of what Jack Kennedy, as presidential candidate, offered in 1960. All three Kennedy brothers embraced it. Robert Kennedy was an enthusiast for immigration reform, in particular for the abolition of the national quotas, which were heavily biased in favor of would-be immigrants from northern Europe. Edward Kennedy was a lifelong advocate of immigration reform and as a freshman senator did much of the heavy lifting needed to pass the immigration bill when it was adopted by Lyndon Johnson. In particular, the youngest Kennedy played an important part in spreading the idea that the Hart-Celler Act, as the Kennedy immigration bill was called after its sponsors, Senator Phil Hart of Michigan and Representative Manny Celler of Brooklyn, would not lead to a massive wave of new immigrants. In fact, the young Ted Kennedy's first assignment as a floor leader for a bill was for Hart-Celler in 1963. He sought to reassure Congress and the country that the bill would not change very much at all. (It is fair to say that LBJ gave similar assurances.) In Senate hearings Kennedy said: "First, our cities will not be flooded with a million immigrants annually. Under the proposed bill, the present level of immigration remains substantially the same. . . . Secondly, the ethnic mix of this country will not be upset. . . . Contrary to the charges in some quarters, [the bill] will not inundate America with immigrants from any one country or area, or the most populated and deprived nations of Africa and Asia . . . the ethnic pattern of immigration under the proposed measure is not expected to change as sharply as the critics seem to think. . . . It will not cause American workers to lose their jobs."[46]

It seems that the Kennedy brothers were thinking in modest terms—of making it easier, for example, for relatively small numbers of Irish farmers and nurses, among others, to move to Massachusetts, where among the many advantages of the American Dream they would be able to vote for Kennedys and other Democratic candidates from the

Bay State. There was no conscious dishonesty in this. The Kennedy family myth, after all, largely evoked the opportunities created by immigration and the triumph of hardworking immigrants over the prejudices of those who feared or opposed immigration.

Neither the Kennedys, the ADL, nor any other of the (mainly liberal) supporters of the legislation anticipated its immense impact, especially the implication of unrestricted immigration for relatives of migrants who had already arrived and of migrants from the Western Hemisphere. Almost every statement Senator Ted Kennedy made proved to be inaccurate. The level of immigration has not remained substantially the same. The ethnic mix has indeed been upset. Whether or not inundation is an appropriate term, the new immigrants have mainly come not from a (relatively) prosperous Europe but from Asia and especially from Central and Southern America. The only prediction the senator made that seems so far to be true is that immigration has not caused American workers to lose their jobs: many American workers have indeed lost their jobs, but that is the consequence of factors other than immigration.

From the 1880s to the 1920s (when immigration dwindled to a trickle), mass immigration from southern and eastern Europe resulted in some 26 million people moving to the United States, of whom roughly two-thirds remained in America.[47] In a second great migration, over the rather more than four decades since the passage of Hart-Celler, more than 30 million have emigrated to the United States. More than half of them have come from Central and South America, at least two-thirds of these from Mexico, and a quarter from Asia. Roughly one-sixth are of European or Canadian origin.

Some population experts have predicted that by 2050 fewer than half of the population will be of European descent.[48] Others believe that this tipping point will come even sooner. Still others point out that, as a result of intermarriage, it may soon be quite unimportant which continent one's ancestors came from. What is not in doubt is that—as a result of Lyndon Johnson's ability to persuade Congress to pass legislation introduced under the Kennedy administration and keenly encouraged by the Kennedy brothers—the ethnic character of the United States, long a country inhabited by the descendants of Europeans and of their African slaves, has radically changed. Soon the United States will be a country where persons of European descent will be in a minority and will probably lose their cultural and political predominance over the others. This may be, for good or ill, the supreme monument to the Kennedy family's political struggles, and probably not what the Kennedys or LBJ had in mind.

As we have seen, Jack Kennedy wanted to "do something" about poverty. All he had time to do before his death was to pass the Area Redevelopment Act in 1961: its funding was voted down in the House in June 1963 as a direct result of southern congressional anger over Kennedy's civil rights speech after George Wallace's schoolhouse door performance at Tuscaloosa. He introduced the War on Poverty bill, but it was not passed until after his death. Kennedy's biographer Ted Sorensen claims that this was one of many bills that would have been passed by the Eighty-seventh Congress, and that Democratic and Republican leaders of both houses of Congress all said as much.[49] Yet the act *was* passed under Johnson, and it did benefit from his incomparable advocacy as well as from the favorable circumstances caused by Kennedy's death.

The contrast between JFK's cautious approach to domestic reform and LBJ's wholehearted commitment in 1964 and after is striking. Yet Johnson's War on Poverty—the bellicose metaphor was as revealing as it was characteristic—flashed only briefly across the political sky. In 1964, it was one of the chief thrusts of a great reforming administration; by 1967, it had largely subsided. It fell victim both to the rival claims of Vietnam on the federal budget and to the discovery, largely occasioned by the Watts riot of 1965 and the vast change it created in the political climate, that eliminating poverty was after all no easy matter. So far from being an unobjectionable work of Christian charity, it touched the most sensitive nerves of American political culture.

Both the embryonic Kennedy plans for a campaign to end poverty and the fully fledged Johnson war respected a deeply held principle of the American political creed: eliminating poverty must be a matter of helping the poor to help themselves, not of offering entitlement to benefits, least of all to cash payments.[50] The two main thrusts of the 1964 act, the Job Corps and the subsequently notorious community action program, both stayed within that tradition.

In 1965, however, events moved fast. The sequence is important. In the early summer, copies began to circulate inside the administration of a document prepared by the assistant secretary of labor, a certain Daniel Patrick Moynihan. It argued that the experience of the African American poor had so grievously damaged the black family that it would take more than a helping hand to abolish poverty in the ghettos. The report was taken to LBJ by his counsel, Harry McPherson, and the president directed his speechwriter, Richard Goodwin, to make that the theme of the major speech he was going to make on June 4 at Howard University.

On August 11 a white policeman, Lee Minikus, arrested a black man, Marquette Frye, on suspicion of drunk driving in the Watts neighborhood of Los Angeles. (It is remarkable how often the spark that ignited a combustible social mix was provided by what was perceived as the high-handed behavior of a cop.)[51] Within minutes, a crowd gathered, first of hundreds, then of thousands, from Los Angeles's deprived South Central district, where trim housing concealed a social pathology of unemployment, poverty, and alcohol and drug abuse. The arrest was a mere trigger: racial tension had been smoldering in South Central for months. The disturbance lasted five days and was on a spectacular scale, bigger than the Detroit race riots of 1943, bigger indeed than any race riot in America since the troubled period after World War I. Almost a thousand buildings were destroyed, three thousand people were arrested, more than one thousand were injured, and thirty-four were killed. It took the deployment of almost fourteen thousand troops from the California National Guard to get the upheaval under control.[52]

The Watts riots shocked political Washington because it confirmed that black anger was just as explosive in northern and western cities as it was in Birmingham or Atlanta. The event shocked Lyndon Johnson personally: he could not accept it. "How is it possible" he asked, "after all we have accomplished?"[53] It provoked a white backlash that shifted the magnetic poles of American politics. And it made politicians, including Lyndon Johnson himself, think twice about the War on Poverty. The shock was reinforced by the publication in the fall of the Moynihan report *The Negro Family: The Case for National Action,*[54] which split the liberal factions in the Democratic Party between those who saw the report as a racist attack on the African American people and those who were inclined to concede its force.

LBJ had originally intended to follow up his Howard University speech with a grand White House conference on the theme "To Fulfill These Rights." To prepare for this, a planning conference was scheduled for October. After Watts, LBJ seemed to have lost interest, or at least taken a more cautious approach. It has been argued[55] that after Watts, LBJ simply gave up on his ambitious project for going beyond equality of opportunity. Certainly he showed a new suspicion and hostility to the more radical people within the civil rights movement. "Black Power," that somewhat hollow slogan, was first shouted out by Stokely Carmichael and his friend Willie Ricks in June 1966. But already by the fall of 1965 elements within the civil rights movement were losing patience with the slow pace of change. LBJ, too, was losing patience with the more aggressive African American leaders, including Martin Luther King, and he sought to exclude King's consigliere, Bayard Rustin, from the White House conference planning and to put it in the "safe" hands of white businessmen.

It goes too far, however, to say that in 1965 LBJ had given up on his dream of racial harmony and equality. What is true is that policy was turning toward the more radical strategy of offering the poor, and specifically the African American poor, money rather than the traditional helping hand. The short-lived fashion for a "guaranteed income" was at hand.

There was another factor. "Community action" was the talisman of the liberal social policy community's thinking about how to abolish poverty, and the administration had adopted the slogan. The poor must not be treated as individuals and helped to stand on their own feet in the traditional American fashion. They must be empowered to demand resources and progress as communities. This led straight to trouble with Lyndon Johnson's own core community, professional elected Democratic politicians, at all levels, but especially in the cities.

As early as January of 1965 the mayor of Baltimore, Theodore McKeldin, had complained to the president that his plans were being jeopardized by "individuals . . . who do not understand the problems and operations of local governments."[56] It was not long before the same point was being made by some of LBJ's closest allies, including James H. Rowe and his budget director Charles Schultze, and by some of his most powerful political allies, including perhaps the most powerful of them all, Mayor Richard Daley of Chicago.[57] Mayors, whatever their personal ideological color, did not appreciate the federal government financing bitter and often personal attacks on them and their administrations, especially when it was a Democratic administration in Washington that appeared to subsidize these rabble-rousers from their own political base.

The achievements of LBJ's Great Society were towering, and several of them—the civil rights and voting rights legislation, Medicare, Medicaid, federal aid for education reform, and immigration reform among them—have become enduring features of the national cultural landscape. Yet the creative phase of the LBJ era was brief.

By 1966 Vietnam was not only absorbing more and more of the president's attention, it was consuming more and more of his budget. The civil rights movement was divided: on the left it tailed off into romantic revolutionism and outright criminality. The Democratic Party itself was divided, both over the war and over "the cities," the euphemism for racial anger in the North. The original philosophy of the War on Poverty was challenged by an aggressive, confrontational "welfare rights" movement.

In his 1966 State of the Union speech, LBJ insisted that the United States was still "strong enough to pursue our goals in the rest of the world" (read: Vietnam) "while still building a Great Society here at home." While some liberal leaders, from the president himself by way of Jacob Javits to Ted Kennedy, continued to insist that the United States was rich enough to have both "guns and butter," many Democratic politicians, including Abraham Ribicoff, Eugene McCarthy, and eventually Robert Kennedy himself, saw opportunities in challenging that proposition. On April 4, 1967, Martin Luther King broke with LBJ by coming out openly against the war at Riverside Church. He deeply angered the president by saying that "the war in Vietnam is but a symptom of a far deeper malady within the American spirit."[58]

As early as the summer of 1966, both support for the war and LBJ's personal popularity had begun to fall precipitously. In the 1966 midterm elections, the administration took what a later generation would call a shellacking. By August 1967 LBJ's rating had fallen below 40 percent,[59] and his unpopularity was so acute that he had to virtually give up traveling around the country because his personal safety could not be guaranteed. The 1968 election was a watershed. It marked not only the end of the Democratic hegemony that had lasted since 1932 but the rejection of liberalism as the dominant public philosophy and the beginning of the conservative ascendancy.

A number of general conclusions can be reached about LBJ's domestic achievements before his attention was fatally diverted to Vietnam, with catastrophic consequences not only for that country and for the standing of the United States in the world but also for Lyndon Johnson's personality and psychic stability.

His achievements were genuine, lasting, and on balance benign. Of all presidents in the twentieth century, only Franklin Roosevelt can claim a comparable record of legislative success. The LBJ reforms were broad, affecting everything: the economy, health care, education at all levels, immigration, poverty, urban and rural beautification, and the environment. They were deep; they tackled problems that both previous and subsequent presidents tried and failed to address. Even if some failed and others were rejected by powerful interest groups, they were on the whole successful. And they have had a lasting effect. Indeed, the reform of immigration law, sketched by JFK but carried through by LBJ, will turn out to have had—as an unintended consequence—an absolutely fundamental effect on the character of the country. Johnson found a country inhabited by the descendants of European immigrants and their African slaves and left it one where citizens of European ancestry would be in a minority.

While Johnson originally sold his policies as a continuation of Kennedy's, not only did he go far beyond what Kennedy intended in many ways, he made it perfectly clear to his colleagues and intimates that this was his deliberate intention. He showed beyond argument that the perception of most northern liberals that Johnson was "to the right" of John Kennedy was plain wrong: LBJ's commitment to radical social reform, and in particular to radical change in the status of African Americans, was far deeper and more personal than JFK's.

LBJ benefited both from JFK's life and from his death. Kennedy was cautious and far more interested in foreign policy than in domestic reform. Yet the style, the ambition, and the personnel of the New Frontier made the pursuit of ambitious social democratic goals more acceptable. Richard Russell was correct when he said that it would be three times harder for the South to resist desegregation under Johnson than it would have been under Kennedy. The Kennedy assassination triggered a mood of national self-examination that prepared the way for the Johnson reforms. The Republicans' choice of Barry Goldwater as their candidate made the Johnson landslide easier. Both Medicare and federal aid to education, still uncertain before the 1964 election, were inevitable after it. Not least, this was because of a change in the judgment of powerful congressional politicians (among them Wilbur Mills, Richard Russell, and Everett Dirksen) that the "rules of the game" had changed: legislation that until Dallas had been unthinkable was now inevitable.

Having said all that, the Johnson reforms were his own doing. They benefited from his vast knowledge and experience of Congress, from the allies he had made and the opponents he had intimidated in his long years on the Hill. They benefited from his skill—for example, from the cunning with which he wooed and outmaneuvered tough opponents such as Mills, Harry Byrd, and Dirksen. Above all, they reflected his passionate personal commitment to health care, to education, to the abolition of poverty, and to social justice, not least for African Americans. Many suspected him when he came to the White House of being conservative, racist, even corrupt. He proved that he was none of those things. Crass he certainly could be, and manipulative, determined enough to use whatever weapon lay to hand to win. He was a prey to self-doubt and pessimism. He was also magnificently brave, confident, and, if tactically crafty and well used to equivocation, he was also, like Bunyan's pilgrim, valiant for truth.

No Umbrella Man

I'm no Chamberlain–umbrella policy man.

—Lyndon B. Johnson at the Democratic

nominating convention, Los Angeles, 1960

I left Washington in the summer of 1965, before Watts. I quit my job with the London *Observer* and went to work as a reporter for British Independent Television. That new work brought me back to the United States several times, for example, to do a formal interview with LBJ at the ranch and also to make a documentary, *The Fire This Time,*[1] about the new northern phase of the civil rights struggle. That involved filming in Brooklyn and Cleveland and a number of interviews, including one with Martin Luther King Jr. At the end of 1967 I moved to the London *Sunday Times* and was soon back in the United States.

In my new job, I no longer spent my days in the newsroom of the *Washington Post* or the West Wing of the White House. But I did continue to see my friends in both places. Friends at the White House had to be discreet: LBJ did not like aides who were not "on the team." I knew some well enough to understand how shaken, unhappy, and unsure they were—a state that became far worse after the Tet offensive at the end of February 1968.

My friends at the *Post* were increasingly skeptical of the war. There were also signs, like ice melt in a warming Arctic, of a general breakup of the liberal consensus. McPherson, Moynihan, and often Meg Greenfield (the last named of the *Post*), and I still sometimes met after work for Rob Roys, a sugary concoction of Scotch whisky and sweet vermouth, at the downstairs bar at the Hay-Adams, across Lafayette Square from the White House. But even in that little school there were now disagreements. Greenfield, future editorial page editor of the *Post*, was beginning to move to the neoconservative right. So, in his complicated way, was Moynihan. (Later as a Democratic senator, he moved back to an eclectic but unmistakably liberal position.) In 1965, he was one of the editors listed on the cover of the first issue of the *Public Interest*, the magazine that first challenged many liberal assumptions. Pat and Meg's former editor at the *Reporter*, Irving Kristol, had been the *Observer*'s New York correspondent when I was its correspondent in Washington. Now he was emerging as the leading impresario of the neocons. Later the *Public Interest* was seen as a neocon manifesto: in the beginning, however, its editors were of many political persuasions. They were brought together by a shared distaste for the new radical politics of the peace movement and the campus. They also shared a suspicion of—as they saw it—the misuse of social science as a guide to public policy.

When I came back in late 1967 to organize coverage of the 1968 presidential election for the London *Sunday Times*,[2] optimism was hard to find, about the war or anything else. Politically, my friends were uncertain, divided, sometimes anguished; in many cases—in a city where politics was an all-consuming obsession—public disillusion translated into personal crisis. Friends were splitting up from their partners. People quarreled angrily at parties. I remember, for example, physically protecting an elderly Canadian diplomat of great distinction from a senior CIA official, stumbling drunk, who kept asking the Canadian why his country didn't become part of the United States.

Alcohol in many forms was part of both the amenity and the stress of pre-Vietnam Washington: martinis the size of flower vases at cocktail parties, oceans of wine at lunch at Chez Camille or at Nora's, long conversations, growing increasingly impassioned and self-pitying as the evening went on, over scotch in someone's apartment late at night. Sexual adventures helped many to cope with the souring of their dreams. Journalists were not the only ones who drank. Lyndon Johnson drank too much. So did the self-controlled patrician Mac Bundy.

I used occasionally to interview the dignified Dean Rusk at the end of his working day in his office at the State Department. Mr. Rusk was considered a model of judgment and sobriety. When I arrived, the secretary would be looking through papers and sipping a scotch. "Would you like a drink?" he would ask, and a Filipino waiter would enter, carrying a second scotch for the secretary. "Thank you," I would say, "I would love a scotch." The waiter would come back with a scotch for me and a third for the secretary. The formula, I saw, was $n = W + 2$, where W was the number of times the secretary's scotch had been replenished.

The war. That was the problem. No one was more agonized about it than Rusk's trusted colleague my quiet friend Ben Read, my very earliest contact in Washington.[3] A Philadelphia Quaker patrician, Ben had served in the Marines in World War II. He was no pacifist, but chance put him at the very vortex of the storm. From 1963 he was executive secretary of the secretary of state. One of his jobs was to approve targets for bombing in North Vietnam. His friends understood that he was painfully traumatized by the conflict between his patriotism and his deep instinct that the war was wrong. No one should speak glibly about the psychosomatic effects of such stresses. Ben died young. His wife, Nan, became an alcoholic. One of his children committed suicide by jumping from one of the bridges over Rock Creek Parkway.

In the two and a half years I had been away from the United States, everything had changed. When I left in 1965, the mood was still on balance optimistic. The assassination had dented confidence in a special American providence, yes, but Lyndon Johnson had revived some of the sense of forward movement that had attended the New Frontier. Few of my friends were enthusiastic about the war, but in 1965 it was still for many of them just one of the things a great power like the United States had to do from time to time.

By 1967 American society was traumatized by the discovery that racism was not confined to the Deep South, as witnessed by urban riots from Watts to Detroit and by the astonishing success of George Wallace in his 1964 forays in Wisconsin, Indiana, and Maryland. That revelation profoundly transformed politics. It was in 1965 that Lyndon Johnson signed the Voting Rights Act, muttering to Bill Moyers as he did so, "There goes the South!"[4]

From that moment on, the whole pattern of American party politics began to shift like a kaleidoscope. As southern conservatives joined the Republican Party, moderates and liberals of the tribe of John Lindsay and Jacob Javits began to leave it. The Democratic Party, too, shed its conservative southern wing and became ideologically liberal, though not as much as the new Republican Party was ideologically conservative.

One of my friends, Marcus Raskin, who had worked briefly on Mac Bundy's national security staff in the White House, became a political radical, perhaps as far to the left as one could go without losing all hope of influence in Washington. Late one night, Marc told me, there was a knock at his front door. It was Bob Moses, most dazzling of all the younger leaders of the civil rights movement. "This black-white stuff," he told Marcus gruffly, "doesn't work."

Moses was off to Africa. He went to Tanzania, where he stayed and taught school from 1969 to 1976 before he came back to the United States.[5] Many who could not go as far to the left as Bob or Marcus nevertheless found that the war and the racial upheavals of the 1960s challenged their deepest assumptions about democratic government: many threw themselves into specific causes such as radical feminism or environmental activism.

The twin scourges that would first frustrate, then destroy the Johnson administration, civil rights and Vietnam, were now the subject of worried discussion almost everywhere. Great as were the political consequences of the racial upheaval of the 1960s, for many of my friends in Washington, the impact of the war was even more painful. It made my friends ask whether the United States was not behaving like the very kind of imperial power they had been brought up to believe it would never be. The war also—and this was even more painful—challenged the assumption, reinforced by victory in World War II, of American invincibility. I remember processing up Massachusetts Avenue to the National Cathedral with several dozen friends from the *Post*, led by Ben Bradlee, to hear Haydn's *Mass in Time of War*.

It was not easy for those at the eye of the storm to separate the impact of the war from that of the civil rights movement. The blows came almost simultaneously. Take the chronology of the summer of 1965. Lyndon Johnson and his staff in the White House, and my friends at the *Post* or on Capitol Hill, could hardly separate the crises in Alabama and in Vietnam into separate boxes. "When sorrows come, they come not single spies / But in battalions."[6] The civil rights movement and the war in Indochina were a double helix, twisted together round the high hopes of the Great Society like a garrotter's knot.

For the first five days of February 1965, for example, Dr. King was in prison in Selma. On February 7 the Viet Cong attacked Camp Holloway, the Special Forces base near Pleiku, killing eight Americans and destroying U.S. aircraft on the ground: that led directly to Operation Flaming Dart, the first American bombing of North Vietnam. On March 7, Alabama state troopers charged into a peaceful protest march of white and black clergy in Selma with clubs, bull whips, and electric cattle prods; the very next day the Marines splashed ashore at Da Nang, the first U.S. combat troops to deploy to Vietnam.

Would JFK have escalated the war in 1965? For many years, it was simply taken for granted by many that he would not have done. The war's growing number of opponents liked to call it "Johnson's war." Kennedy's admirers found it more comfortable to believe that their hero was not responsible for such a painful national reverse and for the killing and destruction it entailed.

The man who was perhaps closer than any other to the decisions of peace and war under both presidents, McGeorge Bundy, is said to have come, at the end of his life, to the conviction that JFK would not have taken the decisions that LBJ took in the spring of 1965. Bundy's former research assistant at New York University, Gordon Goldstein, reports that in his final years Bundy "arrived at a firm conclusion that he shared with me and discussed with various colleagues . . . that Kennedy would not have deployed ground combat forces to Vietnam and thus would not have Americanized the war." Goldstein recorded that in one of his work sessions with Bundy, the latter said, "What he"—that is, Kennedy—"wanted to do about Vietnam—shorthand, in political terms—was flush it. He didn't want it to be a big item. And he didn't think it was a big test of the balance of power. It was a test of American political opinion, but he could stand that in a second term." Goldstein recorded one perceptive, and sharp, aside of Bundy's about his two employers: "Kennedy didn't want to be dumb. Johnson didn't want to be a coward."[7]

Goldstein's book is only secondhand evidence of Bundy's conclusions many years after the event, but it is buttressed by the opinion
of others who were close to Kennedy. Robert McNamara, his defense
secretary, came to share the opinion that Kennedy would have found a
way to withdraw. McNamara published a number of autobiographical
works, apparently motivated by a sense of guilt about his part in the war.
In his 1995 memoir, *In Retrospect: The Tragedy and Lessons of Vietnam*,
he wrote, "I conclude that John Kennedy would have eventually gotten
out of Vietnam rather than move more deeply in." His own view, when
he wrote that book, was that he "seriously questioned" whether without
U.S. intervention in Vietnam Communist hegemony would have spread
further; that "we could and should have withdrawn from Vietnam" in
late 1963 or in late 1964 and early 1965; and he listed eleven major causes
of what he now called "our disaster in Vietnam."[8]

McNamara had once been, at least in public, an unquestioning
hawk. In 1966 he told a meeting of the National Security Industrial Association at the Shoreham Hotel in Washington, "I don't mind it being
called McNamara's war." His biographer Deborah Shapley considers that
he committed himself to a military solution to the war when he signed
off on McGeorge Bundy's memo recommending escalation at a meeting with LBJ on January 27, 1965. However, she also points out that he
suffered a recurrence of bruxism, a painful disease occasioned by stress,
and suggests it was a symptom of agonizing doubt. She quotes LBJ's aide
John Roche as saying that by the summer of 1967 "McNamara was in
a very serious psychological condition," and she reports that LBJ was
afraid of "another Forrestal," a reference to the suicide of the first secretary of defense, James V. Forrestal.[9]

The view that Kennedy might have withdrawn from Vietnam in
a second term was shared by two other well-informed colleagues and
friends of President Kennedy. McNamara's deputy, Roswell Gilpatric,
told an audience at the Kennedy Library, "The president personally dis-
closed his intention to disengage from Vietnam in his second term."[10]
Michael Forrestal, who worked for Bundy on the National Security
Council staff and had responsibility for Vietnam, told a CBS interviewer
that in his last conversation with JFK, twenty-four hours before the
president's death, JFK said, "We have to start a plan for what we are

going to do now in South Vietnam. I want to start a complete and very profound review of how we got into this country, and what we thought we were doing and what we now think we can do. I even want to think about whether we should be there."[11]

Recently two historians, James G. Blight and his wife, janet Lang,[12] have organized a conference, published a book, and collaborated with the production of a documentary, *Virtual JFK,* all of which promote the view that Kennedy, if he had lived, would not have escalated the war. The documentary uses clips of interviews with participants in the policy disputes over the war, including both presidents and Robert McNamara. In the London weekly the *New Statesman,* Blight summarized his view: "We know for certain that JFK's decision not to Americanise the war was wise. His successor, Lyndon B. Johnson, retained virtually the entire team of national security advisers assembled by Kennedy, who gave Johnson the same hawkish advice they had given Kennedy. . . . Unlike JFK, LBJ caved in to his inherited hawks again and again."[13]

In 2013 Thurston Clarke published an account of Kennedy's last hundred days of life.[14] His thesis is that Kennedy had been greatly changed, softened, by two events, one public, the other very personal: his experience of looking into the nuclear abyss in the Cuban missile crisis and the death of his infant son, Patrick, in early August 1963. In this context Clarke argued that Kennedy, had he lived, would not have escalated American involvement in Vietnam and would have withdrawn all American troops.

It may seem rash to question the testimony of so many witnesses, including many who were personally involved in Kennedy's Vietnam policy. Nevertheless, I believe that they are essentially incorrect in asserting a firm belief that JFK would not have escalated the war in 1965. I am emboldened to contradict their conclusions for many reasons. For one thing, friendship and a loyalty to the memory of JFK, which in most cases was far stronger than their loyalty to LBJ, ought to be discounted. (Kenny O'Donnell and Dave Powers, for example, can hardly be offered as expert, unbiased witnesses.) There has rarely been such a posthumous public relations program as that mounted by JFK's widow, brothers, and friends to present him as both a "cavalier without fear and without reproach"[15] and a champion of peace. We now know that in several respects that campaign, however honorably meant, glossed over serious personal limitations.

Second, Bundy and McNamara, at least, changed their opinion over time. Their shades might wish us to accept the later, rather than earlier, expressions of their thinking. Yet in 1978, as Goldstein is fair enough to recall, McGeorge Bundy reminded a meeting of the Massachusetts Historical Society that "the public record has [Kennedy] constantly asserting two propositions that could not have coexisted easily in later years: that we must not quit there [Vietnam] and that in the end the Vietnamese must do the job for themselves. . . . Just what he would have done we shall never know."[16] This is, interestingly, very similar to the conclusion of another man, highly respected for his judgment, who worked very closely with both Kennedy and Johnson, JFK's aide Larry O'Brien, who came to have great respect for LBJ. O'Brien thought that if Kennedy had been reelected in 1964, "he would have found a way of disengaging." But "whatever he might or might not have done if he were reelected none of us will ever know."[17] Robert McNamara's positions were even more changeable. As the Harvard professor Sam Beer, who knew JFK very well, summed it up, "Well, of course the big anti-Vietnam people like Arthur [Schlesinger] and Ken Galbraith say he would never have done it. But he would have. These were all his people."[18]

Third, we should examine rather closely what precisely these defenders of JFK's reputation were and are saying. Goldstein was saying that in Bundy's opinion John Kennedy would not have done *in 1965* what Lyndon Johnson did in that year. But he argues that case (as recorded in Goldstein's book and—according to Goldstein—in fragments of a work by Bundy himself that was never published) largely by recalling what Kennedy said and did in the very different circumstances of 1961–63. Specifically, much is made of Kennedy's repeatedly expressed objections to placing American ground troops in combat in Asia. But the fact that he maintained that position in 1961–63 does not prove that he would have been able to maintain it in 1965. Blight and Lang's portrait of an embattled pacifist president, heroically resisting the pressures of hawkish advisers, does not square with my recollection of conversations with many of the actors at the time and later. Certainly at the time most of Kennedy's advisers, and the same men when they were working for

Johnson, saw themselves as moderates resisting pressure from "hawks" at the Pentagon.[19] Nor is the Blight view supported by such evidence as the Kennedy tapes during the Cuban missile crisis. The thesis largely ignores the vast difference between the circumstances of 1961–63 and the circumstances of 1964–65.

The truth is that Kennedy's position on Vietnam, especially in the crucial weeks between the Buddhist crisis in the spring of 1963 and his death, was conflicted, contradictory, and obscure. He had successfully resisted pressure from the Joint Chiefs of Staff to send American forces to Laos, and when in the spring of 1963 they sent Robert McNamara another memo saying that if the Diem government could not get the Viet Cong under control, there would be no alternative "to the introduction of US military forces," JFK urged Roger Hilsman, the great advocate of counterinsurgency war, newly appointed assistant secretary of state for Far Eastern affairs, to do everything possible to avoid getting the United States directly involved in the war in Vietnam.[20] He told Averell Harriman and Roswell Gilpatric that he was sick of the conflict in Vietnam, and he told Senator Mike Mansfield (an early and persistent critic of the war) that he would bring "troops" (meaning advisers) back in early 1964. He gave a more private and perhaps more realistic opinion to his friend the journalist Charlie Bartlett, "I can't give up a piece of territory like that and then get the American people to re-elect me."[21]

Indeed, one clue to his uncertainty lies in the contrast between his public statements and his private hints. Publicly, he did not waver in his support for American commitment to the war. Privately, he sometimes hinted both at personal doubts about the war itself and at a distinction between what he could do before his expected reelection in 1964 and what he might be free to do after that.

Interviewed by Walter Cronkite of CBS, supposedly then the most influential journalist in America, on September 2, 1963, while on holiday at Squaw Island, Cape Cod, for example, Kennedy raised the question of whether the war could be won without support for the effort from the South Vietnamese population. Thurston Clarke says with some truth that this "effectively pulled the rug out from under Diem."[22] But JFK also said in so many words to Chester Huntley and David Brinkley: "I don't agree with those who say we should withdraw. That would be a great

mistake."[23] After all, pulling the rug out from under Diem, as finally happened a couple of months later, was not the same as withdrawing from
the war. Effectively, one might say, Kennedy went along with those in
Saigon who wanted to get rid of Diem precisely in order to prosecute
the war more successfully, though to be sure Kennedy's attitude to the
coup is uncertain. He regretted the death of Diem and his brother-in-
law Nhu, but that does not mean that he did not also hope for their fall.
Ideally, perhaps, he wished for something impossible: that Diem would
get rid of Nhu and govern in a less authoritarian way.

A week later, he gave the inevitable matching interview to
Cronkite's competitors, NBC's Chet Huntley and David Brinkley. Asked
about the domino theory, he said, "I believe it, I believe it," and went on,
"I think we should stay . . . we should not withdraw." Thurston Clarke
maintains that these plain statements "bore no more resemblance to his
real intentions than Roosevelt's pledge not to involve the US in World
War II."[24]

It is sadly true that statesmen, including John Kennedy, do not always say all that they are thinking. This has been observed for many
centuries. It is all very well for writers like Clarke and James Blight, who
want to believe retrospectively in Kennedy's wisdom and restraint, simply to ignore clear statements of settled policy. The fact that JFK felt
compelled to make them is highly relevant to the question of whether
he could have changed his policy as his admirers maintain he would
have done. Still less can the possibility that these clear statements did
not represent Kennedy's unexpressed thoughts on hard issues be used
to prove how he would actually have behaved in very changed circumstances more than a year later.

The question, to repeat, is not what JFK would have *preferred to
do,* but what he *would have done.* Gilpatric is said to have given it as
his opinion that Kennedy would have wanted to withdraw from Vietnam when he had won a second term.[25] Again, no doubt he would have
wanted to withdraw. He might still have found it impossible, faced with
the military and political realities of 1965, to avoid doing something like
what Johnson did. At no time, after all, did Johnson himself express
a wholehearted desire for victory in the war. He, like Kennedy, settled
for what he and his civilian advisers praised and his military command-

ers bitterly resented, that is, what the latter saw as a moderate policy that fell short of a total commitment to victory.

Again, it has been argued that because Kennedy displayed caution and moderation in his handling of the Cuban missile crisis, he would have avoided escalation in Vietnam in 1965. But in 1962 he thought he faced the danger of nuclear war. In Vietnam in 1965, so long as he was not so reckless as to provoke the rulers of China or the Soviet Union, he would have faced no such risk.

Not all of Kennedy's advisers agree that he would have responded differently from the way Johnson did in the circumstances of 1965. Walt Rostow, for example, told an oral history interviewer that LBJ "inherited a situation disintegrating diplomatically, disintegrating militarily . . . [he had] very simple alternatives in 1965. Acknowledge you've got disaster and pull your men out. Go on doing what you're doing. Or pull your men out."

Given the disintegration of the situation caused by external factors including the collapse of successive governments in Saigon, growing confidence on the part of the Viet Cong, and the growing understanding that North Vietnam could reinforce its order of battle in South Vietnam by way of the Ho Chi Minh Trail faster than the United States could inflict casualties, it seems clear that JFK's advisers would have given him the same advice they gave LBJ.

"My own net judgment, for what it's worth," Walt Rostow said, "is that, if President Kennedy had not been killed, he would have made the same decisions as President Johnson and quite possibly made them earlier."[26] Some would dismiss Rostow's judgment out of hand as worthless. Was he not the high priest of war? Did his colleagues not call him "the Air Marshall"?[27] Was he not a passionate partisan of Lyndon Johnson, full of resentment that because of his loyalty on Vietnam he had not been offered the post he hoped for in a great northeastern university but grateful that the University of Texas offered him a hook to hang his hat? Such judgments, in my opinion, are only a special case of the extraordinary ability of Kennedy's partisans to present a rosy portrait of their hero, his actions, and what they assume would have been his actions had he not been murdered. It is true that Rostow was a classic cold warrior, deeply hostile to Communism, but so was John Kennedy. That was scarcely an unusual attitude in 1950s America. But Rostow was as qualified as anyone to make a judgment. He had been JFK's trusted adviser—specifically on Vietnam—had worked with him, had known him well. It is true that Rostow was so committed to the dream of military victory that I have seen his eyes tear up with sheer exhilaration at a briefing as he read off the latest (no doubt fictional) estimate of Viet Cong casualties. But after Mac Bundy left, Rostow was LBJ's designated national security adviser. He had been a senior official in the National Security staff, working closely with Kennedy too. Few were better informed about the woeful situation in South Vietnam than he was. And he was not alone in this judgment. General Maxwell Taylor, for example, Kennedy's favorite general, shared Rostow's opinion about the necessity of escalation in 1965. So did many senior civilian and CIA officials.

Goldstein frames his case for believing that JFK would not have sent ground troops to Vietnam in the context of a theoretical political science proposition—it is the title of his concluding chapter—that "intervention is a presidential choice, not an inevitability."[28] No doubt, theoretically, "the buck stops" in the Oval Office, as the brass motto on Harry Truman's desk proclaims. (It is now to be seen in his library in Independence, Missouri). Yet no student of the presidency or of American foreign policy from Truman's day to Johnson's (not to speak of more recent examples) can fail to be impressed by the extent to which "presidential choice" is usually the end product of an immense, often raucous sausage machine of "staffing-out," conferences, speechwriters, interagency groups, lobbying, infighting, newspaper leaks, special pleading, drafting, and redrafting.

"I thought I was president," Harry Truman told David Brinkley, "but when it comes to these bureaucracies, I can't make them do a damn thing."[29] Presidents from Franklin Roosevelt on complained of their sense of impotence when confronted with the bureaucracy. For Roosevelt, it was the navy who resisted all pressures. Even a president with as formidable an endowment of will and energy as Lyndon Johnson, or one with the sublime self-confidence of Jack Kennedy, found it hard to ensure that what the government of the United States actually did was precisely what the president of the United States wanted it to do. Jack

Kennedy might have wanted to withdraw from Vietnam. But if, for example, the Speaker of the House of Representatives, the commandant of the Marine Corps, the chairman of the Democratic National Committee, his family, and his own White House staff all told him he couldn't do it, would he have prevailed? In reality, Johnson's civilian advisers (William Bundy is a good example)[30] thought they were taking a moderate stance by escalating the war, and his military advisers were itching to be more decisive. Even if he wanted to pull out, would he have done so if it were plain that to do so would have derailed his presidency and caused him to abandon other cherished political ambitions?

A classic instance of how the bureaucracy can act against a president's wishes—though far from the only one—was the coup that led to the overthrow and murder of non-Communist South Vietnam president Ngo Dinh Diem and his brother Ngo Dinh Nhu, a critical moment in the slide to war in Vietnam. The conspirators in Saigon were greatly encouraged by the famous August 24, 1963, telegram, sent by assistant secretary of state for Far Eastern affairs Roger Hilsman, with the support of Michael Forrestal (son of the first secretary of defense and number two on Vietnam under Mac Bundy at the NSC) and his patron Averell Harriman, to ambassador Henry Cabot Lodge in Saigon. It was taken by dissident South Vietnamese generals as official American encouragement for a coup. Neither Kennedy, nor his national security adviser (Bundy), nor his defense secretary (McNamara), nor even the director of Central Intelligence (John McCone) formally signed off on the message.[31]

It was, after all, the weekend, and in August. Beaches, tennis courts, and golf courses beckoned. The secretary of defense, to be specific, was at Aspen among the cool Colorado mountains. The director of Central Intelligence, McCone, was on a boat in Puget Sound. McGeorge Bundy was at a family summer home on Cape Ann, Massachusetts, Roswell Gilpatric at a farm in the Virginia hunt country, George Ball playing golf. Rusk was in New York, preparing for the general assembly of the United Nations. He did come to the phone and gave some guarded approval to the cable, but it is not clear that he understood the details. The president was at a rented cottage on Squaw Island, on Cape Cod, with his wife and children, his friend William Walton, and a photographer.

He was much concerned with drafting and redrafting a press release about Jackie's forthcoming holiday on Aristotle Onassis's yacht in such a way as to give the (false) impression that Onassis would not be there.[32]

There has been a tendency to interpret this episode to mean that Kennedy wanted to overthrow Diem. It more clearly demonstrates that even a strong president cannot always ensure that his policy is actually at all times carried out. Presidential power is constrained not only by congressional resistance but also by the sheer unwieldy bulk of its own bureaucratic process. In theory, and to the imperious mind of a Kennedy or the autocratic instincts of a Johnson, the president's decision was indeed final. Yet the decisions had to be taken in the prescribed forms and according to a timing that always shaped and often limited presidential freedom. Political considerations, especially the imperative of winning reelection, played their part. Presidential decision was sculpted by the shared assumptions of cold war Washington. And ultimately, it was more influenced by considerations of domestic politics than by diplomatic or strategic logic.

The theory that Kennedy might have avoided the disaster of American commitment to Vietnam in 1965 is not of merely biographical interest. Tragically, the commitment to Vietnam led to Richard Nixon's victory in 1968. By that time, especially in the very circles that would like to believe that Kennedy would have avoided that commitment, the war had become thought of as "Johnson's war." That has prevented many from acknowledging how Vietnam grew from policies and assumptions that were all but universally approved in the United States in the early 1960s, and certainly shared by the Kennedy administration, even if JFK himself did have secret reservations. It is tempting to imagine that, if only John Kennedy had not been killed, that larger tragedy would have been avoided. But the proposition is not much more than wish fulfillment. The wiser judgment is surely Mac Bundy's earlier one, given to the Massachusetts Historical Association: "Just what he would have done we shall never know."

There were three stages to American involvement in Vietnam, each corresponding to a presidency. Each stage demonstrated in different ways how policy could be distorted by the failure of responsible policy makers to make use of accurate information from their subordinates, and each showed the pernicious effect of ignorance, false assumptions, and the primacy of political considerations over reality.

Under President Eisenhower, the United States first seriously considered getting militarily involved in rescuing the collapsing French empire in Indochina and decided, somewhat narrowly, against active military participation. (There was even serious consideration of Operation Vulture, which would have involved using atomic weapons to pull French chestnuts out of the fire of Dien Bien Phu.) Fortunately, the Eisenhower administration decided, thanks to Ike's robust common sense, to do nothing of the kind. "You boys must be crazy!" he told his aide Robert Cutler. "We can't use those things against Asians for the second time in less than ten years. My God!" His administration decided, somewhat narrowly, against active military participation.[33] Then came the Geneva Conference, which dismantled French Indochina into four successor states: Cambodia, Laos, a Communist North Vietnam, and an anti-Communist South Vietnam, whose population was largely Buddhist but whose regime was largely Roman Catholic.[34]

When John F. Kennedy was inaugurated in 1961, the ramshackle new state of South Vietnam was already under political and military attack from North Vietnam and from an insurgency of its own people, led by the Viet Cong, which was neither a wholly domestic insurgency nor a typical foreign invasion. The United States was already committed to defend what was essentially a puppet regime with little popular support. The Kennedy administration seriously considered going to the aid of the (at least equally) fragile regime in Laos, but decided, thanks to the political sophistication of Averell Harriman, not to send American troops to that remote, landlocked. and strategically insignificant nation. When Kennedy was shown Edward Lansdale's report on Southeast Asia by Rostow, he exclaimed: "This is the worst one we've got. You know, Eisenhower never mentioned Vietnam."[35]

In Vietnam, however, the Kennedy administration did commit itself to the support of the Diem regime. This support involved substantial aid and the deployment of military personnel, described as "advisers," to the South Vietnamese military. It was not long before they became involved in combat, command, and communications, in tactical intelligence, contacts with the civilian population, and weapons supply, all coordinated by an imposing headquarters in Saigon, Military Assistance Command Vietnam, or MACV.[36] Under the Kennedy administration the number of American "advisers" rose from under one thousand to over sixteen thousand.[37] So optimistic were the reports sent back to Washington by the American military and civilian authorities in Saigon, however, that by the time Kennedy was assassinated, there was some cheerful talk of the situation improving to the point where a partial withdrawal of American personnel would be possible. Although the Diem government had just been overthrown and intelligence and military officers in the field took a jaundiced view of the capabilities of the South Vietnamese military and government, so stubbornly bullish was the top tier of military and official Americans in Saigon that it became official policy that one thousand American advisers would be withdrawn.[38]

This gap between the profound pessimism of both military and CIA officers on the ground, who understood how corrupt, incompetent, and demoralized the South Vietnam government was, and the buoyant estimates sent back to Washington by their seniors (which were believed by their august recipients there) lasted throughout the American experience of Vietnam. For example, during the Johnson years the ranking commander in Saigon, General William Westmoreland, actually succeeded in insisting that formal estimates of the enemy's order of battle must never rise above three hundred thousand, even though many of the best-informed intelligence officers believed the true number was at least five hundred thousand, and perhaps many more.[39]

When he first became president, LBJ was not thinking much about Vietnam. To be sure, he had scorched through there in 1961, publicly calling the wretched Diem "the Winston Churchill of Asia."[40] It is less often recalled that he sent a shrewder, more pessimistic private assessment to JFK. A decision to support Diem, he said, must be made "with the knowledge that at some point we may be faced with the further decision of whether we commit major United States forces."[41]

His conclusion, however, was orthodox. In general terms, he shared the current assumptions of cold war Washington: that Communism must be challenged wherever it threatened to subvert the American-led

"Free World," that if even minor threats were not robustly met, American "resolve" would be doubted and American face lost, and finally that to respond with anything less than total certainty to such threats would be to invite electoral disaster and the contempt of the American people.

Senators and congressmen of that generation felt obliged to appear fiercely patriotic; they were also, because of the various Red scares of the postwar years, determined that no one should ever question their anti-Communism. The imperative of defeating Communism was a natural extension of the virtuous war against Hitler and the Japanese militarists. Jack Kennedy had learned anti-Communism at his father's knee, and in his early Senate career he repeatedly expressed strong anti-Communist sentiments. But it would be a mistake to imagine that there was anything unusual about his unquestioned assumption of the "twilight struggle." It was shared by labor-backed northern Democrats and bourbon southerners, by Republicans of both the moss-backed and the moderate persuasions, by military men (and many senators were generals in the Reserve)—by all but a dissenting minority of intellectuals and Ivy League professors. That the United States must prevail wherever challenged was common ground, an integral part of the belief system that I have called the "liberal consensus." Its core was an unspoken bargain: most conservatives accepted, however grudgingly, the domestic policies of the New Deal; most liberals accepted the conservative anti-Communist foreign policy.

There has been a natural tendency to emphasize the differences between the approaches of JFK and LBJ. This is understandable, both because, as we have seen, they were indeed very different men, from very different backgrounds, and also because the question of responsibility for Vietnam inevitably becomes an allocation of blame or a defense of one president or the other. The truth is that, different as they were, both men either shared the same basic assumptions or, if they did question one point or another in the general culture, found it politically dangerous to say so plainly.

The Johnson administration came into office when a number of events had made the cheerful confidence of the Kennedy years untenable. The crudely brutal suppression of Buddhist opposition, dramatized by the bonzes' horrific tactic of setting themselves (or their brethren) on fire, revealed how hollow was the attempt to portray the Diem regime as a champion of democracy. The American support of the military coup against Diem and his and his brother's murder by South Vietnamese officers, whether or not it was sanctioned by the president himself, further discredited America's allies in Saigon.

Successive military governments proved no more stable than Diem's. The Buddhists were demonstrating again. The South Vietnamese military's poor performance in the field, especially but not only at the battle of Ap Bac in January 1963, made official optimism look ridiculous. The attempt by the American brass to conceal the realities infuriated the (then) small but talented and irrepressible American press corps in Saigon. The evolution in these reporters' attitude from critical support to angry skepticism and finally to more or less open opposition[42] influenced the withering of political support for the war at home, though there were always others in the Saigon press corps who supported the war through thick and thin.

By late 1964, Lyndon Johnson had won reelection by the greatest margin in American presidential history. (JFK seems to have calculated that he would win reelection easily in 1964, but he could hardly have won by the overwhelming margin LBJ was to achieve, partly no doubt precisely because of Kennedy's assassination.) Johnson's advisers, and especially Walt Rostow and most senior officials, did not acknowledge how bad the situation in Vietnam was. But they did understand that they were not yet winning—indeed, that they might lose.

The pressures that weighed on LBJ would have weighed on JFK too.[43] Politically, Saigon was in even worse chaos in early 1965 than in 1963. Militarily, the situation was far worse: the enemy was rampant, and it was plain that without decisive American support the South Vietnamese government and army were in no condition to resist. Stiffened and supported by North Vietnamese regulars and well armed (with captured American weapons as well as with what the Chinese and the Soviet Union supplied), the Viet Cong were growing bolder and more aggressive.

On November 1, 1964, they launched a meticulously planned sneak attack on the U.S. airfield at Bien Hoa, only twelve miles north of Saigon. Six B-57s were destroyed and twenty other aircraft damaged; five Americans and two South Vietnamese were killed and more than a hundred injured.[44] Because it was three days before the presidential election, LBJ did nothing. On Christmas Eve, with considerable effrontery, not to mention courage, two Viet Cong operatives managed to get into the Brinks Hotel, a billet for American officers in Saigon itself, at "happy hour" and blow up a car bomb that killed two and wounded sixty-five. Four days later a Viet Cong detachment succeeded in working its way round Saigon. They held the town of Binh Gia for eight hours, then withdrew. When the South Vietnamese army responded, they caught them in a merciless ambush, killing two hundred and cutting up seven crack battalions.[45]

The last straw came at Pleiku in February 1965. McGeorge Bundy was in Saigon on a fact-finding tour when the Viet Cong attacked Camp Holloway, an American base near Pleiku, the chief town of the Central Highlands. Ten planes were destroyed, eight Americans killed, and more than a hundred injured.[46] Bundy went to see for himself, cabling LBJ that the Viet Cong's "energy and persistence are astonishing" and that there was a "widespread belief that we do not have the will and force and patience and determination to take the necessary action and stay the course." The only response must be "continuous bombing of North Vietnam."[47] It is worth underlining that in Bundy's mind, as in the minds of his colleagues around LBJ, one decisive factor was the fear that America would lose not battles or territory but *credibility*.

Bundy was in Vietnam at the suggestion of none other than JFK's favorite general, Maxwell D. Taylor, now ambassador in Saigon.[48] Taylor had admitted in early January that "we are presently on a losing track. To take no positive action now is to accept defeat in the fairly near future." There were only two options, in Taylor's judgment: either put in combat troops or bomb North Vietnam in a serious way.

Is one to conclude that, if JFK had been alive, either Taylor or Bundy would have given different advice to him than they gave to LBJ? Only sheer partisanship, surely, would conclude that Kennedy would have rejected advice that a reluctant Johnson found persuasive. In 1965 Johnson faced far stronger pressure to intensify American commitment to the war than ever Kennedy faced. But Kennedy would have had to confront that same pressure in 1965, had he lived. As one historian has put it, "Given the direction and momentum of [Kennedy's] policies as of November 1963, is it more than wishful thinking to assume that the situation in Vietnam and the extent of American involvement there would have been significantly different for him at the end of January 1965 from the way it was for Lyndon Johnson?"[49]

So the Johnson administration turned to the idea of bombing North Vietnam in the hope that the government in Hanoi would be forced to withdraw its support for the insurgency in South Vietnam. This wholly illusory calculation was only one of half a dozen fatal mistakes that governed American policy as it floundered deeper and deeper into the mire of Indochina. Before we can pursue to a conclusion the question before us—whether JFK, if he had lived, would have made the same fatal commitment that LBJ actually did make—we must anatomize those catastrophic errors that were the common ground of both presidents and almost all their advisers.[50]

The first point to be made is that they were the same advisers. LBJ made a conscious decision to keep on as many of the aides and advisers he had inherited from Kennedy as possible, and there was considerable continuity in those involved in Vietnam policy. Secretary of State Rusk and Secretary of Defense McNamara remained in place, in Rusk's case until the end of the Johnson administration and in McNamara's until 1968. McGeorge Bundy resigned on February 28, 1966, but his job passed to Walt Rostow, who as Bundy's deputy and then at the State Department had been influential before he was promoted. Assistant Secretary of State Roger Hilsman left in March 1964, but he was replaced by William Bundy, elder brother of McGeorge, whose background was in the CIA. He had already been involved in policy making as the relevant assistant secretary at the Pentagon and in pressing for a congressional resolution to cover action in Vietnam. He played a key part in drafting policy papers over the winter from LBJ's reelection in November 1964 to the decisions of the spring of 1965.

Bundy senior (he was a little touchy about assumptions that he was younger than Mac) was convinced of the importance of winning the war but pessimistic about the possibility of doing so. He chaired the Vietnam Working Group, which presented LBJ with three options. Option A was to continue "steady as we go." B envisioned dramatic escalation, "a systematic program of military pressures against the North." C called for slower and more gradual escalation. Negotiations for an end to the conflict were not an option. LBJ made that plain, as indeed had JFK.

(One of the most striking aspects of America policy throughout the war was the unwillingness to see what negotiations with Hanoi might offer. Johnson in particular went through the motions of pursuing even the most unlikely potential intermediaries. None of these fruitless approaches had any effect, for the simple reason that LBJ, in this as so much else following JFK, flatly refused to enter any negotiation whose end might involve South Vietnam, at any time or in any way, coming under the authority of Hanoi.)[51]

Subsequently the three options morphed into Phase I (option A) and Phase II (option C). The most aggressive option was dropped. But instead of being alternatives, as option A and option C had been, the two phases were to be adopted serially, one after the other.

There were, of course, as I have stressed, great differences, both of style and of substance, between the two presidents. President Kennedy's admirers pointed to what they claim, with some justification, to have been his temperamental preference for caution. But there was no clear break in policy terms. The fact that one thousand "advisers" were theoretically withdrawn from Vietnam in late 1963 is irrelevant for our purpose; that reflected unjustified optimism on the part of the military, not moderation in the White House. LBJ had after all been JFK's vice president, and as such sent to Vietnam to emphasize the administration's commitment.

There were several ambassadors to Saigon, but the military leadership hardly changed. Maxwell Taylor, an ambassador himself after several other responsible roles, was an influential voice throughout, and Generals Westmoreland, Paul D. Harkins, and the Marine Corps's Victor "Brute" Krulak held their posts under both administrations, as did Admiral Harry Felt and many ranking subordinate officers in both the armed forces and the CIA. This continuity is not in itself conclusive evidence that Kennedy would have taken the same decisions that Johnson did. But it does raise a certain presumption that the same men, responding to the same assumptions and ideas, might well have reached the same conclusions in changed, and much worsened, circumstances.

Of course, if one starts from the notion that Lyndon Johnson was an ignorant Texan, his banausic political cunning to be sharply contrasted at all times with the lofty sophistication, the humanity, and the subtlety of John Kennedy, it must follow that Johnson would necessarily reach different conclusions. But that contrast is a caricature. It reflected the prejudices of the less astute of Kennedy's admirers rather than the actual abilities and experience of the two men.

With the benefit of hindsight, it is easy to see how many of the basic assumptions of the policy that took the United States into a disastrous war were false or at least flawed. Many years ago I myself wrote how depressing it was that the written arguments of men with high reputations for intelligence and clarity were tarnished by "*cliché,* fixed ideas, unexamined assumptions and a persistent tendency to argue backward from predetermined conclusions."[52]

The veteran CIA analyst Harold P. Ford, responsible for many of the National Intelligence Estimates on Vietnam, asked why "the impact of intelligence on the decisions to escalate America's role in the war was slight."[53] The reason, he concluded, was the "deep-rooted" resistance of the consumers of that intelligence to the reality the intelligence and military officers on the ground were reporting. Those consumers were the top military and civilian officials and the presidents themselves. The agency's reporting, Ford wrote, clashed with widely held views, among them the idea that the Vietnam War was a part of a conspiracy run from Moscow and Beijing; the conviction that to make America's commitments credible the country had to take a stand somewhere and that place must be Vietnam; and the "domino theory."[54] It is time to scrutinize some of the most influential of these analogies and assumptions.

One essential constraint on American policy, felt by JFK and even more acutely by LBJ, was the fear, drawn from the experience of the Korean War, of Chinese intervention. Y. F. Khong, a Harvard and Oxford historian who has studied the role of these analogies, believes that "the historical analogy that played the most influential role in the decision-making of the 1960s was that of Korea. This is true not just because George Ball said so, but because however one sifts the record— by quantitative analysis of the public and private use of the analogies, by textual analysis of the documents of the period, or by what former

policy-makers are now willing to say—the 'lessons' of Korea emerge
as a pre-eminent consideration in the minds of those who formulated
America's Vietnam policy."[55]

There were in fact many lessons of Korea. The most important
by far, for Lyndon Johnson, was that, whatever all other calculations
might suggest, the United States must never get into a war with what
was still then called "Red China." From the very beginning, LBJ whole-
heartedly supported America's stand in Korea. Within hours of President Truman's announcement that America would intervene, Johnson
said the president's action "gives a new and noble meaning to freedom,
gives purpose to our national resolve and determination, convincingly
affirms America's capacity for world leadership."[56] It is interesting that
even so early, there was concern for whether the world would query
America's "resolve." Later, however, after the Chinese entrance into the
war and the military reverses that brought, the lesson subtly changed.
Yes, the United States must demonstrate its "resolve." But it must not get
involved in a ground war in Asia, for to do so might lead to a situation
where only nuclear weapons could prevent Chinese victory, and that
might lead to World War III.

Later there were some American officials (not only General Mac-
Arthur) who discounted or were prepared to defy the possibility of Chinese intervention on behalf of North Vietnam. But that was not the majority view, and it was not Lyndon Johnson's. The Kennedy and Johnson
White House's leading expert on China, James C. Thomson, believed
his colleagues saw Asia with a huge lacuna where China should be.
Once when we were talking he grabbed a piece of paper and scribbled
a sketch map to make his point. Vietnam was a large, pendulous shape,
Japan a larger one. Against each, he scrawled a rough population number: 120 million for Japan, 40 million for Vietnam. At the middle of the
page he jabbed an angry dot and wrote after it "1,000,000,000."

Yet if Thomson was right that neither the Kennedy nor the Johnson administration showed much curiosity about what was happening
inside China, China as an ultimate, existential threat, the one country
that might one day be stronger than the United States, was a reality
they brooded on constantly. Although the matter was deliberately not
much discussed, the Johnson administration was impressed by the

view of Allen Whiting, head of the Far East division of the State Department's Bureau of Intelligence and Research. Whiting drew attention
to the buildup of Chinese forces in and along the border with North
Vietnam. His boss, Dean Rusk, who had served as assistant secretary
of state for the Far East, shared Whiting's concern. "The China factor,"
wrote George McT. Kahin in his study of American intervention, "con-
ditioned and constrained American policy throughout the remainder of
the Johnson administration."[57] In a press conference in Manchester, New
Hampshire, on September 28, 1964, LBJ said, "I want to be very cautious and careful and use it only as a last resort, when I start dropping
bombs around that are likely to involve American boys in a war in Asia
with 700 million Chinese."[58] When President Johnson was urged to ignore the danger of Chinese intervention, he replied tersely, "That's what
MacArthur thought."[59]

Another analogy was the Munich comparison. Long before either
John Kennedy or Lyndon Johnson was president, American foreign policy was deeply influenced by an interpretation—in fact a contestable
interpretation—of the origins of World War II. According to that view,
Hitler, Mussolini, and the Japanese war party had been able to get away
with aggression and territorial aggrandizement because the democracies, specifically Britain and France, had not stood up to them. (America
was not so frequently mentioned in that context, though in relation to
Japan it was acknowledged that the United States had failed to intervene
effectively when Japanese forces first invaded Manchuria and bombed
Shanghai.)

Later it was argued that Britain in particular had needed time to
build up its military and especially the Royal Air Force, and that there
is no evidence that the democracies could in fact have deterred Hitler
from his attacks on Czechoslovakia and Poland. In the 1950s and 1960s,
such refinements of analysis were not aired. The lesson was drawn in the
boldest strokes. Chamberlain was a weakling and a fool, Churchill the
heroic model to imitate. World War II happened, and the United States
was drawn into it, on this interpretation, because Britain and France had
failed to stand up to Hitler and his fascist allies, and America, sheltering
under the doctrine of isolationism, had failed too.

Officials of the Kennedy and Johnson administrations were by no means the only Americans to see history through this lens. Henry Cabot Lodge, ambassador to Saigon, for example, said at the time of the Johnson administration's 1965 debates over intervention, "I feel there is a greater threat to start World War III if we don't go in. Can't we see the similarity to our own indolence at Munich?"[60] The Bavarian capital became the label for the policy of appeasing dictators because it was there that Chamberlain met Hitler, after which he returned to London fatuously promising "peace in our time." "The principal lesson we learned from World War II," said Dean Rusk, who had been an undergraduate at Oxford in 1933 and had been shocked when the university's debating society voted not to fight for "king and country," "is that if a course of aggression is allowed to gather momentum it continues to build and leads eventually to a general conflict."[61]

Similar views were widely held on Capitol Hill. In July 1965 Speaker John McCormack said simply, "The lesson of Hitler and Mussolini is clear."[62] LBJ expanded on this thought in many ways and in different formulations when he was still majority leader in the Senate, as vice president, and as president. During the 1960 Democratic convention he infuriated Robert Kennedy and the Kennedy partisans by telling the state of Washington delegation that he was no "Chamberlain–umbrella policy man,"[63] and then rubbed salt in the wound by saying he never thought Hitler was right. This was taken by many, especially Robert Kennedy, as a stinging and unfair allusion to Ambassador Joseph P. Kennedy's association in London with the "Cliveden set" and others who wondered out loud whether it might be wise to do a deal with Hitler the better to fight Stalin. Perhaps the simplest statement of Johnson's long-held view was that "we have learned at a terrible and brutal cost that retreat does not bring safety and weakness does not bring peace."[64]

The Munich analogy, with its assumption that the United States must be ready to fight present incursions to prevent the need to fight later at a disadvantage, was, as Khong points out, part of the intellectual basis for another influential truism of the day, one whose origin can be traced back as far as the Truman administration: the domino theory.[65] As long ago as June 1949, National Security Council paper 48/1 proclaimed that "the extension of Communist authority in China represents a grievous political defeat for us. . . . If Southeast Asia is also swept by communism, we shall have suffered a major political rout the repercussions of which will be felt throughout the rest of the world, especially in the Middle East and in a then critically exposed Australia."[66]

Another National Security Council paper, NSC 64, dated February 27, 1950, still before the outbreak of the Korean War, predicted that "if Indochina were controlled by a Communist-dominated government, . . . the balance of South East Asia would then be in grave hazard." Two years later, in June 1954, with French rule in Indochina tottering, the NSC argued that "the loss of any of the countries of Southeast Asia . . . would have critical psychological, political and economic consequences" for India and the Middle East (except Turkey and, oddly, Pakistan). It is tempting to wonder whether the NSC was using very small-scale maps, perhaps from a school atlas.

In a press conference on April 7, 1954, according to his aide Sherman Adams, Eisenhower "[applied] what might be called the falling domino principle." He compared Indochina to the first of a row of dominoes which, once knocked over, makes the fall of every row a certainty. "The fall of Indochina would lead to the fall of Burma, Thailand, Malaysia and Indonesia. India would then be hemmed in by Communism, and Australia, New Zealand, the Philippines, Formosa and Japan would all be gravely threatened."[67] Throughout the 1950s Eisenhower, Secretary of State John Foster Dulles, and Undersecretary of State Walter Bedell Smith repeatedly used this essentially paranoid understanding of half the world, one that virtually ignored the internal political history and the free will of the nations of Asia. There is one rather amusing exception. After the disastrous French defeat at the siege of Dien Bien Phu in 1954, Dulles conceded at a press briefing that Laos and Cambodia, while important, were "by no means essential." On second thought, he asked for this statement of the obvious to be deleted from the official record.[68]

What is perhaps more surprising, given JFK's keenness to portray himself as a new broom, is that the domino theory continued to be official policy throughout the Kennedy administration. If JFK harbored private doubts about it, so too did LBJ. Those doubts were not, however, strong enough for either one of them to break with what had been government doctrine, under Republicans as well as Democrats, at least since the Chinese revolution and arguably since Stalin made it plain in early 1946 that wartime comradeship was at an end.

In June 1964 Lyndon Johnson asked the CIA formally whether, if South Vietnam came under North Vietnamese control, the rest of Southeast Asia must follow. The agency's Board of National Estimates responded with equal formality and precision: "With the possible exception of Cambodia, it is likely that no nation in the area would quickly succumb to communism as a result of the fall of Laos and South Vietnam."[69] Subtly, that argument was taken on board, only to be discarded in the revised draft of the NSC Working Group's opinion, prepared by William Bundy and John McNaughton: "The so-called 'domino' theory," they wrote, "is over-simplified. . . . Nonetheless Communist control of South Vietnam would almost immediately make Laos extremely hard to hold [Did the United States ever "hold" Laos?], have Cambodia bending sharply to the Communist side, place great pressure on Thailand . . . and embolden Indonesia to increase its pressure on Malaysia . . . [which] could easily . . . tend to unravel the whole Pacific and South Asian defense structure." The voice, so to speak, rose to a hysterical scream: "There would almost certainly be a major conflict and perhaps the risk of nuclear war."[70]

No doubt one should make some allowance for the duty of responsible officials to take into account the worst possible consequences of a policy. Yet one of the most remarkable characteristics of the passage just quoted is the manner in which wild, if all too familiar, prophesies of calamity are qualified with what journalists call "savers": "could easily," "tend to," "almost certainly," "perhaps." The CIA's experts privately dismissed the domino theory. The policy makers, who were supposed to be benefiting from their expertise, reverted to wild prophesies of doom. Of course, this was another example of the gap between analysts who were genuinely knowledgeable about a country they had studied for years, and "generalists"—Walt Rostow was the most egregious but he was far from alone—who squeezed each foreign country into a mold of their own ideological assumptions. There is nothing in the least surprising about that: American policy makers from Eisenhower on believed in the domino theory and it guided their policy more often than not. Yet in

Vietnam the consequences of this failure to learn from those best able to teach were disastrous.

Another dangerous illusion was the idea that the Soviet Union and China constituted what was still often called in official Washington "the Communist bloc." The truth is that—as a band of the more perspicacious analysts at Langley were coming to understand—one of the most important developments in world history in the 1960s was precisely the rapidly widening split between Moscow and Beijing, or Peking or Peiping, as the Chinese capital was still alternatively called. Dean Rusk's use of the phrase "Soviet-dominated Asian Bloc" was an early example of a lurking assumption that experts already knew to be questionable but that was in fact hardly questioned in the debates among LBJ's senior advisers. Walt Rostow in particular was a strong believer in this idea of a "Communist bloc," united in its struggle to establish its domination over the "Free World" through revolution. To be sure, it was not until the late 1960s that Soviet and Chinese forces, in army group strength, actually fought each other on the Ussuri River in the Soviet Far East.[71] Well before 1964, the decision year for U.S. commitment to South Vietnam, it was apparent to many experts in the State Department and the CIA, not to mention scholars at the many American universities that had been encouraged by the federal government to undertake "area studies" of the Soviet Union and China, that Moscow and Beijing saw one another as ideological antagonists—indeed, virtually as enemies.

As we have seen, the background to Khrushchev's management of the Berlin and Cuban missiles crises was the threat to the Soviet leader's position from the "antiparty group" and political competitors who were against him, all but openly supported by the Chinese leadership. It is true that modern scholarship suggests that in 1950 Stalin did know and approve of Chinese support for North Korea in its invasion of South Korea. But a dozen years later relations between the Soviet Union and China were utterly different. We now understand that one of the reasons for China's contempt for Khrushchev was precisely Chinese suspicion that he was seeking an understanding with America in order to leave him free to deal with China.

By February 1962, the National Intelligence Estimate 11-5-62 concluded, "Sino-Soviet relations are in a critical phase just short of an acknowledged and definitive split. There is no longer much chance of a fundamental resolution of differences. In our view, the chances that such a split can be avoided during 1962 are no better than even."[72]

The matter was the subject of considerable controversy. But fortunately we have an authoritative account that makes it absolutely clear that (though there were those who refused to accept the reality of a Sino-Soviet split) by 1962 experts in the CIA were in possession of a mass of excellent evidence that for any practical purposes the "bloc" no longer existed. In 1998 the former CIA analyst Harold Ford published a paper called "The CIA and Double Demonology: Calling the Sino-Soviet Split."[73] Ford pointed out that as early as the mid-1950s, a number of "heretics" in the CIA were reporting and analyzing evidence of serious differences between the Soviet Union and the Chinese Communists. These heretics were a distinguished group. They included Ford himself; Chester Cooper, later to play a significant role in Vietnam diplomacy, who as early as 1954 was bringing groups of CIA officers together to confront them with this evidence; James Billington, author of a classic on Russian history, *The Icon and the Axe,* and currently the librarian of Congress; and Donald Zagoria. As early as 1956 they were officially brought together as the Sino Soviet Studies Group within the agency, but it was the publication in 1962 by Princeton University Press of Zagoria's book *The Sino-Soviet Conflict*[74] that first brought the subject into public knowledge.

Ford concedes that for a long time these "heretics" were disputed and even derided within government. Among their leading disparagers was James Jesus Angleton, head of counterintelligence at the CIA, who insisted that the split was a trick to lull America into vulnerable complacency. Another was Walt Rostow, who was to have so much influence on Lyndon Johnson when he became the president's national security adviser.

Even so, Ford estimates that by 1960 official Washington had every reason to be aware of the split. In the course of 1961, Ford wrote, Washington's knowledge of its details had been enriched by a massive haul of documents from clandestine intelligence. Almost certainly, he was referring to the documents passed to the West by Colonel Oleg Penkovsky, an officer close to Ivan Serov, head of GRU, the Soviet military intelligence, who was turned and set up as an agent by British intelligence before being unmasked and executed by the Soviets in 1963.[75]

By February 1962, when, as we saw, the National Intelligence Estimate judged a Sino-Soviet split almost inevitable, President Kennedy set up a high-level group to study the implications of these judgments, yet it was still many years before they were generally accepted in Washington.

By the time Lyndon Johnson became president, in other words, the CIA's best experts had been preaching for some years that the Sino-Soviet split was indeed real and highly significant; this view was well supported, and senior officials were well aware of it. There should, therefore, have been no excuse for the persisting belief on the part of senior officials such as Walt Rostow that the United States faced in Southeast Asia a united front of two allied Communist powers, the Soviet Union and China. William Bundy in particular, who played a crucial part in charting LBJ's policy, ought, as a former senior CIA officer, to have been aware of the "heretics'" demolition of the concept of the bloc. By 1963, the assumption that the Soviet Union and China constituted a "bloc" was untenable. Yet it was still influential.

Another U.S. supposition involved the very nature of the Vietnam War—was it a conflict of international aggression or a civil war? One of the guiding assumptions of American policy regarding the Vietnam War was that the United States was defending a sovereign nation, South Vietnam, which had been gratuitously invaded by its neighbor, North Vietnam. While that was formally true, it gave a profoundly misleading impression. The two republics dated back only to the 1954 Geneva Conference, which took place only a brief six years before John Kennedy was elected president. Harold Ford's CIA colleague Chester Cooper called the chapter in his book about the origins of the Vietnam War "Birth of a Non-nation," meaning South Vietnam.[76] Before the Geneva meeting, which negotiated what was intended to be a temporary ceasefire rather than a permanent settlement at the end of the Viet Minh's successful war of independence against the French empire, North and South Vietnam had been two different provinces of the same colonial possession. Long before that (the French conquered Annam and Cochinchina in

the mid-nineteenth century), they had been for centuries part of a single, albeit turbulent and often divided, Vietnamese kingdom. Stanley
Karnow, an authoritative historian of Vietnam, described the Geneva
Conference as having produced "no durable solution to the Indochina
conflict, only a military truce that awaited a political settlement, which
never really happened. So the conference was merely an interlude between two wars—or, rather a lull in the same war."[77]

   Much American analysis of the situation in Vietnam assumed that
the North Vietnamese and South Vietnamese were two distinct peoples.
They were not. The South Vietnamese regime was largely composed of
Catholics who had fled from the north, in some cases as recently as after
the Geneva Conference. Roughly 1 million Catholics left the north at
that time. They could be said to include President Diem and the Ngo
Dinh clan that dominated the regime in Saigon and supplied many of
its military officers and officials, though Diem had exiled himself to
America, where he was looked after by Maryknoll nuns and made the
acquaintance of Joseph P. Kennedy's conservative friend Cardinal Spellman of New York.[78]

   Catholics were despised by Buddhists and others in Vietnam as
traitors or at best as timeservers who had profited by supporting French
colonial rule. The peasants of the south, who provided the bulk of the
Viet Cong guerrillas, were mostly Buddhists. (Several millions adhered
to sects such as the Cao Dai and Hòa Hào.) They spoke the same language as the North Vietnamese "regulars" who came down to help them,
albeit with a different accent (like Union and Confederate troops in
another civil war); they belonged to the same ethnic and national group.
There were understandable differences of feeling between North and
South Vietnamese. Northerners tended to look down on southerners
because they had not "made the revolution." No doubt there was resentment among southerners against North Vietnamese cadres and regular
troops, but not the hostility most South Vietnamese felt toward their
American ally.

   Also at stake in the Vietnam conflict were U.S. credibility and resolve. In March 1965 John McNaughton, assistant secretary of defense
and a former Harvard law school professor widely admired for his clar-

ity of thought, expressed his own private estimate of the reasons for American involvement in Vietnam in a memorandum to himself.

70%—To avoid a humiliating U.S. defeat [to our reputation as guarantor].

20% —To keep SVN [South Vietnam] and the [adjacent] territory from Chinese hands.

10%—To permit the people of SVN to enjoy a freer, better way of life.

ALSO—To emerge from crisis without unacceptable taint from methods used.

NOT—To "help a friend," though it would be hard to stay in if asked out.[79]

The historian Fredrik Logevall, in a detailed and very thoughtful study, observes that LBJ and the men Dean Rusk called his "inner cabinet"—Rusk himself, McGeorge Bundy, and Robert McNamara—publicly insisted they chose war to defend South Vietnam from aggression, "but this was false." The key consideration was "credibility and the need to preserve it by avoiding defeat in Vietnam."[80] Logevall shrewdly adds that this credibility was not only national American credibility but also the credibility of the Democratic Party and that of the individuals themselves: that is, the credibility of the Awesome Foursome of LBJ, McNamara, Bundy, and Rusk and of the other officials who took the decisions to escalate the war.

This concern with the credibility of American commitments is found throughout the language of both the Kennedy and Johnson administrations' debates about Vietnam. It was frankly expressed in the crucial cable Mac Bundy sent to LBJ from Pleiku.[81] It is not too strong to say that the major, the decisive reasons for every stage of the commitment, from the Eisenhower administration's tentative willingness to assert American interests in Southeast Asia through the Kennedy administration's decision to keep the anti-Communist government in Saigon alive to LBJ's twin decisions to send American ground forces to

South Vietnam and to bomb North Vietnam, were essentially motivated by the same ideas: that the world doubted the reliability of American commitments, and that its doubts could be laid to rest only by political commitment and military prowess.

It is worth examining this proposition more closely. First of all, what was the audience that must be reassured? What was the composition of the jury that was to be impressed with the iron will of American resolve?

Was it the government of South Vietnam? Certainly America's allies in the country, from the Ngo family and its generals down to the privates fighting in the Delta rice paddies and the highland jungles, must be reassured, if possible. If they concluded that the United States, for all its wealth and military power, would soon give up the struggle and go home, no sensible Vietnamese would continue to fight on alone, especially since a majority probably never much wanted to fight at all, and the consequences of being left in a Hanoi-dominated state from which all the Americans had departed were too horrible to contemplate.

There were, however, wider audiences, too, that must be addressed: first the rulers and the governments of neutral third world countries that might be threatened by "wars of national liberation," as the Kremlin liked to call them, such as Malaysia, Indonesia, and the Philippines in the region, and others farther afield. This was the age of "neutralism," and in particular of the attempt on the part of governments like those of Sukarno's Indonesia, the Nehrus' India, Tito's Yugoslavia, and Mexico, among many others, to create a third world bloc, neutral between capitalist America and the Communist Soviet Union and their allies.

There were other audiences, too, that Washington sought even harder to reassure. There was considerable, perhaps excessive, sensitivity to elite and public opinion in Western Europe. When American statesmen thought about reassuring allies of the reliability of their commitment, they were thinking first and foremost of the more powerful and often fractious allies in Europe: Britain, France (the former colonial power, where knowledge of and interest in Vietnam were naturally greater than elsewhere), and especially Germany. (JFK in particular was concerned to obtain the approval of Harold Macmillan and of Charles de Gaulle, LBJ much less so. He bristled when in a critique of LBJ's policy Harold Wilson, the Labour politician who had succeeded Macmillan, dared to borrow a phrase from the Declaration of Independence, "a decent respect for the opinion of mankind.")[82] After the end of the cold war, the Washington elite could ignore European sensibilities as coming from allies the United States could afford to do without. In the 1960s that was far from the case. Rightly or wrongly, both Kennedy and Johnson, however irritated they could be by European carping or foot-dragging, gave high priority to convincing the West European governments that America's word could be relied on.

Of course Washington under both presidents wanted to convince the antagonists in Moscow and Beijing that it was no paper tiger. But the most important audience of all was the American electorate. Once it was plain that the Viet Cong and its allies in Hanoi were intent on overthrowing the government in Saigon, then no American president dared risk the vengeful rage that—it was almost unquestioningly assumed—would be the fate of the man who "lost Vietnam," as others before them had "lost China." The foreign policy of both JFK and LBJ in Vietnam was essentially domestic policy: both presidents saw that it might decide the next presidential election. And so, in ways neither man could have predicted, it did.

I spent election night, November 5, 1968, in Minneapolis. For a year a team of colleagues from the London *Sunday Times* and I had been covering the presidential election. The year 1968 had been the journalistic assignment of a lifetime—indeed, a professional annus mirabilis. For me, it included a few days in Prague on the eve of the Soviet invasion and a long day watching from a friend's apartment in the Boulevard St Michel as rioting French students shook the foundations of the Republic. But the year's greatest journalistic stories had been in America. I had watched, amazed, as LBJ took himself out of the presidential race. After King's death was announced, I traveled to Memphis with his consigliere, Bayard Rustin. Earlier I had flown to California with Robert Kennedy when he first tested the electoral waters there, and I was in the ballroom of the Ambassador Hotel in Los Angeles when he was shot in an adjoining pantry: I had an appointment to interview him later that night.[83]

I calculated that, however uninspired Hubert Humphrey's campaign had been, if he were nevertheless to win, that would be the culminating journalistic splash of a year of tragedies and miracles. And so I asked my colleagues if I could have the Humphrey beat for the last days of the campaign. Compared with Key Biscayne, where the Nixons were to learn their fate, or with Manhattan or Washington, Minneapolis did not seem attractive: there were few competitors for what my colleagues thought would be a chilly death watch in Minnesota. As things turned out, I came closer than even I believed possible to the ultimate twist in the tail of our story.

"It was about ten past eleven, Minneapolis time—ten past midnight in New York," I reported, "when CBS reported that Humphrey had carried New York, and not just carried it, but swept it by a margin that turned out to be half a million votes. An hour earlier, when CBS predicted he would take the state, Humphrey had said, 'By golly, we might do it!' and for the next five hours the result was in real doubt."[84]

Just before midnight, Senator Fritz Mondale agreed to come down to the press room in the basement of the Leamington Hotel. He looked happy. "We still have strong hope," he told us, "that the Vice President will receive a majority of the Electoral College voters, but it's too early to predict that in the light of the fact that the returns from the West Coast are just beginning to come in." The first returns from California would be from the San Francisco Bay area, habitually more liberal than the south of the state, and a lead there meant little. Still, Mondale could fairly say, "We are encouraged by the fact that at least at this point the Vice President is ahead in California, he's ahead in Texas, and we've carried Pennsylvania, and we carried the state of New York by a remarkable margin, and wherever we look we are doing at least as well—in many places far better—than many have predicted."[85]

I went on to report that Larry O'Brien was to be seen, beaming like a large and happy ginger cat, and Hubert Humphrey himself was briefly observed by the watchers at the Leamington, shaking the snow off his shoulders and "trying hard to hide the hope not even he had expected to feel so solidly at this stage."[86]

That was as close as it got. Sometime near the end of that vigil, my friend Ben Read (executive secretary to Secretary of State Dean Rusk) told me in deepest confidence the story of how Anna Chennault, widow of the hero of the World War II Flying Tigers and a prominent Republican fund-raiser in Washington, had acted as an intermediary to urge President Thieu of South Vietnam to delay accepting LBJ's last-throw offer of a bombing halt. He would, to put the proposition at its bluntest, get a better deal from President Nixon. My coauthors and I used the story in our book, though we also reported (on the basis of my interview with a key Nixon aide, Richard V. Allen) that the Nixon campaign had nothing to do with this gambit.[87] Later I learned that Read's boss, Dean Rusk, and LBJ himself had both seriously considered leaking the Chennault story, but decided in the end not to make use of it because it was simply too damaging to the fabric as well as to the reputation of American democracy.

It is time to return to the two counterfactual questions I asked myself at the outset.

> Would John Kennedy, reelected in 1964, have achieved the legislative successes Lyndon Johnson conjured out of the Eighty-eighth and Eighty-ninth Congresses?

That is surely the easy question. JFK made little secret of the fact that his priority was to get reelected, and in that cause he would "postpone the postponable." If his own failure to appreciate the historic grandeur of the civil rights movement and of the crisis over the issue of racial equality diverted him from that plan, he made only limited progress with domestic reforms before his death. LBJ took over and then surpassed his agenda in a manner that unmistakably demonstrated his prowess—not matched by any subsequent president—at legislative leadership. So, no, it is not likely that JFK would have come even close to equaling LBJ's legislative achievements. At best, he might have succeeded with two major measures: Medicare, which had fair prospects before the assassination, and immigration reform, a pet project of his and his brothers.

> Would JFK have avoided the trap of escalation in the Vietnam War, confronted with the same circumstances that persuaded LBJ to send half a million Americans to fight and to bomb North Vietnam so severely?

That question, as readers will have noticed, I find harder to answer. For one thing, a historian needs evidence that prevails on one side of an argument more than it seems to do in this difficult case. We are dealing, too, with questions that are not only counterfactual but psychological.

Kennedy's admirers, and many of those who knew him best, persuaded themselves that his personal attributes would have saved him from what they, like most of us, have come to see as tragic historical errors. Kennedy was too intelligent, it is said, too temperamentally moderate, too sophisticated to have blundered into the Big Muddy like the big fool in the song.[88]

They may be right. I have to conclude that there is no certainty to be found here. What I have argued, and what I do believe, is that the two men, Kennedy and Johnson, shared a political culture, a set of assumptions and beliefs, a group of advisers, a too-simple patriotism, and an estimate of the effect of their decisions on their own personal political fortunes. Both of them believed that their first necessity was to be reelected, and that their supreme duty must be to preserve American reputation and credibility. It goes without saying that this duty also embraced their own personal and political credibility. John Kennedy was capable of seeing beyond conventional belief systems, as he showed in his great American University speech. But Lyndon Johnson, too, for all his lack of personal delicacy, aimed high all his life, not least in his vision of a Great Society.

After Bien Hoa, Binh Gia, Pleiku, one frustration and humiliation after another, with allies untrustworthy, negotiations taboo, defeat unthinkable but victory elusive, I think JFK, in his own terms, would have had no option but to do what the man he privately despised also did reluctantly. I think he would have gone to war, wryly cynical in private and boldly chivalrous in public, to prove American credibility and his own.

Conclusion

I did not expect to see LBJ again. In 1972, however, I was back in Washington working on another book. I was delighted to be invited to a conference to be held in December at the LBJ Library on the campus of the University of Texas at Austin to discuss the civil rights movement. Many of the paladins of that great struggle were to be there, and so were many of my friends in the Johnson circle.

What no one could be sure of was whether LBJ himself would be there. His health had been terrible. As soon as he stepped onto the plane to fly home to Texas in 1969, he had taken up smoking again. He began to drink his favorite Cutty Sark scotch again: in truth, he had never really given it up. At first he suffered from depression, but with the help of Lady Bird and old friends he recovered his morale and threw himself into running the ranch and other ventures, including writing his memoirs with the help of Doris Kearns, a former White House intern, who later published a much livelier portrait of him, not long after marrying his (and JFK's) speechwriter Richard Goodwin.

As his spirits recovered, his body, battered by sixty years of tension, self-indulgence, and sheer hard work, began to fall apart. In March 1970 it was severe chest pain. In the summer of 1971 he was in hospital with viral pneumonia, and in the spring of 1972 there was a second major heart attack. For the rest of his life he suffered from agonizing angina and every afternoon relied on oxygen and nitroglycerin tablets to help with racking breathlessness and acute pain.

None of these infirmities could keep him from his Last Hurrah. As he climbed onto the platform, I was momentarily shocked. His hair had gone white, but that was not surprising in a man of sixty-four. What was amazing was its length. It almost reached his collar, and it curled upward, giving him the air of a tough nineteenth-century dandy, a riverboat gambler, or a gentleman desperado from the postbellum South.[1] The symbolism was striking. In the 1950s almost all men in America had their hair shorn into crew cuts, or at least very short. Anyone who did not was an aesthete, an old-timer, or gay, though at the time less friendly words were used. Johnson's decision to let his hair grow long was a gesture. What precisely it was meant to convey was not so certain. Did LBJ simply want young people, perhaps his daughters, to think he was not "square"? Was LBJ showing that for the first time in his life he simply didn't care what people thought?

He spoke quietly, not with the rhetorical orotundity of his presidential efforts to match Ted Sorensen's best scripts for JFK, but with an intensity of feeling—of love, even—for us, his friends. Most of the company at the LBJ Library that night (though not this writer) were recruited from those who had taken his shilling, who had ridden with him in his great venture to make America whole and healthy, and had shared first his triumphs, then his failure and humiliation. At his best moments, in his first State of the Union address or at Howard on June 4, 1965, he equaled and even surpassed JFK's oratorical grandeur. This now in Austin was a more human figure, diminished and defeated but still proud. "I'm kind of ashamed of myself," he said, "that I had six years and couldn't do more."[2] He returned to his master theme: the races must overcome unequal history before they could overcome unequal opportunity. Even now, he had to take one of his nitroglycerin pills before he could finish.

We shall never know whether JFK would have lived to achieve that resolution, in the musical sense, of all the themes of a life of striving and strife. That day among his friends and admirers, LBJ seemed to have accomplished it. Less than six weeks later he was dead.

The Vietnam War was Lyndon Johnson's tragedy. I have attempted to persuade my readers that it would have been John Kennedy's tragedy too if he had lived; that for all his cool judgment and his proven military and civil courage, he would not have been able to overcome the assumptions of the day or the limitations of his human sympathy. In part, I have written this book because I do believe that history and the public's memory have been unjust to Lyndon Johnson. But the book has a larger, more important and more topical point. For Vietnam was America's tragedy too. With Kennedy's death, and then with Johnson's abdication and Nixon's victory in 1968, an era in American life ended. Another and very different era was about to begin. Although the past half century has seen its victories and its successes, most Americans, I suspect, would agree with me that, with the passing of my two heroes and their time, something was lost that must be regretted.

As we have seen, that time and those two presidents were marked with not one historical crisis but two. The war was one. The other was the crisis triggered by the civil rights revolution. It was about race, of course, but not only about race. It came to affect almost every aspect of what Americans believe and how they behave.

The war ended the era of political hope in which both JFK and LBJ were true believers. Both meant to fulfill the New Deal agenda that had been interrupted by the election of Dwight Eisenhower in 1952, and especially by the mood of tired reaction after 1956. Who shall say whether Kennedy's or Johnson's vision was the more realistic? Johnson's ambition to create what he called a Great Society was genuine and heartfelt. No doubt Kennedy's commitment to reform was also genuine, but it had a lower priority for him than his dreams of defeating Communism and winning international glory.

They shared, LBJ passionately and JFK with a certain ironic detachment, commitment to a liberal faith—a social democratic faith—in the power of democratic government to transform the life of a great people for the better. The Vietnam War did put an end to the strategic project for domestic reform that LBJ called the Great Society. By 1967, LBJ had in practice lost much of his enthusiasm for domestic reform. (His rancid response to Martin Luther King's coming out against the war in his sermon at Riverside Church in April 1967 was a sign of the times.) Partly it was a straightforward competition for resources: the war was costing so much that there was not enough money to spend at home. Partly it was a matter of inflation: LBJ was afraid the war would cause unmanageable economic problems. Partly it was simply a test of presidential attention: not even a man with Johnson's extraordinary energy, it seemed, could build a Great Society and fight a major war at the same time.

The effect of the war, though, was apparent not only on the man Lyndon Johnson—it showed also on the temper and the priorities of the American people. In 1964, Johnson had been elected in his own right by a record margin: he carried forty-four of the fifty states and won 43 million votes, compared to the 27 million who voted for Barry Goldwater, or 61 percent of the vote. No one since has come close to that achievement. Without the war, no doubt he would have been reelected in 1968. Few remember how close Hubert Humphrey came to beating Nixon that year. With 13.5 percent of the vote cast away on George Wallace, Nixon won 43.4 percent, Humphrey 42.7 percent. The political impact of the war did not come mainly from the actual course of the fighting in Indochina. The consequences of the war for the United States were caused by things that happened in America, not Indochina—among them, draft cards burned, draft-aged men moving to Canada, rioting on university campuses, students shot down at Kent State and Jackson State.

I remember flying over from England in May 1970 to cover the frenzied response to President Nixon's decision to attack Viet Cong sanctuaries across the border of South Vietnam in Cambodia. The moment I got in from the airport I called Pat Moynihan, now working for Nixon in the White House. Where did I want to meet? he asked. For old times' sake, and in all innocence, I suggested the downstairs bar at the Hay-Adams, just across Lafayette Park from his new place of work. When I got there, the park was ringed with buses, parked nose to tail as a laager, protected by dozens, perhaps hundreds of policemen. The streets were crammed with demonstrators in a state of febrile excitement. Some of them had smeared themselves with the blood of a slaughtered lamb. A tall figure, his Irish tweed hat bobbing above the crowds, pushed through the protesters to meet me. I realized with a shock that it was an act of real physical courage on Pat's part to have agreed to meet me at that place on that day.

By that date—May 1970—a national panic, almost an incipient national breakdown, seemed to be taking place in the most historically confident of all nations. The war ended dreams of a New Frontier or a Great Society. The legacy of the New Deal, for Kennedy and even more for Johnson, had been the conviction, held by a majority of Americans, that a democratic government could solve the nation's problems. By 1970, that belief was shattered.

The crucial achievement of the conservative ascendancy that began that snowy election morning in Minneapolis in 1968 has been to mock and destroy that faith. Half a century on, a Republican leader can say, in a moment of political triumph, that what pleases him most is that the people are now tired of big government.[3] But in truth many Americans do still yearn for a government that will be both benevolent and effective. Barack Obama's election in 2008 reflected their numbers and their aspirations. I remember watching President Obama's inauguration with friends under a stuffed moose's head in front of a blazing log fire on another snowy day, this time in the Tennessee mountains. Many felt there was light at last at the end of a very long tunnel. But as the *New Yorker* put it during the Vietnam War: they were right about the tunnel, wrong about the light.

What JFK and LBJ and their supporters believed in was not big government for the sake of it. They wanted government effective enough to carry out the policies it had been elected to act on. And government, by the way, is still big: expenditure is still immense, the defense establishment is still enormous. Conservatives talk about shrinking the size of government. Some of them are philosophically committed to the idea that government in itself is an evil, that taxes are theft. What most conservative politicians mean, though, is that they want to shrink only the parts of government that serve the interests of those citizens they disapprove of: they have no objection to money being spent on weapons or on bailing out banks.

Opposition to the Vietnam War grew steadily until those against it were in a large majority. But that majority was not exclusively made up, as it seemed to many at the time, of people who wanted the war ended because it was wrong. At least as many wanted it ended because it could not be won—and in fact it was not being won. So the war did change American public opinion, but not unilaterally. Some drew from it the lesson that the United States should not fight to make the world conform to its wishes. Others drew a very different conclusion: that the United States should fight wars only if it could be sure of winning them.[4]

The Vietnam War was one precondition for the new conservative mood. It focused both radical dissatisfaction with Great Society policies and conservative reaction against them, which in the end was stronger because more widely shared: after 1968, both the Left and much of the Right, to use those treacherous terms, opposed the war. The disillusion the war engendered in the American people and the impact it had on inflation and on the economy generally frustrated LBJ's dreams of going beyond the New Deal agenda and bringing the whole nation under the Big Tent of his social democratic dream.

Even as Lyndon Johnson triumphed in 1964, the seeds of a new conservatism, at once more populist and more intellectual than the political philosophy of a Robert Taft or a Richard Russell, were beginning to germinate. It reflected not only dissent from the liberal consensus and the desire to repeal the New Deal but a response to the perceived chaos of ethical confusion and social turmoil. It took time for the new conservatism to take the shape it would present when it came to power, fully fledged, with Ronald Reagan in 1981. (Here Watergate, anecdotal as the episode might seem from the long perspective, played a critical part. Before the Ervin hearings, many conservative Democrats, some northerners as well as southerners, were thinking about becoming Republicans. The Reagan Revolution might have come after Nixon's second victory in 1972—might have been, in fact, a Nixon Revolution, if it had not been for the Plumbers and their dirty tricks.)

The defeat of the Democratic administration in 1968, however, was not exclusively the consequence of the Vietnam War. Others things that had happened in the turbulent years since John Kennedy's inauguration had played at least as important a part in bringing the years of New Deal liberalism to an end. Chief of them no doubt was racial upheaval. If the American political system started from the assertion of grand principles, among them liberty, democracy, equality, and the rule of law, the 1960s had been the decade when that system was compelled to answer a practical but vital question left unanswered for a hundred years: How far would these principles be extended to that roughly one-eighth of the population who were "black"? African Americans themselves, with great courage, demanded that this question be answered. Many white people, too, once the contradiction between their ideals and the realities of racial relations had been squarely made clear, agreed that there must be a great change.

Once again, as with the war, the response was not simple. In physics, every action must have an equal and opposite reaction. In politics, the reaction may be opposite, but more than equal. The turmoil of the 1960s came about not only because the great question in its simple form touched deeply held beliefs and prejudices but also because the full scope of the change implied by confronting it was not apparent immediately. It took a while, for example, for it to become clear that the change would affect the North, and in particular its great cities, not just the South. Again, it took a moment for it to sink in that "race relations" could not be treated as an isolated issue to be dealt with, like other shortcomings, by the application of a few reform programs and a certain amount of money. It took time for people to understand that the whole political system would be affected. The reality of the Congress, for example, was that it was structured around two great political parties whose underlying principles arose out of the unsolved racial dilemma. The liberal policies that the Democratic Party, hegemonic since the New Deal of 1933, professed to believe in could not be passed into law, let alone effectively carried out, because the real dominant power in Congress was not the formal alliance between northern and southern Democrats but the effective coalition between southern conservatives, ostensible Democrats, and their allies among conservative Republicans. To solve the racial conundrum it would be necessary to change that fundamental reality of party politics. This too would have practical implications that were not by any means all immediately apparent: for the seniority system in Congress, for example, for the rules of procedure of the Senate, and for many areas of the law, not least for replacing a liberal majority with a conservative one in the Supreme Court. Nor would the necessary changes be limited to workings of the political system as such. They would affect churches, schools, universities, corporations, labor unions: the list came to seem almost infinite. The new emotional turmoil in politics was already producing a social revolution: it changed attitudes to authority everywhere, from the barracks room to the bed-room, and from the campus to the courts.

Indeed, the whole subject matter of the political process would be changed. Before the civil rights revolution, political conflict largely cen-tered on issues of economic interests and economic justice: now those is-sues seemed less urgent than those concerning the rights and status not of economic groups or classes but of "minorities": African Americans, "Hispanics," women, homosexuals. By an awkward metaphor, these mi-norities both imitated and were seen as imitating the African American movement for justice. Women, for example, though a statistical majority of the population, saw nothing strange about adopting some of the language and the tactics of the racial minority. So in myriad ways over the 1960s and the 1970s, the ripples from the movement for African American rights and justice transformed the wider shores of American life in ways hardly imagined initially even by those keenest on the need for change in 1960.

As with the war, so with the racial upheaval and the challenge to traditional forms of authority. The transformation of American politics was no simple matter. Everywhere the reaction to change was as signifi-cant as the change itself. In a literal sense, the new conservatism was re-actionary. Already in the 1960s when the federal government responded to the demands of African Americans for justice, action evoked a more than equal reaction. In the very year the Kennedy-Johnson ticket won the White House, a new breed of conservatives was outraged by the Fifth Avenue pact between Richard Nixon and the liberal Republican Nelson Rockefeller, and William F. Buckley was founding Young Americans for Freedom. By the time of Lyndon Johnson's death, the new conserva-tism was rampant everywhere, shocked not just by big government or Keynesian economics but by long hair, marijuana, rock music, women's liberation, and black power.

It is worth recalling that the conflict between the old ways and the new was not limited to the United States. From Berlin to Johannesburg, from Prague to Paris, in Communist states as well as Western socie-ties, many in a new generation rejected the norms of their elders, and their elders pushed back. Views of Communism, which had still seemed attractive to many in the 1930s, turned to fear and hatred as the real-ity of Communist rule sank in and the cold war threatened cataclysm.

Around the world there was a reaction against the perceived failures of social democratic policies. Business challenged labor unions. Taxpayers demanded relief. As the memory of the Depression and world war began to fade, government, once seen as a protector, was perceived as an incubus. Everywhere, around 1970, the new conservatism was winning and the "Thirty Glorious Years" of the postwar period were ending.

This international perspective reinforces what is plain from the American experience, different as that was in many ways: the great political questions would be decided not by the personalities of "great men" but by the collective activity of political organizations. In the United States, as in Europe, technology and economics, ideology and practical considerations constrained the freedom of democratic politicians. In the middle of the twentieth century, "great men," like them or loathe them—Roosevelt and Churchill, Hitler and Mussolini, Stalin and Mao, Tito and de Gaulle—did seem to personify great nations. New nations emerging from colonial rule followed the fashion: Gandhi, Nehru, Sukarno, Castro, and the rest.

Jack Kennedy and Lyndon Johnson had grown up in that world. But once you left the bleak and chilling perspectives of cold war and nuclear confrontation, the issues of political struggle were becoming less heroic and more domestic. Kennedy was a master of a formal rhetoric that Johnson tried to match, but in 1960 he owed more to an informal style. Political polling was giving new leaders new tools to work out what the voters wanted; television was giving them a new way of communicating with the people. Where the great leaders of the middle of the century had been masters of radio, a medium that enabled the solitary leader to speak to the millions, Kennedy owed more to his cool, more intimate style, which spoke not to the masses but to the individual, the style of the debate, the interview, the walkabout. Paradoxically, the new politics were also dramatically more expensive: they involved not the cozy intimacy of FDR's speeches[5] and whistle-stop appearances in small towns but logistics to fly planeloads of aides, speechwriters, and journalists around the country. Journalists hailed the new politics as favoring the young and the poor. But it was the Kennedys and the Rockefellers who could afford the mainframe computers, the polling and analysis of the new national political campaigns. The Kennedy campaign of 1960 and the Johnson campaign of 1964 were part of the new corporate Madison Avenue style, distinct from both the patriotic revivalism of wartime and the clubby machismo of Tammany and its imitators. Politics cost money, more and more money, as politicians vied with one another until, after fifty years of escalation, raising money has become an indispensable part of what politicians do.

Here, perhaps, is the key to a paradox. Both Kennedy and Johnson —especially Kennedy—were hailed as great men, and both had many of the attributes of the role. But they had learned to operate—to lead— in the new world of polling and jet aircraft, computers and the teleprompter.[6]

We come back to Thomas Carlyle, the Sage of Ecclefechan, and his "great man theory of history." Were great issues in history essentially decided by individuals, by "great men"? Or are the climate, the atmosphere of an age, institutional constraints or a political culture so powerful that even the strongest individuals cannot resist their influence? The key that links the idea of personal charisma to the realities of political organization is the concept of leadership. In the world of sailing ships and cavalry charges, even in the world of eminent Victorians, the lone great man really could make history. In the late twentieth century that was an obsolete memory. But the deep undercurrents of history could still be steered by men who knew how to lead.

In their very different ways, both John Kennedy and Lyndon Johnson were natural leaders. Kennedy possessed the apparently effortless appeal of a child born to the purple. Johnson had the willpower of a man who identifies his own ambitions with the common good. Most of those who have succeeded those two in the White House were men of surpassing talent; none were great leaders. Gerald Ford, Jimmy Carter, and the younger Bush never even seemed to be. Nixon was intelligent as well as cunning. The elder Bush managed foreign policy with great skill, though like Kennedy he was little interested in the humdrum concerns of those not born to great wealth: people noticed that he had never bought his own tennis socks. Clinton had brains, personal magnetism, and real empathy, but he lacked self-discipline. Only Ronald Reagan was a natural leader, a man with an instinct for empathy and a gift for the in-spiring phrase and the uniting gesture, but he was limited by ideological rigidity and in the end by fading powers. The preeminence of Kennedy and Johnson among recent presidents, though, cannot be put down to personal gifts alone. To lead from the White House was still easier in the 1960s than it has become since.

We have seen that far more people believed that they had voted for John Kennedy in 1960 than did so. Lyndon Johnson understood that this was what he was up against. He had to overcome the view of many Americans that they had lost an incomparable leader. That view was held with special intensity by the emerging elite of a nation newly fused into greater unity than ever before by national newspapers and news magazines, coast-to-coast television, and jet air travel.

Lyndon Johnson from the Texas Hill Country might demonstrate a deeper sympathy with the poor, with racial minorities, with ordinary citizens than the Harvard-educated Boston patrician with his trust fund and his network of influential friends from Hollywood by way of Wall Street to Georgetown and even London. LBJ might have had the deter-mination and the political skill to carry through a program of reform his wary predecessor did not even venture to undertake until his reelection to a second term was certain. LBJ might have accepted—indeed, in-ternalized—the foreign policy of the American establishment, with its commitment to bringing American ideals as well as American interests to as much of the globe as possible. He would still remain, in the opin-ion of large and influential sections of public opinion, a provincial: an inelegant symbol of the old politics, a usurper, even an embarrassment. That was what many felt. It was also what he, in his skinless pride, feared they would feel.

It would take a major work of social science investigation and of the imagination to explain why Kennedy appealed to the new elite. In part it was surely because he was seen as embodying that class's new, assertive confidence in America's Augustan Age, as poor Robert Frost didn't get to say. Lyndon Johnson, only nine years younger, recalled memories of want and conflict of which the new class did not want to be reminded. Kennedy, to put it at its simplest, said good things about America, good and comfortable things that Americans wanted to hear;

Johnson said true but critical things, about equality and especially about race, that were not comfortable.

Part of Kennedy's appeal to the intelligentsia and the new class was that he was favorably contrasted with Dwight Eisenhower. To be sure, to trade stereotypes, Kennedy insiders were young millionaires who had inherited their money, played tennis, and wore blue suits, whereas those in Ike's "Gang" were elderly millionaires, "self-made" men who wore brown suits and played golf. (Jack Kennedy, as it happens, loved golf and played it much better than Ike: so much for stereotypes!) JFK was young for a presidential candidate, delivered elegant oratory with ringing eloquence, and was the master of an acerbic yet essentially reassuring wit; Ike looked elderly and in his second term infirm, and he garbled his syntax, sometimes on purpose. Yet Ike had a far better claim than Kennedy to represent American power and success in the world. He had, after all, been the supreme commander of a triumphantly successful "crusade" in Europe, whereas JFK could claim at most to have been a gallant junior officer who behaved with exemplary courage in a minor action. It is no longer unorthodox to point out that Ike was in many respects a highly successful American president. Yet in the last years of Eisenhower's second term, a whole library of highly influential books—by Neustadt and many others—ridiculed him as inert and called for a new strenuous activism in the presidency.[7]

Among professional historians, the great man theory of history is long dead. Yet it lives on in the way John F. Kennedy is remembered, at least in the popular mind. Serious historians may insist that history moves through the interplay of vast, impersonal forces: demographic bulges like the baby boom or the great new immigration after the 1965 reform, economic forces like energy resources, international competition, or globalization. Yet these forces do tend to be attached to individual figures, and in America supremely to presidents, rather in the same way as the fortunes of a great corporation with a hundred thousand employees with an infinite variety of skills are symbolized by the name of a Jack Welch or a Steve Jobs. Whatever its deeper causes, the end of the liberal era was associated with the death of JFK and the abdication of LBJ.

Each of the two figures who are the subject of this book can be called a great man by all standards except the very highest. They were both men of rare character, ambition, and achievement who dared to be leaders. They were something more than the mere embodiments of impersonal forces. Their story is more than an anecdote, half a century old. It has urgent, continuing relevance. Indeed, the political history of the last half century is haunted by their twin ghosts. To a remarkable extent that history has been an extended debate on the events of the years from Kennedy's death to Johnson's. The liberal, social democratic creed that was the public philosophy of the United States from the election of Franklin Roosevelt until that of Richard Nixon was subverted by the strategic recovery of the business class and by its success in selling its ideology, aided by an intellectual (or anti-intellectual) counterrevolution. Liberal democracy was abandoned by many in the working class who had been its beneficiaries as well as by many of the intellectuals who had been its advocates.

Lyndon Johnson's ultimate failure was due to the Vietnam War, and specifically to his decision to escalate American involvement so as to avoid what he saw as unacceptable damage to America's reputation for reliability as the world leader. Yet it was Kennedy, after all, not Johnson, who in the public mind symbolized the assertion of American power and destiny. Where Johnson could claim to have succeeded was in completing and even in vital respects surpassing the New Deal. The paradox is elegant in its simplicity. Kennedy was a foreign policy president forced to confront the unavoidable domestic issue of civil rights. Johnson was a domestic agenda president brought down by the necessity, as he saw it, of matching and completing Kennedy's foreign policy.

Between them, they carried forward an ideal of the presidency that was essentially the legacy of Franklin Roosevelt. Theodore Roosevelt and Woodrow Wilson had foreshadowed how a presidency at the apex of a democratized American system might fit the realities of the twentieth century by appealing over the heads of intermediate institutions to the people. FDR left a model that both Kennedy and Johnson consciously followed. Since their passing, the presidency has seemed increasingly isolated and so increasingly powerless to deliver what the citizens expect of it.

One of the dubious merits of the great man theory is that it does provide convenient symbols for what are in reality complex, contradictory events. So it has been temptingly easy to see JFK as the symbol of a golden age of heroic American unity and international glory, and to cast LBJ as the emblematic villain of overambitious government and its unintended consequences.

We see what we want to see. Both men were gifted leaders. Yet in reality, neither was wholly a free actor. Both were prisoners of that unruly plasma of ideas, assumptions, accidents, and illusions that make up the spirit of an age. Many of government's blunders in the last fifty years—and they have included at least two repetitions of the never-to-be-repeated Vietnam War—can be put down to the misunderstandings of the five hinge years from 1963 to 1968, the brief years of JFK and LBJ. Camelot those years were not. The dream of a Great Society was elusive. Yet whatever the failures and errors of those years, they were arguably the time when the American government did better than before or since to serve the best interests of the American people. That is the true epitaph for JFK and LBJ, the last two great presidents.

Notes

Introduction. A Parting of the Ways

1. This was the great German sociologist Max Weber's term for followers drawn by the promise of reward—in this world or the next—to the service of charismatic leaders.

2. Thomas Carlyle, *On Heroes, Hero-Worship and the Heroic in History* (London: James Fraser, 1841).

3. Sir Lewis Namier, born in Poland, member of the British delegation to the peace conference in Paris in 1919, political adviser to the Jewish Agency, and from 1931 to 1953 professor of history at Manchester University. His major works include *The Structure of Politics at the Accession of George III, England in the Age of the American Revolution*, and *History of Parliament*. He was interested in the role of individuals and small groups, their concerns and the links between them. The journal *Annales d'histoire sociale et economique* was founded by the historians Marc Bloch and Lucien Febvre, professors at Strasbourg, in 1929. It attacked the traditional emphasis on rulers and elites and focused on "mentalities" and "the long run" as well as on the lives of ordinary people and new sources for investigating their lives.

The importance of la longue durée, the long run, was present in Bloch's early work. Fernand Braudel, one of the second generation of the Annales school, analyzed the concept in an article in *Annales* (of which he had become editor) in 1958. Fernand Braudel, "Histoire et sciences sociales: La longue durée," *Annales: Sciences sociales* 13, no. 4 (1958): 725–53. He returned to the subject in an article (written with A. Coll) in *Réseaux* 5, no. 27 (1987): 7–37.

4. Marc Bloch, *Apologie pour l'histoire; ou, Métier d'historien* (Paris: Armand Colin, 1949).

5. *Public Opinion Quarterly* 28, no. 2 (1964): 189–215.

6. Arthur M. Schlesinger Jr., *A Thousand Days: John F. Kennedy in the White*

House (Boston: Houghton Mifflin, 1965); Theodore C. Sorensen, *Kennedy* (New York: Harper & Row, 1965).

7. Theodore White, *The Making of the President, 1972* (New York: Harper, 1973). The genesis of the Camelot myth is examined in a later chapter.

8. Eric F. Goldman (1916–89) worked as a consultant in the White House from 1963 to 1969. His best-known book was *Rendezvous with Destiny* (New York: Knopf, 1952).

9. Robert A. Caro, *The Years of Lyndon Johnson* (New York: Knopf): vol. 1, *The Path to Power* (1982), vol. 2, *Means of Ascent* (1990), vol. 3, *Master of the Senate* (2002), vol. 4, *The Passage of Power* (2012).

10. Robert Dallek, *Lone Star Rising*, vol. 1, *Lyndon Johnson and His Times, 1908–1960* (Oxford: Oxford University Press, 1991); Robert Dallek, *Flawed Giant* (New York: Oxford University Press, 1998); Irving Bernstein, *Guns or Butter* (New York: Oxford University Press, 1996); Randall B. Woods, *LBJ: Architect of American Ambition* (Cambridge, Mass.: Harvard University Press, 2006).

11. Tom Wicker, *JFK and LBJ* (New York: Morrow, 1968).

12. Ibid., 278, quoting his own article in *The Times* written the day Johnson announced his "abdication."

13. Godfrey Hodgson, "Morley's Lives of the Kennedys," *Crossbow* l9, no. 34 (1966).

14. Thomas Babington, Lord Macaulay, *Horatius,* in *Lays of Ancient Rome* (London: Longman, 1847), verse 60.

15. Hodgson, "Morley's Lives of the Kennedys."

16. Godfrey Hodgson, *Observer* [London], November 24, 1963.

17. The late Joseph Kraft, in front of a group of fellow White House correspondents in the bar of the Driskill Hotel in Austin, Texas, upbraided me harshly for those very words. The British newspapers, he said, had been in the habit of sending to Washington a very different class of correspondents, the sort of men who had been properly educated—and he mentioned the very institutions where I had in fact been educated myself. Snobbery was never very far from the spirit of Camelot.

18. *Public Papers of the Presidents: John F. Kennedy, 1961* (Washington, D.C.: Government Printing Office, 1962), 1:2.

19. Theodore H. Sorensen, oral history, March 26, 1964, 1:1, John F. Kennedy Presidential Library and Museum, Boston.

20. The phrase, from St. Augustine's *Confessions,* was famously quoted in John Henry Newman's *Apologia pro Vita Sua* as forming his conviction that the Church of England was schismatic and therefore he should convert to Catholicism.

21. *Public Papers of the Presidents: John F. Kennedy, 1961,* 1:1.

22. Ibid.

23. Michael Harrington, *The Other America* (New York: Macmillan, 1962).

24. White, *The Making of the President, 1972,* xix.

25. According to the U.S. Bureau of the Census, the population of the United States in 1960 was just under 180 million. The population of the eleven states of the former Confederacy was 43.8 million. The population of the "South" region was 55 million.

26. Fredrik Logevall, *Choosing War: The Lost Chance for Peace and the Escalation of War in Vietnam* (Berkeley: University of California Press, 1999), 72: "From late August onward, Kennedy's actions indicate that he had resigned himself to the necessity of removing Diem."

27. George McT. Kahin, *Intervention: How America Became Involved in Vietnam* (New York: Knopf, 1979), 79.

28. There is a good account of some of these in Evan Thomas, *The Very Best Men* (New York: Simon & Schuster, 1996).

29. For example, school desegregation in the South.

30. The reading copy, in the LBJ Library, is attributed to Goodwin. Both McPherson and Moynihan, whom I saw frequently at this time, discussed their contributions with me.

31. *Public Papers of the Presidents: Lyndon B. Johnson, 1965* (Washington, D.C.: Government Printing Office, 1966), no. 301, pp. 635–40.

32. *Public Paper of the Presidents: Lyndon B. Johnson, 1963–64* (Washington, D.C.: Government Printing Office, 1965), vol. 1, no. 357, pp. 704–7.

33. Kenneth O'Donnell and David Powers, *"Johnny, We Hardly Knew Ye": Memoirs of John Fitzgerald Kennedy* (Boston: Little, Brown, 1972), 267.

34. Walt Rostow, oral history, 1:2. Lyndon Baines Johnson Library and Museum, Austin.

35. Horace Busby, oral history, 6:6, LBJ Library. It seems Duckworth did not use the material: he was simply trying to rile Johnson's liberal aide Horace Busby. But he was tapping into a widespread instinct in the South at the time.

36. George Reedy, oral history, 5:11, 8:54, LBJ Library.

37. Ibid., 6:54.

38. Only some: the very Catholic Prince von Solm established colonies for conservative German settlers too.

39. Busby, oral history, 1:6.

40. William Manchester, *The Death of a President* (London: World Books, 1967), 386.

41. Reedy, oral history, 7:9.

42. In Britain and Europe, a liberal was originally one who defended freedom in religion, society, and economics, or what came to be called a "Manchester liberal," and to this day *libéral* in French (and its equivalent in other European languages) means approximately what "conservative" means in America, where "liberal" came to be a euphemism for "on the left," or "social democratic."

43. Richard Reeves, *President Kennedy: Profile of Power* (New York: Simon & Schuster, 1993), 62.

44. Johnson was not always so nice with Robert Parker, a black sharecropper's son who worked for him as a waiter in the 1940s; occasionally he humiliated him. But then he occasionally humiliated even his closest white professional staff. Dallek, *Lone Star Rising*, 277.

45. I was present as a reporter both when Barnett declared his love for the State

of Mississippi at halftime in the Ole Miss–Kentucky football game that weekend and on the Ole Miss campus during the riot.

46. The fullest account of this episode is in Taylor Branch, *Parting the Waters: America in the King Years, 1954–63* (New York: Simon & Schuster, 1988), 650–52.

47. Sorensen, oral history, 5:123, JFK Library. I was also present at the "school-house door," actually a building on the University of Alabama campus.

48. Nick Bryant, *The Bystander: John F. Kennedy and the Struggle for Black Equality* (New York: Basic Books, 2006), 472–73.

49. Both jokes from the author's personal knowledge.

50. Stewart Alsop, "Johnson Takes Over: The Untold Story," *Saturday Evening Post,* February 15 1964, 17–23.

51. Theodore H. White, *The Making of the President, 1964* (New York: Atheneum, 1976), 19.

52. Arthur Schlesinger, more perceptive than many liberals, wrote in his journal as early as December 5, 1963: "On the whole, it is hard to fault the new President thus far on issues," though he added, "On taste, there is the expected infusion of corn." Arthur M. Schlesinger Jr., *Journals, 1952–2000* (New York: Penguin, 2007), 210.

53. "Beyond Vietnam," April 4, 1967, text in *A Call to Conscience: The Landmark Speeches of Dr. Martin Luther King Jr.,* ed. Clayborne Carson and Kris Shepard (New York: IPM/Warer Books, 2001). Audio: http://mlk-kpp01stanford.edu/index.php/encuy clopedia/doc_beyond_vietnam. Online: "Beyond Vietnam: A Time to Break Silence," *Common Dreams,* September 30, 2014, www.commondreams.org/views04/0115-13.htm.

54. Joseph W. Alsop, oral history interview, June 10, 1971, RFK #1, JFK Library.

55. *Camelot* opened on Broadway in 1960 and ran for more than eight hundred performances. With music by Frederick Loewe and book by Alan Jay Lerner, the musical was based on T. H. White's version of the Arthurian legend, *The Sword in the Stone.*

56. Joan Blair and Clay Blair Jr., *The Search for JFK* (New York: Putnam, 1976), 616.

57. The reference, to Sir James Frazer's *The Golden Bough,* first edition 1890, third edition in twelve volumes, 1906–15, was surprisingly frequent.

58. Kevin Phillips, *The Emerging Republican Majority* (New Rochelle, N.Y.: Arlington House, 1969).

59. Weber's work has been irregularly translated into English. His theory of charisma was laid out in *Wirtschaft und Gesellschaft* (1933). The relevant section was first published in English by A. M. Henderson and Talcott Parsons, *The Theory of Social and Economic Organization* (Glencoe, Ill.: Free Press, 1947).

Chapter I. Life Is Unfair

1. King Hassan II of Morocco had discussions with President Kennedy on March 29, 1963. *Public Papers of the Presidents: John F. Kennedy, 1963* (Washington, D.C.: Government Printing Office, 1964), no. 116, p. 293.

2. I cannot resist an anecdote about the opening of the White House briefing

room in 1969. Nixon's press people wanted to invite a respected reporter to be the guest of honor at the opening of this facility, which is located where FDR's swimming pool used to be, that is, roughly beneath the presidential offices. They chose Eddy Folliard, the veteran *Washington Post* White House correspondent, who had seen many presidents come and go. "I'll have a drink," said Eddy, "but I won't go upstairs."

3. John O'Donnell, father of Doris O'Donnell (a great friend of mine and my wife's) and husband of the influential liberal columnist Doris Fleeson, could not be described as liberal.

4. Theodore H. White's *The Making of the President, 1960* (New York: Atheneum, 1961), played an extraordinary role in persuading his numerous readers that Kennedy was a new and good thing.

5. Ibid., 22.

6. Joan Blair and Clay Blair Jr., *The Search for JFK* (New York: Putnam, 1976), 612–13.

7. Ibid., 613.

8. Ibid., 616.

9. Nigel Hamilton, *JFK: Life and Death of an American President,* vol. 1, *Reckless Youth* (New York: Random House, 1988); Seymour Hersh, *The Dark Side of Camelot* (New York: HarperCollins, 1998).

10. Richard J. Whalen, *The Founding Father* (New York: New American Library, 1964).

11. Hamilton, *Reckless Youth,* 725.

12. Ibid.

13. Richard Reeves, *President Kennedy: Profile of Power* (New York: Simon & Schuster, 1993), 43 and notes on 668–70.

14. Robert Dallek, *John F. Kennedy: An Unfinished Life* (Boston: Little, Brown, 2003), 704.

15. Wikipedia has assembled a compendious collection of these ratings, both among the general public and by groups of academics and other specialists. Nate Silver's Five Thirty Eight survey, for example, in January 2013, placed JFK ninth and LBJ twelfth among presidents.

16. I once had occasion to visit there and was startled by the sheer number of employees keeping track of the family's money and investments of every kind.

17. Werner Sombart, *Why Is There No Socialism in the United States?* trans. Patricia Hocking and C. T. Husband (London: Macmillan, 1976). It is interesting that Sombart's sentence, short and simple in the original, has been expanded by his translators. Sombart actually wrote nothing about "reefs" or doom: he wrote, "An Roastbeef und Apple-Pie werde alle sozialistichen Utopien zuschanden," that is, "On roast beef and apple pie all socialist utopias are destroyed." The German version is: *Warum gibt es in die Vereinigten Staaten keinen Sozialismus?* (Tübingen: Mohr, 1906), 126.

18. Weber did not define charisma with his usual care. The concept is described in chapter 3 of his *Wirtschaft und Gesellschaft* (Economy and Society). It was translated into English by A. M. Henderson and Talcott Parsons, *The Theory of Social and Economic*

Organization (Glencoe, Ill.: Free Press, 1947). It is best known through Weber's *The Protestant Ethic and the Spirit of Capitalism,* 1905, translated into English in 1930.

19. Senator Kennedy did not campaign for president in 1956, but he came quite close to being nominated as the Democratic candidate for vice president. At one point on the second ballot he was actually ahead of the man eventually chosen, Senator Estes Kefauver of Tennessee. After Senator Albert Gore Sr. released his candidates, there was a surge for Kefauver. But Kennedy came within thirty-eight and a half votes, or even fewer on some accounts, of being nominated.

20. For example: Edward S. Corwin, *Presidency, Office and Powers* (New York: New York University Press, 1957; earlier edition 1948); Herman Finer, *The Presidency: Crisis and Regeneration* (Chicago: University of Chicago Press, 1960); E. S. Corwin and Louis Koenig, *The Presidency Today* (New York: New York University Press, 1956); Richard E. Neustadt, *Presidential Power* (New York: Wiley, 1960); Rexford G. Tugwell, *The Enlargement of the Presidency* (Garden City, N.Y.: Doubleday, 1960).

21. Personal information from Bundy.

22. The same, confirmed by records of the Army Signals Corps. As lieutenant, then captain and major, he was commanding officer of 6813th Signal Security Detachment at Bletchley Park.

23. Maxwell Taylor, *The Uncertain Trumpet* (New York: Harper, 1960).

24. John Hersey, "A Reporter at Large: Survival," *New Yorker,* June 17, 1944, 31. Joseph Kennedy chose Hersey in part because he was married to Frances Ann Cannon, a former girlfriend of JFK. This article was important in bringing into prominence the second Kennedy son after his brother was killed. The story was given further publicity by Robert Donovan, *PT 109* (New York: McGraw-Hill, 1961).

25. These ideas were first deployed in Richard Scammon and Ben J. Wattenberg, *The Real Majority* (New York: Coward, McCann & Geoghegan, 1970). They were later summarized in Ben J. Wattenberg, *The Massive Middle Class Majority and What It Thinks* (New York: Family Circle, 1973).

26. See Godfrey Hodgson, *America in Our Time,* rev. ed. (Princeton, N.J.: Princeton University Press, 2005), 83. I owed the confidence of my disagreement with the "Everyone is now middle class" thesis to a large degree to the work of Andrew Levison, *The Working Class Majority* (New York: Coward, McCann & Geoghegan, 1974).

27. Tom Brokaw, *The Greatest Generation* (New York: Random House, 1998).

28. I may add that on the occasions I was taken to South Boston by my Boston Irish friend David Nyhan of the *Boston Globe,* I was always treated with friendliness and even warmth.

29. Thomas Pakenham, a friend of mine who inherited an Irish estate in the mid-1960s, told me that he was horrified to learn that a discriminatory policy of this kind had existed under his Protestant uncle. (His parents were converts to Catholicism.)

30. Arthur M. Schlesinger Jr., *Journals, 1952–2000* (New York: Penguin, 2007), 205.

31. Tom Hayden, *Irish Inside* (New York: Verso, 2001), 26.

32. Tip O'Neill, *Man of the House* (New York: Random House, 1987), 1.

33. Galbraith, brought up as a Scot in Ontario, had studied in England at Cambridge. Price and Beer were Rhodes scholars at Oxford, and Schlesinger, who had also studied at Cambridge, was a lifelong Anglophile.

34. Henry Adams, *The Education of Henry Adams*; Amanda Foreman, *A World on Fire* (New York: Random House, 2011).

35. Including Canon Hardwick Rawnsley, one of the three founders of Britain's National Trust for conservation.

36. Godfrey Hodgson, *Woodrow Wilson's Right Hand* (New Haven, Conn.: Yale University Press, 2008).

37. Lawrence E. Gelfand, *The Inquiry: American Preparations for Peace, 1917–1919* (New Haven, Conn.: Yale University Press, 1963); Hodgson, *Woodrow Wilson's Right Hand.*

38. Godfrey Hodgson, "The Establishment," *Foreign Policy,* no. 20 (Spring 1973).

39. Robert Dallek, *John F. Kennedy: An Unfinished Life* (Boston: Little, Brown, 2003), 310.

40. After writing this paragraph I discovered that Arthur Schlesinger Jr. had also noticed the similarity between his friend JFK and the British Whigs. *A Thousand Days: John F. Kennedy in the White House* (Boston: Houghton Mifflin, 1965), 83.

41. Ibid., 83, 105. There have been several lists of President Kennedy's favorite books. Most give John Buchan's *Montrose* (London: Hodder & Stoughton, 1928) and Winston Churchill's life of his ancestor, the first Duke of Marlborough, *Marlborough: His Life and Times,* 4 vols. (London: George Harrap, 1933–38). Others mention his affection for Ian Fleming's James Bond novels. Possibly Professor Schlesinger thought the president's most loved book must be the Bible?

42. Conrad Russell, *The Fall of the British Monarchies* (Oxford: Oxford University Press, 1991).

43. Steve Pincus, *1688* (New Haven, Conn.: Yale University Press, 2009).

44. Caroline Robbins, *The Eighteenth Century Commonwealthmen* (Cambridge, Mass.: Harvard University Press, 1959).

45. I was reminded of the significance of Robert Frost's prediction of an Augustan Age by a highly original paper by Emile Bojesen of the University of Winchester, read at a conference at the University of Sussex, May 15, 2014.

46. There has been controversy about the role of the father's friend Arthur Krock of the *New York Times* in the writing of the thesis and its publication in book form. It would appear that the young JFK did exploit his father's press secretary, James Seymour, to provide him with documentation that no other Harvard undergraduate could have acquired: Krock's part was limited to suggesting a title and finding a publisher for an undergraduate thesis.

47. He may not have sailed on the *Mayflower,* but he knew the pilgrims before they left Leiden, and joined them in Plymouth on the very next voyage on *Fortune.*

48. Califano, Levinson, Nimetz, Robinson, and Stanford Ross from Harvard Law, Bohlen from Princeton. Levinson, oral history, 1:9, Lyndon Baines Johnson Library and Museum, Austin.

49. Reedy, oral history, 19:29, LBJ Library.

50. George Reedy, *Lyndon B. Johnson: A Memoir* (Kansas City: Andrews McMeel, 1982), 23.

51. Walter Isaacson, obituary of McGeorge Bundy, *Time*, September 30 1996; Robert Dallek, *Flawed Giant* (New York: Oxford University Press, 1998); and Richard Goodwin, *Remembering America* (Boston: Little, Brown, 1988).

52. Horace Busby, oral history, 1:15–16, LBJ Library.

53. Robert Dallek, *Lone Star Rising*, vol. 1, *Lyndon Johnson and His Times, 1908–1960* (Oxford: Oxford University Press, 1991), 14. Dallek sources this remark to Ronnie Dugger, *The Politician: The Drive to Power, from the Frontier to the Master of the Senate* (New York: Norton, 1982).

54. Reedy, oral history, 12:16.

55. The following brief account of the Johnson family background is based on Randall Woods, *LBJ: Architect of American Ambition* (Cambridge, Mass.: Harvard University Press, 2006); Robert A. Caro, *The Years of Lyndon Johnson*, vol. 1, *The Path to Power* (New York: Knopf, 1982); T. R. Fehrenbach, *Lone Star: A History of Texas and Texans* (New York: Da Capo, 2000).

56. The Southwest Texas State Teachers College, now the San Marcos campus of Texas State University.

57. The author has visited Cotulla. Even today it has fewer than four thousand inhabitants, widely spread, 84 percent of them Hispanic, and the average income is less than $11,000 a head.

58. The King ranch is not the biggest in the world: that honor belongs to an Australian property of 6 million acres. It is not even the biggest in the United States. Still, at 825,000 acres it is not small, and the Kleberg clan also owns large spreads in northern Australia and substantial oil properties in Texas.

59. Louis Gomolak, "Prologue: LBJ's Foreign Affairs Background, 1908–1948" (Ph.D. diss., University of Texas, 1989).

60. Woods, *LBJ*, 128.

61. Dallek, *Lone Star Rising*, 160.

62. According to "Simpson Thacher's Client Care Lesson," *Lawyer*, January 28, 2008, the firm had "a longstanding Lehman brothers relationship." Weisl's son Edwin Weisl Jr. was closely connected with the Robert Lehman foundation. The most prestigious, long-established Wall Street law firms, such as Sullivan & Cromwell and the "Cravath firm," have been called "white shoe firms" after a 1950s Ivy League fashion for white buck shoes.

63. This is one of the themes of Michael Janeway, *The Fall of the House of Roosevelt* (New York: Columbia University Press, 2004), especially 28–43. Michael Janeway was one of the two sons of Eliot Janeway, an influential journalist with the Luce publications and economic commentator.

64. Arthur B. Krim, a New York entertainment lawyer who was chairman of United Artists, chairman of the Democratic Party Finance Committee, and a close friend of the Johnsons. He actually lived in the White House for a time.

65. McGeorge Bundy, oral history 1:33, LBJ Library.

66. Reedy, oral history 10:7.

67. Dallek, *Lone Star Rising,* 6–7.

68. Woods, *LBJ,* 290, citing Jan Jarboe Russell, *Lady Bird: A Biography of Mrs. John-son* (New York: Scribner, 1991), 172–73.

69. Dallek, *Lone Star Rising,* 10.

70. Woods, *LBJ,* 219.

71. Robert A. Caro, *The Years of Lyndon Johnson,* vol. 2, *Means of Ascent* (New York: Knopf, 1990), xxvi–xxvii.

72. Woods, *LBJ,* 233.

73. Caro, *Means of Ascent,* xxxiv.

74. Woods, *LBJ,* 155.

75. Dallek, *Lone Star Rising,* 224, citing Dugger, *The Politician,* 235.

76. Woods, *LBJ,* 155.

77. Later part of Halliburton, Inc.

78. Woods, *LBJ,* 135.

79. George N. Green, *The Establishment in Texas Politics* (Westport, Conn.: Greenwood, 1979).

80. One is reminded of the brilliant political device of General de Gaulle. When the Republic was threatened by the murderous fury of the Algerian settlers and their political allies, De Gaulle went on television and said, "Je vous ai compris": I have understood you. He had indeed, but not in the way they hoped, and he proceeded to destroy them politically without mercy.

81. Robert A. Caro, *The Years of Lyndon Johnson,* vol. 3, *Master of the Senate* (New York: Knopf, 2002), 231–91. This gives an extended account of LBJ's conduct of hearings that ended Olds's career.

82. Harry McPherson, oral history, 1:16, LBJ Library.

83. Reedy, oral history, 9:18.

84. Horace Busby, oral history, 5–6, LBJ Library.

85. *New York Times,* March 4 1956.

86. Robert A. Caro, *The Years of Lyndon Johnson,* vol. 4, *The Passage of Power* (New York: Knopf, 2012), 9, speaks of "a monumental feat of legislative maneuvering, of bullying, cajoling, threatening, of lightning tactical decisions . . . of parliamentary genius on a grand scale." See also Caro, *Master of the Senate,* especially 786–88.

87. Woods, *LBJ,* 304.

88. McPherson, oral history, 1:11–12.

89. Reedy, oral history, passim.

90. Tom Wicker, "Remembering the Johnson Treatment," *New York Times,* May 9, 2002.

91. The pictures were taken by George Tames of the *New York Times* in 1957. Similar pictures survive, however, of LBJ in equally dominant posture with two of his most respected friends, Abe Fortas and Richard Russell. This was just his natural mode of discourse.

92. Anthony Bergen, "The Johnson Treatment," deadpresidents.tumblr/com/10 21745/lbj-day-the-johnson-treatment.

93. McPherson, oral history, 1:13.

94. Reedy, oral history, 17:44.

95. Ibid.

96. Arthur Krim, oral history, 2:1–4, LBJ Library.

97. Reedy, oral history, 12:13.

98. Ibid., 26:12.

99. Krim, oral history, 2:29.

100. Author's conversations with McPherson.

101. Doris Kearns, *Lyndon Johnson and the American Dream* (New York: Harper, 1976), 63.

102. Larry Levinson, oral history, 1:25, LBJ Library.

103. Woods, *LBJ*, 32–33.

104. *Report on the Economic Conditions of the South* (1938). Among those who worked on it were Clifford and Virginia Durr, Hugo Back, Aubrey Williams, and Arthur Goldschmidt. The original report is out of print but it has been published as *Confronting Southern Poverty in the Great Depression*, ed. David L. Carlton and Peter A. Coclanis (Chapel Hill: University of North Carolina Press, 2012).

Chapter II. One Brief Shining Moment

1. The description of the interview below is based on the article that resulted: Theodore H. White, "An Epilogue for President Kennedy," *Life*, December 6, 1963, 158–59.

2. I should declare an interest, or at least an ancient resentment. In 1968, when I and my colleagues Lewis Chester and Bruce Page were getting ready to write the account of the 1968 election that was published by Viking as *An American Melodrama*, we were asked for a drink by Blair Clark, a friend of mine and manager of Senator Eugene McCarthy's campaign for the Democratic nomination, to meet Teddy White. He greeted me with the words, "So you're one of the three monkeys who think if you type long enough you'll be Shakespeare." It was not said as a joke, rather a declaration of war. Our book was better reviewed than White's and probably sold more copies. Until this boorish encounter I had been an admirer, even arguably an imitator, of his 1960 *Making of the President*.

3. Anthony Sampson, *Anatomy of Britain* (London, Hodder & Stoughton, 1962).

4. Evan Thomas, *The Very Best Men* (New York: Simon & Schuster, 1995).

5. The first successful U.S. test of an ABM was in November 1960, and the first test of an ABM with a live warhead was in March 1961, a mere few weeks before my interview with Hitch. Widespread discussion of ABMs began in 1966–67.

6. When Mr. Wiggins retired to Maine he was irritated by how long it took the U.S. mail to deliver his complimentary copy of the *Post* to his home every day. So he hired a cart with a pair of mules and demonstrated in person that it could reach Maine quicker than the U.S. Post Office.

7. Indeed, Katharine Graham invited Bruce Page and myself from *The Sunday Times* to lunch to ask us what would be involved if the *Post* were to take up this investigative journalism. We said good lawyers and a willingness to allow reporters to work for weeks on a single story.

Chapter III. Doctor Fell

The epigraph is a traditional English rhyme (originally written by Thomas Brown in 1680), cited by George Reedy about LBJ's relations with Robert Kennedy: George Reedy, oral history, 20:211, Lyndon Baines Johnson Library and Museum, Austin.

1. The phrase is from William Manchester, *The Death of a President* (London: World Books, 1967), 385.

2. Ibid.

3. Arthur M. Schlesinger Jr., *A Thousand Days: John F. Kennedy in the White House* (Boston: Houghton Mifflin, 1965), 92–93.

4. S. Douglass Cater, interviewed by David McCullough on PBS, *American Experience,* November 7, 2011.

5. Bobby Baker, *Wheeling and Dealing: Confessions of a Capitol Hill Operator* (New York: Norton, 1978), 116.

6. Smathers's Senate offices were noted for the suntanned Florida beauties who answered the phone there. Before JFK married (and perhaps afterward), he and Smathers used to disappear for dinner with attractive women they'd invited to watch late-afternoon debates in the visitors' gallery of the Senate.

7. There is a sprightly account of the Bashir episode in Reedy, oral history, 19:30–36.

8. Steven M. Gillon, *The Kennedy Assassination 24 Hours After* (New York: Basic Books, 2009).

9. Larry O'Brien, oral history, 1:13, LBJ Library.

10. Jeff Shesol, *Mutual Contempt* (New York: Norton, 1977), 77.

11. Arthur Schlesinger Jr., *Journals, 1952–2000* (New York: Penguin, 2007), 49.

12. Shesol, *Mutual Contempt,* 77, citing Kenneth O'Donnell, oral history, LBJ Library.

13. Liz Carpenter, oral history, 1:11, LBJ Library.

14. Randall Woods, *LBJ: Architect of American Ambition* (Cambridge, Mass.: Harvard University Press, 2006), 400.

15. Gillon, *The Kennedy Assassination,* 332.

16. Reedy, oral history, 21:4.

17. Ibid., 21:56.

18. On my thirtieth birthday, which I had spent at the UN covering some story, I was staying at the Beekman Tower Hotel, across East Fiftieth Street from RFK's apartment. To my amazement, he and a friend, Bill vanden Heuvel, showed up with a bottle of whisky. After we had drunk some of it and discussed, among other things, the supernatural, they took me out to dinner.

19. Robert Dallek, *Lone Star Rising,* vol. 1, *Lyndon Johnson and His Times, 1908–1960* (Oxford: Oxford University Press, 1991), 559. The incident is recounted in Bobby

Baker, *Wheeling and Dealing*, 42–43, and was witnessed by LBJ's friend Judge A. W. Moursund. See Dallek's footnote at 964.

20. Lady Bird Johnson, oral history, 40:36–37, LBJ Library.

21. Woods, *LBJ*, 358, citing Shesol, *Mutual Contempt*, 39, which cites *New York Times*, July 15, 1960.

22. Baker, *Wheeling and Dealing*, 123.

23. One invaluable, though by no means unchallenged, account of the dealings over the vice presidential nomination is the memo written soon after the events by Philip Graham, publisher of the *Washington Post* and a good friend of both LBJ and the Kennedys. He called it *Notes on the 1960 Democratic Convention;* it is often referred to as the Graham memorandum. The original is in the LBJ Library at Austin. The most accessible version is perhaps that printed as an appendix to Theodore White, *The Making of the President, 1964* (New York: Atheneum, 1975), 407–15.

24. Shesol, *Mutual Contempt*, 44.

25. Baker, *Wheeling and Dealing*.

26. Arthur M. Schlesinger Jr., *Robert Kennedy and His Times* (Boston: Houghton Mifflin Harcourt, 1978), 208.

27. Shesol, *Mutual Contempt*, 49, citing Robert F. Kennedy, oral history (interviewed by Arthur Kennedy, February 2, 1965), John F. Kennedy Presidential Library and Museum, Boston. Evan Thomas, *Robert Kennedy: A Life* (New York: Simon & Schuster, 2000), 97, quotes the same phrase, attributing it to Robert Kennedy's oral history interview with Arthur Schlesinger; Thomas shrewdly calls this the Kennedy version of what happened. In his 1965 *A Thousand Days*, Schlesinger reports only that Robert Kennedy had told Phil Graham "that Johnson would not be considered" (43), that John Kennedy "was certain, on the basis of Johnson's multitudinous declarations and attitudes, that there was practically no chance that Johnson would accept" (45), that "to Kennedy's astonishment," Johnson "grabbed at" the offer of the Vice-Presidency" (48), and that he returned to his suite saying, "You just won't believe it . . . He wants it!" (49). It is fair to say that the master historian also added that "the confusion of that afternoon defies historical reconstruction . . . including this one."

28. Shesol, *Mutual Contempt*, 45.

29. Dallek, *Lone Star Rising*, 580. Dallek quoted JFK as telling his aide Mike Feldman, "We will never know the full story of how Johnson became the vice-presidential nominee."

30. Schlesinger, *Robert Kennedy*, 220.

31. Shesol, *Mutual Contempt*, 54, quoting the "Graham memo."

32. Robert A. Caro, *The Years of Lyndon Johnson*, vol. 4, *The Passage of Power* (New York: Knopf, 2012), 115, citing [Ralph G.] Martin, *A Hero for Our Time* (New York: Macmillan, 1983).

33. Baker, *Wheeling and Dealing*, 133–34.

34. Shesol, *Mutual Contempt*, 63; and see Merle Miller, *Lyndon: An Oral Biography* (New York: Putnam, 1980), 276. It appears, however, that this is an old political joke, often attributed to the Arizona congressman Mo Udall. It is not to be found in Baker,

Wheeling and Dealing, who would surely have included it if he thought it was used by his former boss.

35. Reedy, oral history.

36. Woods, *LBJ,* 412, citing "Marshal Probers Wait File," *Dallas Times Herald,* May 28, 1962, and Walter Jenkins Memoranda of Conversation with Deke DeLoach of the FBI, May 31 and June 1, 1962, Pre-presidential Confidential File, box 1, LBJ Library.

37. Baker, *Wheeling and Dealing,* 77.

38. Ibid., 79–80.

39. It is suggested by Thurston Clarke, *JFK's Last Hundred Days* (New York: Penguin, 2013), 80, that Rometsch might have been an employee of the Stasi, the East German secret police, but would have come under the KGB once she was in the United States, as the Soviet Union controlled all espionage in North America.

40. Rometsch was deported on August 22, 1963. Seymour Hersh, *The Dark Side of Camelot* (New York: HarperCollins (paperback edition), 399. He explains that Rometsch was escorted out of the country by La Verne Duffy, a former associate of Robert Kennedy on the Senate Rackets Committee who was a lover of Rometsch's. Hersh also claims, on the basis of interviews with Duffy's brother Wayne, that Rometsch was paid substantial sums. The story was originally broken by a well-known investigative journalist, Clark Mollenhoff, in the *Des Moines Register,* October 26, 1963.

41. Memorandum in Kennedy Library, POF.

42. Twenty-four in 1960, twenty-five in 1964, thirty-four in 2008.

43. Woods, *LBJ,* 413–14. The institution is now part of Texas State University.

44. Manchester, *The Death of a President,* 176–77.

45. Ibid., 423.

46. Woods, *LBJ,* 25, citing Orville Freeman diary, presidential papers, box 9, LBJ Library.

47. Shesol, *Mutual Contempt,* 122.

48. This is the document as printed in ibid. Special File on the Kennedy Assassination, box 1, LBJ Library.

49. Shesol, *Mutual Contempt,* 117, citing Rowland Evans and Robert Novak, *Lyndon Johnson: The Exercise of Power* (New York: Signet, 1966), 336.

50. Stewart Alsop, oral history, 1:9, LBJ Library.

51. It appears that LBJ "fell in love" with Fehmer, a youthful University of Texas graduate, but that Fehmer rejected his advances because of her Catholic faith. Woods, *LBJ,* 404–6, based on an interview with Fehmer.

52. Shesol, *Mutual Contempt,* 120.

53. The episode loses nothing in its extended telling by Manchester, *The Death of a President,* 337–45.

54. Daniel P. Moynihan, *Coping* (New York: Vintage, 1973), 5.

55. Schlesinger, *Journals, 1952–2000,* 205.

56. Manchester, *The Death of a President,* 527.

57. Shesol, *Mutual Contempt,* 119, citing an interview by William J. Jorden for the LBJ Library.

58. Ibid., 203ff.

59. With the exception of Arthur Schlesinger, *Journals, 1952–2000*, 207, November 25, 1963: "He has made a general request that everyone stay and has followed this up with personal calls to most of the staff (notable exception: me)." However, LBJ did decline to accept Schlesinger's letter of resignation at first and he did say the next day, as he said to others: "I need you far more than John Kennedy ever needed you."

60. Caro, *The Passage of Power*, 399, 410.

61. Address to Joint Session of Congress, November 27 1963, in *Public Papers of the Presidents: Lyndon B. Johnson, 1963–1964* (Washington, D.C.: Government Printing Office, 1965), vol. 1, no. 11, p. 10.

62. Ibid., 1:8; Woods, *LBJ*, 436.

Chapter IV. Rumors of War, Rumors of Peace

1. The phrase comes not from Holy Scripture but from James Joyce's parody of it at the end of the Cyclops episode in *Ulysses*, when Leopold Bloom is ejected from Donohoe's in Little Green Street, Dublin, "like a shot off a shovel."

2. Evan Thomas, *The Very Best Men* (New York: Simon & Schuster, 1995), 207.

3. Nigel Hamilton, *JFK: Life and Death of an American President*, vol. 1, *Reckless Youth* (New York: Random House, 1988), 787.

4. Thomas, *The Very Best Men*, 246–47. Arthur Schlesinger was present at the March 11 meeting when, in front of the top civilian and military officials of the administration, the CIA's Richard Bissell briefed the president on the invasion plan. Schlesinger said Kennedy thought it was too "spectacular." "He did not want a big amphibious invasion in the manner of the Second World War; he wanted a 'quiet' landing, preferably at night. And he insisted that plans be drawn on the basis of *no United States military intervention*." Arthur M. Schlesinger Jr., *A Thousand Days: John F. Kennedy in the White House* (Boston: Houghton Mifflin, 1965), 242.

5. Richard Reeves, *President Kennedy: Profile of Power* (New York: Simon & Schuster, 1993), 95.

6. Ibid., 103.

7. Tom Wicker, J. W. Finney, Max Frankel, and E. W. Kenworthy, "CIA: Maker of Policy or Tool?" *New York Times*, April 25, 1966.

8. Marcus Porcius Cato, known as Cato the Censor and Cato the Elder to distinguish him from his great-grandson, ended every speech with the words *Delenda est Carthago*: Carthage must be destroyed.

9. The Kennedy brothers were obsessed with getting rid of Castro. See, for example, "John Kennedy was disgusted with the . . . disaster at the Bay of Pigs, but he was more than ever determined to get Castro" (Thomas, *The Very Best Men*, 270). Thomas also records that "Robert Kennedy had become consumed with avenging his brother's embarrassment at the Bay of Pigs. . . . RFK had declared that Castro was the administration's top priority . . . no time, money, effort—or manpower is to be spared" (287).

10. William Cavendish, eldest son of the Duke of Devonshire, had the "courtesy

title" (i.e., a title held only as long as his father was alive) of Marquess of Hartington. If he had lived, he would have succeeded as Duke of Devonshire, head of perhaps the most distinguished and one of the richest aristocratic families in England.

11. Evan Thomas, *Robert Kennedy: A Life* (New York: Simon & Schuster, 2000), 136.

12. The public documents, including speeches of the 1961 Berlin crisis, are conveniently published in *Foreign Relations of the United States, 1961–1963*, vol. 7, *Arms Control and Disarmament*, ed. David W. Mabon and David S. Patterson (Washington, D.C.: Government Printing Office 1995); and vol. 14, *Berlin Crisis, 1961–1962*, ed. Charles S. Sampson (Washington, D.C.: Government Printing Office, 1993). In a rich historiographical literature, I found especially helpful Robert M. Slusser, *The Berlin Crisis of 1961: Soviet American Relations and the Struggle for Power in the Kremlin* (Baltimore: Johns Hopkins University Press, 1973).

13. Aleksandr Fursenko and Timothy Naftali, *Krushchev's Cold War* (New York: Norton, 2006), 248.

14. *Public Papers of the Presidents: John F. Kennedy, 1962* (Washington, D.C.: Government Printing Office, 1963), 1:476.

15. Slusser, *Berlin Crisis*, 44.

16. *Public Papers of the Presidents: John F. Kennedy, 1962* 1:534.

17. *Foreign Relations of the United States, 1961–1963*, vol. 7, *Arms Control and Disarmament*.

18. Roswell L. Gilpatric, October 21, 1961, Options on the Berlin Crisis, new documents from the Kennedy administration, September 25, 2001, document 6, National Security Archive, Washington, D.C.

19. I remember flying into Berlin to cover the Wall going up to be greeted by a West German tabloid newspaper that expressed the fears of the German Right in bold letters on the front page: *Was Khrushchev willt: Ganz Berlin! Ganz Deutschland! Ganz Europa!* (What Khrushchev Wants: All Berlin! All Germany! All Europe!).

20. Slusser, *Berlin Crisis*, 185. An Anglo-American proposal had been formulated in Secretary Rusk's office by a small group of British and American officials. It was apparently an idea proposed by Kennedy and endorsed by Macmillan, intended to embarrass the Soviet Union.

21. Ibid., 207, citing *New York Times*, September 8 and 11 (two of Sulzberger's columns); and Pierre Salinger, *With Kennedy* (New York: Doubleday, 1966), passim, regarding his dealings with Mikhail Kharlamov, one of Khrushchev's press secretaries.

22. Slusser, *Berlin Crisis*, 339, 342, 344.

23. Robert F. Kennedy, *Thirteen Days* (New York: Norton, 1969).

24. McGeorge Bundy, *Danger and Survival: Choices about the Bomb in the First Fifty Years* (New York: Random House 1988), 431.

25. Ernest R. May and Philip D. Zelikow, *The Kennedy Tapes* (Cambridge, Mass.: Harvard University Press, 1997), 204.

26. Bundy, *Danger and Survival*, 402–3.

27. "In the details, Keating was probably mistaken; he was most likely basing his claims on reports by Cuban émigrés that they had seen SA-2 antiaircraft missiles that

were large and looked to the untrained eye as if they might be nuclear missiles." David G. Coleman, *The Fourteenth Day* (New York: Norton, 2012), 203.

28. May and Zelikow, *The Kennedy Tapes*, 46; Bundy, *Danger and Survival*, 395.

29. Bundy, *Danger and Survival*, 412. Bundy argues that this was something more than hostility to Castro or cold war policy. "It was something different: a visceral feeling that it was intolerable for the United States to accept on nearby land of the Western Hemisphere Soviet weapons that could wreak instant havoc on the American homeland . . . simply intolerable."

30. Andrei Andreyevich Gromyko was Soviet ambassador in Washington as early as 1943. He was Soviet foreign minister from 1945 to 1985. An old-line Communist who had come up under Stalin, he was known to some in Washington as Grim Grom.

31. Thomas, *Robert Kennedy*, 214, citing Jean Stein and George Plimpton, *American Journey: The Times of Robert Kennedy* (New York: Harcourt Brace Jovanovich, 1970), 132. At the time for some reason the group was known as ExComm; later the second "m" was often dropped. They were: Secretary of State Dean Rusk; Secretary of Defense Robert McNamara; Secretary of the Treasury Douglas Dillon; director of Central Intelligence John McCone; national security adviser McGeorge Bundy; presidential counsel (and speechwriter) Theodore Sorensen; Undersecretary of State George Ball; Deputy Undersecretary of State U. Alexis Johnson; chairman of the Joint Chiefs of Staff General Maxwell Taylor; Assistant Secretary of State for Latin American Affairs Edwin Martin; Charles Bohlen, an expert on Soviet affairs who left to become ambassador to France after one day and was replaced by Llewellyn Thompson, another Soviet expert; Deputy Secretary of Defense Roswell Gilpatric; and Assistant Secretary of Defense Paul Nitze. Among those who attended intermittently were Vice President Lyndon Johnson (!); former cabinet members Dean Acheson and Robert Lovett; UN ambassador Adlai Stevenson; special assistant Kenneth O'Donnell; and USIA director Don Wilson. After the crisis was over, JFK presented all these men and some other close advisers with a small gold tiepin as a memento. Thomas, *Robert Kennedy*, 210.

32. May and Zelikow, *The Kennedy Tapes*, 197. The military had prepared a series of five graduated options, from a strike at missile and nuclear storage only to a strike at all military sites preparatory to an invasion, requiring from 52 to 2,002 sorties. McGeorge Bundy, after a sleepless night, concluded that an air strike was necessary, and put in a paper so arguing. But McNamara did not agree, and the tide of opinion moved away from air strikes to a blockade/quarantine, at least as an initial move.

33. Ibid., 131–32.

34. Bundy, *Danger and Survival*, 398.

35. May and Zelikow, *The Kennedy Tapes*, 143: "that's like Pearl Harbor." "Later that night" (Tuesday), according to Thomas, *Robert Kennedy*, 215, "Ball had written his fellow members of ExCom a passionate memo: 'We tried Japanese as war criminals because of the sneak attack on Pearl Harbor.'"

36. JFK speech, October 22, 1962, in *Public Papers of the Presidents: John F. Kennedy, 1962*, 806–8.

37. Coleman, *The Fourteenth Day*, published a picture of this press conference.

There was a confusion, he explained, about the date, given in one Defense Department release as "November." But elsewhere it is made clear that this was the conference given by Robert McNamara, as secretary of defense, at which the pictures were shown, and that it took place on October 23.

38. Bundy, *Danger and Survival,* 427.

39. May and Zelikow, *The Kennedy Tapes,* 358. Attempts have been made (by the British writer Michael [Lord] Dobbs and others), to portray this anecdote as a myth. They are right in that no immediate naval confrontation occasioned this aside. The tape records merely that Bundy laughed at a whispered remark from Rusk. The words are supplied in an account given by Dean Rusk's son Richard, as recorded in Daniel S. Papp, ed., *As I Saw It* (New York: Norton, 1990), 237. This is in effect Secretary Rusk's memoir as dictated to his son. Rusk's remark broke the tension, which Robert Kennedy records in *Thirteen Days* as having been the most acute of the entire crisis, because of the pent-up uncertainty about how the Soviet leadership would respond to the quarantine.

40. May and Zelikow, *The Kennedy Tapes,* 485–91. The version printed there (cited here) is the unofficial translation read and relied on by JFK and his ExCom. It apparently differs "in various, subtle ways" from the official State Department translation.

41. Ibid., 490.

42. Author's personal recollection of Holborn's account.

43. May and Zelikow, *The Kennedy Tapes,* 504. The editors believe that Rusk got hold of some copies of the text of the Khrushchev message that was being broadcast and reported in the press in the United States and elsewhere.

44. Bundy, *Danger and Survival,* 425.

45. Ibid., 426.

46. Stewart Alsop and Charles Bartlett, "In Time of Crisis," *Saturday Evening Post,* December 8, 1962.

47. May and Zelikow, *The Kennedy Tapes,* 607–9. This text is based on a memo from Robert Kennedy to Rusk, October 30, 1962, which is in the President's Office Files in the John F. Kennedy Library in Boston. It is essentially reliable, especially as it is "substantively identical" with Dobrynin's account in his report to Moscow, published in *Bulletin of the Cold War International History Project,* no. 5 (Spring 1995): 79–80.

48. It was a British diplomat, Sir Henry Wotton, as long ago as the reign of James I, who wrote (in Latin) that a diplomat was a gentleman who was sent abroad to lie for his country. Incidentally, McGeorge Bundy said (*Danger and Survival,* 451) that in the 1980s Soviet former officials told Americans that while Gromyko did know of Khrushchev's intention to put the missiles in Cuba, Dobrynin did not, and was therefore not lying.

49. May and Zelikow, *The Kennedy Tapes,* 582.

50. The evidence for this is in Dobrynin's report to Moscow, recently released. Thomas Blanton, "The Cuban Missile Crisis Just Isn't What It Used to Be," *Cold War International History Project Bulletin* 17/18 (fall 2012): 13.

51. Bundy, *Danger and Survival,* 418, quoting Khrushchev's memoirs, *Khrushchev Remembers.*

52. During the Carter administration there were several occasions when Soviet

forces in Cuba were said to include a "combat brigade." In 1992 both the *Washington Post* and the *New York Times* published reports that Robert McNamara, after meeting with Soviet and Cuban officials, said that the Soviet Union had forty-three thousand troops in Cuba, far more than U.S. intelligence knew. In September 1991 the *Los Angeles Times* reported that Mikhail Gorbachev had said that eleven thousand Soviet troops would be leaving Cuba, and that would leave at least eight thousand behind. Quite apart from Soviet forces in Cuba, of course, the Soviet Union equipped large Cuban forces that fought for Soviet-backed cases in Angola and Ethiopia.

53. The version in this paragraph and the next is from Centre visuel de la connaissance de l'Europe, an international organization based in Luxemburg.

54. Theodore C. Sorensen, *Counselor* (New York: HarperCollins, 2008), 325–28.

55. "A Strategy of Peace," June 10, 1963, in *Public Papers of the Presidents: John F. Kennedy, 1963* (Washington, D.C.: Government Printing Office, 1964), vol. 3, no. 232, pp. 459–64.

Chapter V. Other Americas

1. LBJ's family was well known and had once been prosperous, but when he was growing up his father had fallen on hard times. Although the family was better off than most in the Texas Hill Country, LBJ knew hardship. See Robert A. Caro, *The Years of Lyndon Johnson,* vol. 1, *The Path to Power* (New York: Knopf, 1982), 87–90, 114–16, 146–47; Randall Woods, *LBJ: Architect of American Ambition* (Cambridge, Mass.: Harvard University Press, 2006), 26, 38.

2. Richard Blumenthal, "Community Action: The Origins of a Government Program" (senior B.A. thesis, Harvard University, 1967), 54, referred to in Daniel Patrick Moynihan, *Maximum Feasible Misunderstanding* (New York: Free Press, 1969), 100. Blumenthal cited an interview with David Hackett, a friend of Robert Kennedy who played a key role in the development of the War on Poverty. Blumenthal's remarkable thesis was written when the future U.S. senator from Connecticut was a student of future U.S. senator from New York Daniel Patrick Moynihan, who opened the doors for Blumenthal to interview most of the players in the creation of the War on Poverty.

3. Sadly, it seems that this classic exchange is largely apocryphal. One version is that it was Hemingway himself who said, at lunch with his editor Max Perkins, that the rich were different, and the writer Mary Colum, who was present, who added that they had more money. Fitzgerald subsequently used the exchange in a short story, "The Rich Boy."

4. Oscar Lewis introduced his theory of the "culture of poverty" as a critique of the work of an earlier American anthropologist in a Mexican village, Tepoztlán. He published this in *Five Families: Mexican Case Studies in the Culture of Poverty* (New York: Basic Books, 1959). He developed this work in *Tepoztlán: Village in Mexico* (New York: Holt, 1960). He then studied the urban poor in a suburb of Mexico City, publishing his findings in *Children of Sanchez* (New York: Random House, 1961).

5. Michael Harrington, *The Other America* (New York: Macmillan, 1962), 161.

6. Leon H. Keyserling, *Progress or Poverty: The US at the Crossroads* (Washington, D.C.: Conference on Economic Progress, 1964).

7. See James T. Patterson, *America's Struggle against Poverty, 1900–1985* (Cambridge, Mass.: Harvard University Press, 1981), 117.

8. Benjamin Fine, *1,000,000 Delinquents* (Cleveland: World, 1955).

9. Keyserling, *Progress or Poverty*, 3–7.

10. James L. Sundquist, ed., *On Fighting Poverty* (New York: Basic Books, 1969), 20 (Sundquist's introduction). This is the second volume of Perspectives on Poverty, sponsored by the American Academy of Arts and Science.

11. Godfrey Hodgson, *America in Our Time*, rev. ed. (Princeton, N.J.: Princeton University Press, 2005), 172, 512.

12. Michael B. Katz, *The Undeserving Poor* (New York: Oxford University Press, 2013), 108.

13. Frances Fox Piven and Richard A. Cloward, *Regulating the Poor: The Functions of Public Welfare* (New York: Pantheon, 1971).

14. Quoted in G. Calvin Mackenzie and Robert Weisbrot, *The Liberal Hour* (New York: Penguin, 2008), 86. Neustadt's memoranda of advice to a long series of presidents have been published in Charles O. Jones, ed., *Preparing to Be President* (Washington, D.C.: AEI, 2000).

15. Mackenzie and Weisbrot, *The Liberal Hour*, 87.

16. Ibid., 89–90.

17. Nick Bryant, *The Bystander: John F. Kennedy and the Struggle for Black Equality* (New York: Basic Books, 2006), 473.

18. Richard Reeves, *President Kennedy: Profile of Power* (New York: Simon & Schuster, 1993), 55–57.

19. Robert Dallek, *John F. Kennedy: An Unfinished Life* (Boston: Little, Brown, 2003), 333.

20. Patterson, *America's Struggle against Poverty*, 132.

21. In October 1961 President Kennedy called a panel of experts to the White House to discuss legislation on behalf of mentally retarded people. On October 24, 1963, he signed the Maternal and Child Health and Mental Retardation amendment to the Social Security Act of 1935. www.jfklibrary.org/JFK/JFK-in-history/JFK-and-People-with-Intellectual-Disabilities.aspx.

22. Reeves exaggerates, but not much, when he writes: "Whenever he could get away with it, Kennedy shrugged off congressional concerns, and most domestic issues too to Sorensen, O'Brien, and Myer Feldman." *President Kennedy*, 276–77.

23. This is the theme of Gareth Davies, *From Opportunity to Entitlement: The Transformation and Decline of Great Society Liberalism* (Lawrence: University of Kansas Press, 1996), especially 3: "This book asks how American liberals came to repudiate a venerable and politically valuable individualist tradition in favor of radically 'un-American' definitions of income entitlement."

24. There was no time for a National Service Corps to emerge before JFK's death. In the Economic Opportunity Act of 1964, there was provision for VISTA (Volunteers in Service for America). In 1970 VISTA merged with the Peace Corps. In 1994 President Clinton created AmericaCorps and VISTA survived as part of that project.

25. Homer Bigart, "Kentucky Miners: A Grim Winter," *New York Times,* October 20 1963, 1.

26. Harry Caudill, *Night Comes to the Cumberlands* (Boston: Little, Brown, 1963).

27. Cited by Patterson, *America's Struggle against Poverty,* 105, citing a 1961 article by Meg Greenfield in the *Reporter.*

28. Patterson, *America's Struggle against Poverty,* 107.

29. Laurence F. O'Brien, oral history, 6:24, Lyndon Baines Johnson Library and Museum, Austin.

30. When I interviewed Kenny O'Donnell, then JFK's principal aide for domestic policy, early in 1962, I asked him when the president would issue an executive order banning discrimination in federally owned and impacted property, something he could do without congressional approval. He replied: "Where do these people go?" They went, of course, into the streets.

31. Reeves, *President Kennedy,* 125.

32. Dwight Macdonald, "Our Invisible Poor," *New Yorker,* January 19, 1963. Macdonald started as a Trotskyite, became a democratic socialist, and remained all his life a radical.

33. Although the phrase is one of the best known of Galbraith's many aphorisms, in the book it was "private opulence" he compared with public squalor. *The Affluent Society* (Boston: Houghton Mifflin, 1958), 203.

34. Harrington, *The Other America.*

35. Ibid., 191.

36. The following account owes much to the proceedings of the conference on poverty held jointly by the Kennedy Library and Brandeis University on June 16, 1973. It owes much also to the remarkable Harvard undergraduate thesis by Richard Blumenthal, "Community Action." See also Moynihan, *Maximum Feasible Misunderstanding.*

37. Date is illegible in my copy of Blumenthal, "Community Action."

38. Principally by Capron and Burton Weisbrod of the CEA staff.

39. Capron interview with Blumenthal, November 22, 1966, Blumenthal, "Community Action," 47n.

40. Irving Bernstein, *Guns or Butter* (New York: Oxford University Press, 1996), 95.

41. Blumenthal, "Community Action," 61.

42. Ibid., 69, quoting Bureau of the Budget, "Specifications for a Bill to Combat Poverty," January 16, 1964.

Chapter VI. Surpassing Kennedy

1. *Public Papers of the Presidents: Lyndon Baines Johnson, 1965* (Washington, D.C.: Government Printing Office, 1966), vol. 2, no. 301, p. 636.

2. Nick Kotz, *Judgment Days: Lyndon Baines Johnson, Martin Luther King Jr., and the Laws that Changed America* (New York: Houghton Mifflin, 2005), 16, based on Kotz's interview with Jack Valenti.

3. Randall Woods, *LBJ: Architect of American Ambition* (Cambridge, Mass.: Harvard University Press, 2006), 423.

4. Richard N. Goodwin, *Remembering America* (Boston: Little, Brown, 1988), 269.

5. Kotz, *Judgment Days*, 96.

6. Kotz, *Judgment Days*, 100, citing *Public Papers of the Presidents: Lyndon Baines Johnson, 1963–64* (Washington, D.C.: Government Printing Office, 1965), 1:228.

7. Kotz, *Judgment Days*, 106.

8. Ibid., 107, 108.

9. Lucy (Mrs. S. W.) Smith Price was elected to the state House of Delegates for Fayette county in 1934. Ibid., 110; Chronology of Women Delegates, www.legis.state.wv.us/publications/legi_women.pdf.

10. Kotz, *Judgment Days*, 111.

11. Ibid., 67.

12. Irving Bernstein seems to disagree. "If Byrd seriously entertained the notion of holding the tax cut hostage to the civil rights bill, he did not mention it publicly." *Guns or Butter* (New York: Oxford University Press, 1996), 35. But what Kotz and others suggest is that Byrd wanted not to hold the tax cut hostage to the civil rights bill but to hold the civil rights bill hostage to the tax bill, that is, to hold up the tax bill so long that there would not be time to pass the civil rights bill.

13. Taylor Branch, *Pillar of Fire* (New York: Simon & Schuster, 1998), 187, citing Branch's interview with Jack Valenti. It is worth noting that this dramatic exchange is not otherwise attested. The first half of the interview, a phone call between LBJ and Russell, is recorded in Michael Beschloss, ed., *Taking Charge* (New York: Simon & Schuster, 1998), 944–95. LBJ then invited Russell to the White House pool: Valenti told Branch that it was there that LBJ threatened to "run down" his old friend.

14. Nick Katzenbach, oral history, 1:18, Lyndon Baines Johnson Library and Museum, Austin.

15. Both LBJ and Katzenbach said they must get their nine votes from fourteen senators, but the list they gave had seventeen names on it.

16. Katzenbach, oral history.

17. Beschloss, *Taking Charge*, 380 (phone calls between RFK and LBJ and between LBJ and Dirksen, May 13, 1964).

18. Woods, *LBJ*, 474–75.

19. The Central Arizona Project, to bring water from the Colorado River to Phoenix and Tucson and their rapidly growing suburbs and to millions of acres of agricultural land, was disputed by California. After the Supreme Court found for Arizona in *Arizona v. California* in 1963, California governor "Pat" Brown said he would not continue resistance. However, the project was not finally initiated until 1968. In effect LBJ threatened to oppose the water project unless Hayden voted for the civil rights bill, but when Hayden's vote was not needed he withdrew his threat to do so.

20. Beschloss, *Taking Charge*, 450.

21. I was present at Miami University, Ohio, and watched with admiration as Robert Parris Moses held his demoralized young troops together and urged them "once more into the breach."

22. This was to be the thesis of, for example, John Egerton, *The Americanization of*

Dixie: The Southernization of America (New York: Harper's Magazine, 1974); and much later of Peter Applebome, *Dixie Rising: How the South Is Shaping American Values, Politics, and Culture* (New York: Random House, 1996).

23. Dan T. Carter, *The Politics of Rage: George Wallace, the Origins of the New Conservatism, and the Transformation of American Politics* (Baton Rouge: Louisiana State University Press, 1995), 197–98.

24. For results, en.Wikipedia.org/wiki/Democratic_Party_presidential_primaries, 1964Results. There is an authoritative narrative of his campaign in Carter, *Politics of Rage.*

25. Carter, *Politics of Rage,* 466.

26. According to http://www.eagleforum.org/about/bio.html.

27. Donald T. Critchlow, *The Conservative Ascendancy: How the GOP Right Made Political History* (Cambridge, Mass.: Harvard University Press, 2007), 41–76.

28. Godfrey Hodgson, *More Equal Than Others: America from Nixon to the New Century* (Princeton, N.J.: Princeton University Press, 2004), 157.

29. *Public Papers of the Presidents: Lyndon B Johnson 1963–64,* 1:704.

30. *Public Papers of the Presidents: Lyndon Baines Johnson, 1965* vol. 2, no. 301, p. 636.

31. Woods, *LBJ,* 465.

32. Goodwin, *Remembering America,* 269.

33. I have borrowed this wonderful description from ibid., 269; and Woods, *LBJ,* 465–66, where it is sourced to Robert Dallek, *Flawed Giant* (New York: Oxford University Press, 1998), 80–81.

34. Graham Wallas, *The Great Society* (London: Macmillan, 1914).

35. Tom Wicker, *JFK and LBJ: The Influence of Personality upon Politics* (New York: Morrow, 1968), 131.

36. The phrase is traditionally attributed to St. Augustine, who happens to have been my special subject at Oxford in the 1950s! Since then, it has been pointed out that only the first half of the phrase can be found in Augustine's Sermon 131. Modern Catholics dislike the way the phrase is used to buttress the intellectual authority of the Vatican.

37. Mirabeau Lamar, second president of the Republic of Texas, to a joint session of the Texas Congress, 1838, cited in Charles A. Gulick, ed., *Papers of Mirabeau Buonaparte Lamar* (New York: AMS, 1973). This sonorous sentence is inscribed in the Hall of Noble Words, part of the main building of the University of Texas in Austin, in English and in a shorter version in Latin.

38. Woods, *LBJ,* 566–67.

39. Michael Pentecost, *Journal of the American College of Radiology,* December 6, 2006.

40. See Stephen P. Strickland, *Politics, Science, and Dread Disease* (Cambridge, Mass.: Harvard University Press, 1972).

41. This account is based on Bernstein, *Guns or Butter,* 156–82; Dallek, *Flawed Giant,* 203–11; Woods, *LBJ,* 568–73.

42. Bernstein, *Guns or Butter,* 179.

43. Dallek, *Flawed Giant,* 209–10.

44. New America Foundation website under "Federal Education Budget Project."

45. Mae M. Ngai, *"A Nation of Immigrants": The Cold War and Civil Rights*, 5, https://www.sss.ias.edu/files/papers/paper38.pdf.

46. U.S. Senate, Subcommittee on Immigration and Naturalization of the Committee on the Judiciary, Washington, D.C., February 10, 1965, 1–3.

47. Samuel Eliot Morison and Henry Steel Commager, *The Growth of the American Republic* (New York: Oxford University Press, 1980), 2:174, say that total immigration from 1830 to 1920 was 37.8 million, of whom 11.6 million, or slightly under one-third, returned to the "Old World." Interestingly, the U.S. Bureau of the Census calculates that 25 percent of the immigrants who entered the United States in the 1980s and 1990s would eventually leave the United States (George J. Borjas and Bernt Brasberg, "Who Leaves? The Out-migration of the Foreign-Born," *Review of Economics and Statistics*, January 1996, 165–76).

48. For example, James P. Smith and Barry Edmonston, *The New American Economics: Demographic and Fiscal Effects of Immigration* (Washington, D.C.: National Academy Press, 1997), 121.

49. Theodore C. Sorensen, *Kennedy* (New York: Harper & Row, 1965), 753. It is interesting, however, that in his six long oral history interviews with Carl Kaysen for the Kennedy presidential library, Sorensen mentioned only legislation about Appalachian poverty; he did not mention a war on poverty, let alone claim that it would have been passed in 1964.

50. This is the theme of Gareth Davies, *From Opportunity to Entitlement: The Transformation and Decline of Great Society Liberalism* (Lawrence: University of Kansas Press, 1996), especially 75–130.

51. This was true of the New York riots in 1965 and of the Detroit riot of 1967, started after a raid by police on a "blind pig" drinking club. It was true of the 1991 Rodney King riot in Los Angeles and, for that matter, among many examples, of rioting in Clichy-sous-Bois near Paris in 2005 and in Tottenham, London, in 2011. It can be argued that an incident of high-handed policing is the typical trigger for urban rioting.

52. The McCone Commission report says, "The full commitment of 13,900 guardsmen was reached by midnight on Saturday." www.usc.edu/libraries/archives/cityinstress/mccone/part4.html.

53. Doris Kearns, *Lyndon Johnson and the American Dream* (New York: Harper & Row, 1976), 319. Kearns quotes Joseph Califano as saying that LBJ could not even bear to read the cables from Los Angeles reporting events there.

54. Moynihan gave me one of 160 early copies in March 1965, shortly before I returned to Britain. I must admit I was taken completely by surprise by the vehement response to the report in some "liberal" quarters.

55. Notably by Lee Rainwater and William Yancey, *The Moynihan Report and the Politics of Controversy* (Cambridge, Mass.: MIT Press, 1967).

56. Davies, *From Opportunity to Entitlement*, 91.

57. Ibid.

58. Dallek, *Flawed Giant*, 467. LBJ believed King "had joined the crackpots."

59. http://www.ropercenter.uconn.edu/CFIDE/roper/presidential/webroot/pres idential_rating_detail.cfm?allRate=True&presidentName=Johnson.

Chapter VII. No Umbrella Man

1. It was a half-hour film, aired on July 13, 1967, in the *This Week* series on British Independent Television. http://www.imdb.com/title/tt1741134/.

2. Coverage that turned into a book: Lewis Chester, Bruce Page, and Godfrey Hodgson, *An American Melodrama* (New York: Viking, 1969).

3. I had known friends and family of his in Philadelphia, where I did a master's degree in history at the University of Pennsylvania.

4. I have not been able to find a solid reference for this well-known quotation. In a recent post, a self-identified Alabama conservative, Dr. Steven J. Allen, goes so far as to assert, "Of course, Johnson didn't say that." I can only report that I remember hearing it said that these were LBJ's words when he signed the Civil Rights Act of 1964. When I asked the late Harry McPherson about it, he responded he believed LBJ had said it to Bill Moyers.

5. Moses, who has a Ph.D. in math from Harvard, started the Algebra Project, an inspired scheme for helping kids who had no language skills through math.

6. William Shakespeare, *Hamlet,* act IV, scene v.

7. Gordon M. Goldstein, *Lessons in Disaster: McGeorge Bundy and the Path to War in Vietnam* (New York: Times Books, Henry Holt, 2008), 231, 3.

8. Robert S. McNamara, *In Retrospect: The Tragedy and Lessons of Vietnam* (New York: Times Books, 1995), 96.

9. Deborah Shapley, *Promise and Power: The Life and Times of Robert McNamara* (Boston: Little, Brown, 1993).

10. Goldstein, *Lessons,* 238, citing Kenneth O'Donnell and David Powers, *"Johnny, We Hardly Knew Ye": Memoirs of John Fitzgerald Kennedy* (Boston: Little, Brown, 1972), 118.

11. Kai Bird, *The Color of Truth* (New York: Touchstone Books, 2000), 260–61, citing the transcript of a CBS interview, only part of which was used on air.

12. Dr. Lang got into the habit of spelling her name with a lowercase initial to distinguish it from her husband's on student papers.

13. James G. Blight, janet Lang, and David Welch, eds., *Virtual JFK,* documentary directed by Koji Matsutani; James G. Blight and janet Lang, "The JFK Anniversary: What if Kennedy Had Lived?" *New Statesman,* August 15, 2013.

14. Thurston Clarke, *JFK's Last Hundred Days* (New York: Penguin, 2013).

15. Pierre Terrail, Sieur de Bayard, cavalry leader who fought for Charles VIII, Louis XII, and François I of France, was revered as the *chevalier sans peur et sans reproche,* the knight without fear and without reproach.

16. McGeorge Bundy, "The History Maker," *Massachusetts Historical Society* (1978), cited in Goldstein, *Lessons,* 229. Goldstein also points out that Bundy told an audience at Hofstra University in 1985: "I don't know what he would have done."

17. Robert Dallek, *Flawed Giant* (New York: Oxford University Press, 1998), 99.

18. Samuel Beer, oral history, November 7, 2002, 19, John F. Kennedy Presidential Library and Museum, Boston.

19. This is particularly true of William Bundy.

20. Clarke, *JFK's Last Hundred Days,* 63.

21. Ibid., 64.

22. Ibid., 136–37.

23. Ibid., 158.

24. Ibid.

25. Roswell Gilpatric, oral history, JFK Library.

26. Walt W. Rostow, oral history, 1:41–42, LBJ Library.

27. There have been many references in print to this sobriquet. One of the earliest is perhaps in Christian G. Appy, ed., *Cold War Constructions, 1945–1966* (Amherst: University of Massachusetts Press, 2000), 132.

28. Goldstein, *Lessons,* 229.

29. Truman to Brinkley on bureaucracies, Thomas Cronin, *The State of the Presidency* (Boston: Little, Brown, 1990), 18.

30. Shortly after her husband's death, his widow, Mary Bundy, stressed this point in a private letter to the author.

31. There is considerable academic debate about who saw and/or agreed. Some suggest that JFK knew more and approved more than most historians have believed.

32. Clarke, *JFK's Last Hundred Days,* 88ff.

33. Jean Edward Smith, *Eisenhower in War and Peace* (New York: Random House, 2012), 615.

34. Substantial numbers were also devotees of syncretistic cults such as Cao Dai and Hòa Hào. The proportion adhering to various religions in the 1960s is obscured by the insistence of the Communist authorities that 81 percent of the population was atheist.

35. John M. Newman, *JFK and Vietnam* (New York: Warner Books, 1992), 3, citing Rostow's interview by Richard E. Neustadt in the Kennedy Library, and *Pentagon Papers,* Department of Defense edition, book 10.

36. MACV replaced MAAG (Military Assistance Advisory Group) on February 8, 1962.

37. Dallek, *Flawed Giant,* 98.

38. *Pentagon Papers,* Gravel edition, 2:171, March 1964: "Although 1,000 men were technically withdrawn, no actual reduction of US strength was achieved. The December figure was not 1,000 less than the peak October level." The *Pentagon Papers* writer adds that the one thousand withdrawal was "essentially an accounting exercise" (160).

39. The matter is discussed in great detail in Harold P. Ford, *CIA and the Vietnam Policymakers: Three Episodes, 1962–1968* (Washington, D.C.: History Staff, Center for the Study of Intelligence, Central Intelligence Agency, 1998), 86–104.

40. Randall Woods, *LBJ: Architect of American Ambition* (Cambridge, Mass.: Harvard University Press, 2006), 387.

41. Ibid., 389, citing LBJ to JFK, May 30, 1961, Presidential Office Files, Special: Correspondence, box 30, John F. Kennedy Presidential Library and Museum, Boston.

42. This shift is particularly well charted by Neil Sheehan, *A Bright Shining Lie: John Paul Vann and America in Vietnam* (New York: Random House, 1968).

43. Robert McNamara, Maxwell Taylor, and McGeorge Bundy all concluded in late January and early February that unless American military effort escalated, the war would be lost. Fredrik Logevall, *Choosing War* (Berkeley: University of California Press, 1999), 317–18.

44. *Foreign Relations of the United States, 1964–1968*, vol. 1, *Vietnam, 1964*, ed. Edward C. Keefer and Charles S. Sampson (Washington, D.C.: Government Printing Office, 1992), 873–74.

45. Stanley Karnow, *Vietnam* (New York: Viking, 1983), 418, 423–25, 427–28.

46. George McT. Kahin, *Intervention: How America Became Involved in Vietnam* (New York: Knopf, 1979), 276.

47. Karnow, *Vietnam*, 428.

48. Taylor was one of the very few senior officers liked and trusted by the Kennedy brothers. JFK had a junior officer's contempt for the brass, but not for Taylor. Robert Kennedy was so close to Taylor that he named one of his sons after him.

49. Kahin, *Intervention*, 147.

50. In and before 1965 George Ball, undersecretary of state, was almost alone in his dogged skepticism about the war. Some congressional leaders, including Senators Fulbright, Morse, and Mansfield, were also skeptical.

51. The whole question of whether American commitment to the war could have been avoided is the theme of Fredrik Logevall's careful study, *Choosing War*. The most succinct discussion of the issue is on 335: "By the early spring of 1965 the last chance to prevent another full-scale war in Indochina had passed. Negotiating efforts did not cease . . . diplomatic activity would grow intense in the late spring and summer [of 1965] . . . but thereafter these efforts would be about ending a major military conflict rather than preventing one."

52. Godfrey Hodgson, *America in Our Time*, rev. ed. (Princeton, N.J.: Princeton University Press, New York, 2005), 237.

53. A recent book by Paul Pillar makes the same point with much detail. Paul R. Pillar, *Intelligence and U.S. Foreign Policy: 9/11, Iraq and Reform* (New York: Columbia University Press, 2003).

54. Ford, *CIA and the Vietnam Policymakers*, 82. Gordon Goldstein has claimed (*Lessons*, 139–40) that the domino theory was destroyed by a paper written by the CIA's Sherman Kent in June 1964. Goldstein himself admits that the paper was ignored by the White House.

55. Y. F. Khong, *Analogies at War* (Princeton, N.J.: Princeton University Press, 1992), 97.

56. Woods, *LBJ*, 235.

57. Kahin, *Intervention*, 341.

58. Ibid., 226. Kahin also cites Eric F. Goldman, *The Tragedy of Lyndon Johnson* (New York: Knopf, 1969), 235–37.

59. Kahin, *Intervention*, 339.

60. Khong, *Analogies,* 175.

61. Dean Rusk, *As I Saw It* (New York: Norton, 1990), 55.

62. Khong, *Analogies,* 179.

63. Woods, *LBJ,* 358.

64. LBJ, news conference, July 28, 1965, *Pentagon Papers,* Gravel edition, 4:632–63.

65. Khong, *Analogies,* 184.

66. NSC 48/1 June 1949. Drawn up by Secretary of Defense Louis Johnson, *Pentagon Papers,* Gravel edition, vol. 1, chapter 2.

67. Ibid., 82–87, 106, 593–600.

68. Ford, *CIA and the Vietnam Policymakers,* 159–63.

69. *Foreign Relations of the United States, 1964–1968,* vol. 1, *Vietnam, 1964,* 485. This is the Sherman Kent paper cited by Goldstein as evidence that the domino theory was dead. In reality, it strengthened the domino theory's persuasiveness by shearing away its more absurd exaggerations.

70. Document 241, "Revised Draft 11/21/64 WPBundy/JMcNaughton," *Pentagon Papers,* Gravel edition, 3:658.

71. More than 800,000 Chinese troops faced Soviet forces more than 650,000 strong.

72. National Intelligence Estimate 11-5-62, quoted in Harold P. Ford, "The CIA and Double Demonology: Calling the Sino-Soviet Split," CIA Center for Intelligence Studies, *Studies in Intelligence* (Winter 1998–99), https://www.cia.gov/library/center-for-the-study-of-intelligence/kent-csi/vol42no5/pdf/v42i5a05p.pdf, citing "Political Developments in the USSR and the Communist World," *Foreign Relations of the United States, 1961–1963,* vol. 22, *North East Asia,* ed. Edward C. Keefer, David W. Mabon, and Harriet Dashiell Schwar (Washington, D.C.: Government Printing Office, 1996), 207–8.

73. Ford, "The CIA and Double Demonology." Also published in Sharad S. Chauhan, *Inside CIA: Lessons in Intelligence* (New Delhi, APH, 2004).

74. Donald Zagoria, *The Sino-Soviet Conflict* (Princeton, N.J.: Princeton University Press, 1962).

75. There is, as might be expected, much mystery about the Penkovsky affair. Apparently he first offered himself as an operative to CIA agents, who refused the bait. He was then developed as an agent by a British "businessman," Greville Wynne, and managed by two MI6 officers, Ruari and Janet Chisholm. He was betrayed in 1962 and executed early in 1963, probably not by the gruesome method described by some accounts, which suggest he was cremated alive. Some reports suggest he was a double agent, that he gave the West false information about Soviet nuclear capabilities, and that he was not executed. On balance it is probable that he did provide the British with a large quantity of information, much of it genuine; that the British passed this on to the CIA (in part in an effort to wipe out the black marks earned by the defection of the "Cambridge spies," Philby, Maclean, Burgess and Co.); and that this information included substantial evidence of the depth of the Sino-Soviet split.

76. Chester Cooper, *The Lost Crusade: The Full Story of US Involvement in Vietnam from Roosevelt to Nixon* (New York: Dodd Mead, 1970), chapter 6.

77. Karnow, *Vietnam,* 215. As a former *Time* magazine correspondent in the Far East who knew Saigon well and then moved to Washington and later interviewed many participants both in South and North Vietnam, Karnow had insights not necessarily shared by academic historians.

78. Diem went to the United States in 1950, where he made many influential friends, including Joseph P. Kennedy and Dr. Wesley Fishel, a professor at Michigan State University who became his adviser. Most influential of all was Cardinal Francis Spellman, archbishop of New York (and a friend of Joseph Kennedy), who offered Diem lodging at the Marynoll seminary in Lakewood, New Jersey, and later at Ossining, New York. See *Time,* April 4, 1955; and Seth Jacobs, *Cold War Mandarin* (Lanham, Md.: Rowman & Littlefield, 2006), 29. Diem remained in the United States for about two years before touring Europe, where he met powerful Catholics, including Pope Pius XII.

79. *Pentagon Papers,* Gravel edition, 3:694–702.

80. Logevall, *Choosing War,* 387–88.

81. The one great weakness in the U.S. policy was "a widespread belief that we do not have the will and force and patience and determination to take the necessary action and stay the course." Karnow, *Vietnam,* 428.

82. Information from Harry McPherson to author.

83. Dan Moldea, the author of a book about Robert Kennedy's murder that I reviewed unfavorably in the *Washington Post* maintained online that I had not been in the hotel that night: I was in fact accompanied there by a whole team of highly respected reporters who were my colleagues and who could and would vouch for my presence.

84. Chester, Page, and Hodgson, *An American Melodrama,* 758–59.

85. Ibid.

86. Ibid.

87. Ibid., 732–33.

88. The radical folk singer Pete Seeger wrote "Waist Deep in the Big Muddy" in 1967. Loosely based on a real episode in 1956, it tells the story of a gung-ho lieutenant who insists on marching his men on a training exercise in Louisiana into a river that, swollen by a tributary, is too deep for them. The refrain of each verse is "The big fool said push on," until the last verse, which ends, "The big fool dead and gone." The song was taken up on campuses across the nation, as of course it was meant to be, as a reference to LBJ and Vietnam. When Seeger taped the song for the *Smothers Brothers* show in September 1967 CBS refused to air it, but in February 1968 (in the context of the Tet offensive), CBS relented and aired the song.

Conclusion

1. Even with LBJ's hair cut short back and sides, Jack Kennedy saw the likeness and nicknamed him "Riverboat."

2. Randall Woods, *LBJ: Architect of American Ambition* (Cambridge, Mass.: Harvard University Press, 2006), 883–84.

3. So said Senator Mitch McConnell after the 2014 elections.

4. That was what both the Weinberger doctrine (1984) and the Colin Powell doctrine (2009) boiled down to.

5. The making of a Roosevelt speech is unforgettably described in Samuel I. Rosenman, *Working with Roosevelt* (New York: Harper, 1952).

6. The teleprompter was invented in 1950. It was first used in a political campaign by Dwight Eisenhower in 1952, and improved in 1953 by Jess Oppenheim of *I Love Lucy*.

7. For example, E. S. Corwin and Louis Koenig, *The Presidency Today* (New York: New York University Press, 1957); and in 1960 alone Herman Finer, *The Presidency: Crisis and Regeneration* (Chicago: University of Chicago Press, 1960); Louis W. Koenig, *The Chief Executive* (New York: Harcourt, Brace & World, 1964); Richard E. Neustadt, *Presidential Power* (New York: Wiley, 1960); Clinton Rossiter, *The American Presidency* (New York: Harcourt, Brace, 1956); Rexford G. Tugwell, *The Enlargement of the Presidency* (Garden City, N.Y.: Doubleday, 1960). Fred I. Greenstein led the reassessment of Eisenhower in *The Hidden-Hand Presidency* (New York: Basic Books, 1982). Jean Edward Smith, *Eisenhower in War and Peace* (New York: Random House, 2012), takes this reassessment further.

Acknowledgments

This book is a hybrid. It is an attempt to reevaluate two great American presidents by the device of endeavoring to answer two counterfactual questions: Would Kennedy have been as successful as Johnson in completing the New Deal by leading Congress in the passage of a great structure of social and political reform? Would Kennedy have been able to avoid the damage to that era of reform caused by the war against Communism in Vietnam? It is also an anecdotal memoir of how I, as a young British journalist more than fifty years ago, became fascinated by these two men and tried to understand one of the most consequential eras in recent American history.

I have dedicated the book to my friend Harry McPherson because he was for decades, as well as a close personal friend, my single most patient and inspiring teacher about the great game of Washington politics—with thanks to Trisha for not minding when we talked and talked and talked. But of course Harry was not alone in mentoring me. Others, many of them sadly no longer with us, like Laurence Stern of the *Washington Post*, Benjamin H. Read, Daniel Patrick and Elizabeth Moynihan, Bayard Rustin, Charles Morgan Jr., Michael Janeway, John and Diana Zentay, Doris O'Donnell, Blair Clark, and Philip Bobbitt made generous contributions to my education.

So too did literally hundreds, if not thousands, of American politicians, officials, academics, intellectuals, students both in the United States and at Oxford, and citizens of every kind whom I have had occasion to meet or to interview over the years since I arrived in Philadelphia as a graduate student in the fall of 1955. It would be absurd and arbitrary even to try to name more than the above handful of my instructors, including very many who have strongly disagreed with some of my conclusions. And of course my education was not wholly oral. I have been reading American history and American news with an appetite approaching obsession for decades.

I should name a number of institutions that have helped me in this process, among them the University of Pennsylvania and the three former Rhodes scholars who funded my scholarship to study there in the first place; the London *Observer,* the London *Sunday Times,* and the London *Independent* and their editors, David Astor, Sir Harold Evans, and Andreas Whittam-Smith; my friend Andrew Marshall and my colleagues in the coverage of the 1968 election, Bruce Page and Lewis Chester; the *Washington Post,* especially its editors Russell Wiggins and Ben Bradlee, and Meg Greenfield; the Woodrow Wilson International Center for Scholars, especially the late Michael Lacey; Harvard University, especially Richard Neustadt and Marvin Kalb; the University of California at Berkeley, where I taught for a happy semester; the BBC, especially Simon Coates; Channel Four television in London; Pierre Nora, formerly of Juilliard, the publisher who persuaded me to write my first book (in French, about Reconstruction).

I thank all the publishers who have commissioned me to write for them since then; my main researcher, Ed Adkins; my three agents, Michael Sissons, Peter Matson, and Robert Ducas, to whom I have often been a worry and a trial; and with special gratitude I thank Chris Rogers, Robin DuBlanc, and the other excellent editors and staff of Yale University Press, for which this is the third book I have written.

Thank you to my dear son Pierre, who had the temerity to make a feature film about my efforts to understand the Deep South, *Daddy, Daddy, USA;* and to my other children, all beloved: to Francis, Jessica, and Laura for tolerance and curiosity, and to Hilary for patience and love.

To these and others too numerous to be named, I owe the gratitude of a lifetime, and I have tried sincerely to understand what they had to teach.

Index

Acheson, Dean, 45, 50, 59, 76

Adams, Henry, 44

Adams, Sherman, 205

Affluent Society, The (Galbraith), 143

Albania, 113, 115

Albert, Carl, 74

Alexander the Great, 3, 17

Alger, Bruce, 95

Allen, Richard V., 215

Alphand, Hervé, 81

Alsop, Joseph, 19, 32, 73, 88

Alsop, Stewart, 18, 32, 100, 126

Alsop, Susan Mary, 73

American Broadcasting Company (ABC), 30

American Medical Association (AMA), 142, 167, 168, 169–71

Anderson, Clinton, 92

Anderson, Rudolf, 121, 125, 133

Andrews, Avery, 78

Andrews, Emily, 78

Angleton, James Jesus, 208

antiballistic missiles (ABMs), 76–77

Anti-Defamation League (ADL), 171, 173

Area Redevelopment Act (1961), 174

Arnold, Thurman, 52

Arvad, Inga, 33

Associated Press (AP), 29, 30

Astor, David, 71, 75–76, 81–82

Astor, Nancy, 45

Astor, William, 81–82

Auerbach, Carl A., 60

Augustine, Saint, Bishop of Hippo, 8

Augustus, emperor of Rome, 47

Baines, Joseph Wilson (LBJ's maternal grandfather), 51

Baker, Bobby Gene, 84, 88, 89, 93–94

Baker, Russell, 53

Ball, George, 38, 75, 117, 120, 126, 192, 201

Barnett, Ross, 16–17

Bartlett, Charles, 18, 32, 126, 188

Bay of Pigs invasion, 108–10, 129

Beer, Samuel, 43, 101, 187

Beloff, Max, 71

Beloff, Nora, 71

Bergen, Anthony, 61

Berlin, Isaiah, 17

Berlin crisis, 110–16

Bernstein, Carl, 79

Bernstein, Irving, 4

Bible, Alan, 156

Bigart, Homer, 141
Billings, Kirk LeMoyne "Lem," 80
Billington, James, 208
Bissell, Richard, 107, 108, 110
Blair, Clay, Jr., 20, 33–34
Blair, Joan, 20, 33–34
Blight, James G., 186, 187–88, 189
Bloch, Marc, 3
Blumenthal, Richard, 148
Bohlen, Charles "Chip," 111
Boulding, Kenneth, 136
Bowles, Chester, 73
Bradlee, Ben, 18, 32, 33, 79, 81, 183
Brandeis, Louis D., 43
Brandt, Willy, 113
Brezhnev, Leonid, 116
Brinkley, David, 188, 189, 191
Brokaw, Tom, 41
Brown, George, 55, 68
Brown, Herman, 55, 68
Brown & Root (engineering firm), 55
Brownell, Herbert, 58
Brown v. Board of Education (1954), 57, 58, 143
Buchan, Alastair, 71
Buchan, John, 71
Buckley, William F., Jr., 162, 224
Bundy, McGeorge, 2, 19, 52, 77, 80, 131–32, 183, 191, 192, 198; during Cuban missile crisis, 118, 122, 125–26, 133; drinking habits of, 181; as establishment figure, 45, 49, 76; on JFK's moderation, 122; on JFK's Vietnam plans, 184, 187, 193; LBJ grudgingly admired by, 103; LBJ's accession and, 100–101; on LBJ's intellect, 66; military service of, 38, 75, 76; Vietnam escalation recommended by, 185, 198, 211
Bundy, William, 38, 75, 77, 192, 198, 206, 209
Burma, 212
Busby, Horace "Buzz," 15, 49–50, 57, 78, 150–51

Bush, George H. W., ix, 226
Bush, George W., x, 226
Byrd, Harry, 14, 155, 170, 179

Califano, Joseph, 49, 64
Callas, Maria, 20
Cambodia, 194, 205, 206
Camelot (Lerner and Loewe), 20, 69, 70
Cannon, Howard, 156, 157
Cannon, William, 145, 147
Capron, William, 145, 146
Carey, Hugh, 164
Carlson, Frank, 155
Carlyle, Thomas, x, 2–3, 226
Carmichael, Stokely, 176
Caro, Robert, 4, 53, 54, 55, 58, 65
Carpenter, Liz, 85–86
Carter, Clifford, 15, 93, 150
Carter, Dan T., 161
Carter, Jimmy, ix, 226
Casals, Pablo, 80
Castro, Fidel, 11, 49, 107–10, 124, 129, 225
Cater, Douglass, 78, 84, 166
Catholic Worker, 143
Cato's Letters (Trenchard), 47
Caudill, Harry, 141
Cavendish, Billy, Marquis of Hartington, 42
Cecil, David, 46
Celler, Emanuel, 152, 172
Central Intelligence Agency (CIA), 11, 74–75, 198; Bay of Pigs invasion and, 107–10; during Cuban missile crisis, 117–18; Southeast Asia viewed by, 206–9
Chamberlain, Neville, 88, 180, 203, 204
Chambers, Whittaker, 72
Chancellor, John, 63
Chappaquiddick incident, 20, 33
Charles I, king of England, 46
Charles II, king of England, 46
Chennault, Anna, 214–15
China, 113–14, 115, 131, 190, 201–2, 206, 207–9, 213
Choice, Not an Echo, A (Schlafly), 162

Chou En-lai, 114, 115
Churchill, Winston, 203, 225
Civil Rights Act (1964), 6, 12, 17, 22, 23, 103, 152–54
civil rights movement, 10, 16, 151, 158, 159–60, 183–84, 219, 222–24
Civil War, 7, 10, 14
Clark, Joe, 78
Clarke, Thurston, 186, 188, 189
Cline, Ray, 118
Clinton, Bill, x, 226
Cloward, Richard, 136, 141, 145
Cohen, Albert K., 136, 141
Cohen, Benjamin V., 52
Cohen, Wilbur, 145, 147, 168, 169
Colmer, William, 138, 153
Columbia Broadcasting System (CBS), 29–30
Comprehensive Nuclear Test Ban Treaty, 133
Conein, Lucien "Lou," 10–11
Connally, John, 87, 88, 90, 91, 94–95, 96
Cooper, Chester, 208, 209
Corcoran, Tommy "the Cork," 52, 88
Council on Foreign Relations, 44
Cousins, Norman, 131
Cromwell, Oliver, 46
Cronkite, Walter, 188
Cuban missile crisis, 90, 112, 116–31, 186, 188, 190
Curtis, Carl, 155
Cushing, Harvey, 167
Cutler, Robert, 194

Daley, Richard, 177
Dallek, Robert, 4, 35, 53
Dark Side of Camelot, The (Hersh), 34
Davidson, Stewart, 72–73
Davies, Joseph W., 78
Day, Dorothy, 143
Deadrich, Katie, 166
Dealey, Edward, 95
de Gaulle, Charles, 20, 76, 111, 212, 225

Delaney, James J., 165
Deutscher, Isaac, 71
Devonshire, Dukes of, 42, 46, 47
Diefenbaker, John, 77
Diem, Ngo Dinh, 10, 188–89, 192–93, 194, 195, 196, 210
Dillon, Douglas, 38, 80, 139
Dingell, John, 167
Dirksen, Everett, 156–57, 179
Dobrynin, Anatoly, 126–27, 128, 129
domino theory, 189, 201, 204–6
Donovan, James B., 110
Douglas, Helen Gahagan, 63
Douglas, Melvyn, 63
Douglas, Paul, 53–54
Douglas, William O., 52
Duchin, Peer, 80
Duckworth, Allen, 14
Dugger, Ronnie, 50
Dulles, Allen W., 107, 110
Dulles, John Foster, 205
Dungan, Ralph, 85, 94, 101
Dutton, Fred, 38, 75

Eastland, James, 14, 57, 159
Edmondson, J. Howard, 155, 157
education policy: during JFK's presi-
    dency, 169; during JFK's Senate career,
    137, 140; LBJ's achievements in, 6, 23,
    104, 151, 164–67, 177, 179
Edwards, India, 87–88
Eisenhower, Dwight, 58, 92, 119, 219;
    blandness of, 7, 19, 37, 228; domino
    theory espoused by, 205, 206; Indo-
    china policy of, 194, 211; recession
    under, 135; as war hero, 38, 228
Elementary and Secondary Education
    Act (1965), 166
Engle, Clair, 157
English Civil Wars, 46–47
Enthoven, Alain, 80
Equal Rights Amendment (ERA), 154,
    162–63

Estes, Billie Sol, 93
Evans, Cecil, 65
Everson v. Board of Education (1947), 165

Fay, Paul B. "Red," 33, 80
Fehmer, Marie, 100
Felt, Harry, 200
Feminine Mystique, The (Friedan), 162
feminism, 7, 154–55, 162, 224
Fine, Benjamin, 136
Fitzgerald, F. Scott, 135
Fitzgerald, John F. (JFK's maternal grand-
    father), 39–40, 42, 51
Fleming, Ian, 107–8
Forand, Aime, 167–68
Ford, Gerald, x, 226
Ford, Harold, P., 201, 208, 209
Ford Foundation, 141, 145
Forrestal, James V., 185
Forrestal, Michael, 185, 192
Fortas, Abe, 52, 59
Fox, Charles James, 47
France, 44, 194, 205, 203, 209–10, 212
Frank, Jerome, 52
Fraser, Hugh, 46
Freedom Rides, 142, 158
Freeman, Orville, 38, 87
Friedan, Betty, 162
Frost, Robert, 47, 227
Frye, Marquette, 175
Fulbright, William, 15

Galbraith, Catherine, 81, 101
Galbraith, John Kenneth, 38, 43, 75, 80,
    81, 85, 101–2, 143, 187
Gandhi, Mohandas, 225
Garner, John Nance, 89
General Motors, 135
George, Walter, 56
Georgetown, 71–74
Germany, 8, 15, 45, 128, 212
Gershon, Barbara, 18
Ghaddafi, Muammar, 3

Gilligan, Thomas, 160
Gilpatric, Roswell, 76, 113, 115–16, 126, 185,
    188, 189, 192
Glass, Alice, 63
Goldberg, Arthur, 97
Goldman, Eric, 4
Goldstein, Gordon, 184–85, 187, 191
Goldwater, Barry, 162, 169, 179, 220
Goodwin, Richard, 12, 85, 101, 147, 151,
    163, 164, 175, 217
Gordon, Thomas, 47
Gore, Albert, Sr., 155
Grady, Henry, 67
Graham, Katharine, 73
Graham, Philip, 73, 88, 90–91
Grant, Ulysses S., 14
Great Britain, 8, 42, 43–46, 203, 212
Green, Edith, 147, 166
Green, Theodore Francis, 61
Greenfield, Meg, 74, 180–81
Gromyko, Andrei, 119, 128
Guthman, Ed, 97

Hackett, David, 141, 146, 147
Haffner, Sebastian (pseud. of Raimund
    Pretzel), 71
Halleck, Charles, 152
Hamer, Fanny Lou, 159
Hamilton, Nigel, 34
Handlin, Oscar, 171–72
Hansen, Clifford, 155
Harkins, Paul, 200
Harriman, Averell, 45, 73, 80–81, 132, 188,
    192, 194
Harrington, Michael, 134, 136, 143–44, 145
Hart, Phil, 172
Hartington, Billy, 111
Harvard University, 42–44
Hassan II, king of Morocco, 27
Hayden, Carl, 156, 157
Hayden, Casey, 162
health care, 23, 142, 151, 167–71, 179
Heller, Walter, 101, 139, 144, 145–46, 147

Hemingway, Ernest, 135
Hersey, John, 39
Hersh, Seymour, 34
Hickenlooper, Bourke, 155
Higher Education Act (1965), 166–67
Hill, Clint, 83
Hilsman, Roger, 188, 192, 198
Hiss, Alger, 72
Hitch, Charles, 76
Hitler, Adolf, 3, 45, 88, 196, 203, 204, 225
Hodgson, Alice, 73, 74
Hodgson, Francis, 28, 74
Hodgson, Pierre, 28, 74
Holborn, Fred, 124
Holt, Harry, 65
Hoover, J. Edgar, 96
House, Edward, 44
housing policy, 140
Howard University, 12–13, 15, 150, 164,
    175, 218
Hoxha, Enver, 113
Hruska, Roman, 155
Hughes, John, 164
Hughes, Sarah, 100
Humphrey, Hubert, 52, 101, 102, 156–57,
    159, 213–14, 220
Hunt, David, 145
Huntley, Chet, 188, 189
Hussein, Saddam, 3

immigration, 6, 7, 23, 151, 171–74, 177, 178,
    215, 228
Immigration and Naturalization Act
    (1965), 171–72
Indochina, 194
Indonesia, 11, 205, 212
In Retrospect (McNamara), 185
Ireland, 41–42
Italy, 8, 128

Jackson, Henry "Scoop," 87, 119
Jackson, Robert, 52
Jacobson, Max, 35

James II, king of England, 46–47
Janeway, Eliot, 52
Japan, 8, 196, 202, 203
Javits, Jacob, 10, 177, 183
Jefferson, Thomas, 31, 159
Jenkins, Roy, 82
Jesus Christ, 2, 17
JFK (Hamilton), 34
Job Corps, 174
John Birch Society, 162
Johnson, Andrew, 157
Johnson, Lady Bird (wife), 51, 55, 63–64,
    67, 87, 88, 95, 217
Johnson, Luci (daughter), 62
Johnson, Lyndon B.: accession of, 2, 83;
    Berlin visited by, 113; caricaturing of,
    66, 201; Chamberlain wisecrack by,
    88, 204; China feared by, 201–3; civil
    rights stressed by, 16, 56–57, 150–58,
    175–76; Congress addressed by, 103–4;
    contradictions of, 53–56, 59; during
    Cuban missile crisis, 129; declining
    popularity of, 177–78; drinking habits
    of, 61–63, 66, 84, 181, 217; education
    policies of, 165; election fraud linked
    to, 54; elites resented by, 49; European
    opinion disregarded by, 212–13; Great
    Society proclaimed by, 163–64; How-
    ard commencement speech of, 12–13,
    15, 150, 164, 175, 218; hypochondria of,
    65; idealism of, xii, 49; intimidation
    by, 60–61; Israel backed by, 52–53;
    JFK's legacy continued by, 6, 12–13,
    18–19, 133, 134–45, 147–49, 150–51,
    163–64, 178, 215, 229; JFK's selection
    of, 88–91; JFK's similarities with, 196,
    219, 226, 228–30; Kennedys' animosity
    toward, 14, 83, 84–89, 97; legislative
    skill of, 58–60, 179, 227; liberalism
    of, ix; Medicare and Medicaid created
    by, 168–71; Nazi threat recognized by,
    51; optimism revived by, 182; paranoia
    of, 102; philandering by, 63–64;

Johnson, Lyndon B. (*continued*)
  populism of, 67; realism of, 56;
  reappraisals of, 4; reelection of, 162,
  197, 198, 220, 222, 226; in retirement,
  217–18; rusticity of, 13–14, 21, 49, 53,
  227; scandals surrounding, 54, 93–94;
  as schoolteacher, 15–16, 51; staff abused
  by, 64; undervaluing of, ix, x, 4, 5; as
  vice president, 23, 62, 63, 84, 85, 91–93,
  107; Vietnam war escalated by, 116, 177,
  186, 189–90, 195–200, 211–12, 218–20,
  229; waning Texas influence of, 94–96;
  War on Poverty waged by, 134–35, 137,
  140, 147–49, 175; Watts riot viewed by,
  175; withdrawal from presidential race
  of, 213
Johnson, Rebekah (mother), 50
Johnson, Sam Ealy, Jr. (father), 51
Johnson, Sam Ealy, Sr. (paternal grandfather), 50
Jones, Clarence, 154
juvenile delinquency, 140–41, 147

Kaganovich, Lazar, 115
Kahin, George McT., 203
Karnow, Stanley, 210
Katzenbach, Nicholas, 38, 75, 100, 155–57
Kearns [Goodwin], Doris, 65, 217
Keating, Kenneth, 117
Keeler, Christine, 82, 94
Kennedy, Carolina (daughter), 118
Kennedy, Edward (brother), 20, 33, 172,
  173, 177
Kennedy, Ethel (sister-in-law), 96
Kennedy, Eunice (sister), 140
Kennedy, Jacqueline (wife), 32, 72, 83–84,
  97–98, 99–100, 103, 107, 193; Camelot
  myth created by, 20, 69–70, 80; cultural
  sophistication of, 80, 111; LBJ despised
  by, 84–85; social circle of, 80–81
Kennedy, John F.: Anglophilia of,
  43–46, 48; anti-Communism of, 196;
  anti-poverty policies of, 134–49, 174;
  assassination of, 1–2, 4, 17, 19; during
  Berlin crisis, 110–16; Boston Irish
  background of, 39–40, 41; Bowles disliked by, 73; cabinet and entourage of,
  38–39; Canadian visit of, 77; cautiousness of, 6, 179, 200; changing media
  landscape and, 29–30, 35, 225–26, 227;
  China feared by, 201–2; civil rights
  slighted by, 10, 16–17, 48–49, 133, 138;
  confidence embodied by, 5, 8, 227;
  during Cuban missile crisis, 116–31;
  cultural change and, 36, 158; Diem
  regime backed by, 194–95; education
  bill of, 165; European approval cultivated by, 212–13; far right attacked by,
  162; foreign policy of, 107–33; gossip
  and speculation surrounding, 4, 19;
  Harvard influence on, 42–44, 46;
  idealism of, xii, 7; ill health of, 19–20,
  34–35, 87; immigration reform backed
  by, 171–73; inaugural address of, 6–8,
  12, 137; internal struggles of, 54; LBJ
  despised by, 84–85; LBJ selected by,
  88–91; LBJ's similarities with, 196,
  219, 226, 228–30; middlebrow tastes
  of, 80; military service of, 33–34,
  39; news media entranced by, xi, 18,
  32–33; nuclear test ban proposed by,
  131–32; O'Donnell upbraided by, 85;
  overvaluing of, ix, x, 3–4, 5, 35, 186–87,
  190; personal style of, 13, 22, 37, 228;
  philandering by, 20, 63; as presidential candidate, 31, 36–36, 80, 137, 141,
  172, 226; press conferences of, 28–29,
  30–31; privileged background of, 32,
  39–40, 81, 227; reappraisals of, 19,
  20–21, 33–34; as senator, 137; Sino-
  Soviet split viewed by, 209; social circle
  of, 80–81; tax cuts by, 13; as vice presidential candidate, 37; Vietnam policies
  of, 23, 116, 184–93, 197, 198–200, 215–16,
  218–19; Whiggism of, 45–48, 140
Kennedy, John, Jr. (son), 21

Kennedy, Joseph P. (father), 42, 51, 90,
196, 210; as ambassador to Britain, 41,
45, 88, 204; JFK's career promoted by,
36–37; LBJ's attack on, 88; legend of
PT 109 crafted by, 33–34
Kennedy, Joseph P., Jr. (brother), 31, 33, 70
Kennedy, Joseph P., II (nephew), 41
Kennedy, Kathleen "Kick" (sister), 31, 42, 111
Kennedy, P. J. (paternal grandfather), 39
Kennedy, Patrick (son), 70, 186
Kennedy, Robert F. (brother), 9, 28, 41,
101, 112, 140–41; assassination of, 213;
Bay of Pigs invasion and, 109, 110;
civil rights bill and, 156–57; civil rights
slighted by, 8, 10, 16–17, 151–52; during
Cuban missile crisis, 116–17, 119, 120,
126–27, 129; immigration reform
backed by, 12; JFK's assassination and,
1, 96–98, 100; LBJ disliked by, 14, 97,
204; LBJ's selection and, 86–87, 88, 89,
90, 91; LBJ's suspicions of, 102; vice
presidency coveted by, 159; Vietnam
War questioned by, 177
Kennedy, Rose (mother), 45
Kennedy, Rosemary (sister), 31, 140
Kepel, Francis, 165
Kerr, Robert, 14, 16, 89, 93
Kerr-Mills bill, 168
Keyserling, Leon, 136
KGB, 123–24
Khong, Y. F., 201–2, 204
Khrushchev, Nikita, 90; during Berlin
crisis, 110–16, 207; during Cuban
missile crisis, 118, 121–31, 207; nuclear
test ban accepted by, 132–33
Kilduff, Malcolm, 100
Kilgore, Harley, 57
Kim Jong-Il, 3
King, Martin Luther, 19, 58, 154, 157, 176,
177, 180, 184, 219
King, Mary, 162
Kissinger, Henry, ix
Kleberg, Richard, 51

Kopechne, Mary Jo, 20
Korea, 201–2, 207
Kozlov, Frol, 115
Kraft, Joseph, 18, 32, 138
Krim, Arthur, 52, 63, 64
Kristol, Irving, 181
Krulak, Victor "Brute," 200
Ku Klux Klan, 159

Lady of Shalott, The (Tennyson), 69
Lamar, Mirabeau Buonaparte, 165–66
Lampman, Robert, 144, 145
Lang, Janet, 186, 187–88
Lanin, Lester, 80
Lannoy, Philippe de, 49
Lansdale, Edward, 194
Laos, 11, 188, 194, 205, 206
Lasker, Mary, 169
Lausche, Frank, 156
Lawford, Peter, 36
Lawrence, David, 29
Lederer, Lajos, 71
Lee, Robert E., 14
Leinsdorf, Erich, 51
LeMay, Curtis, 119, 121
Lerner, Alan Jay, 69
Levinson, Larry, 66
Lewis, Oscar, 135–36
Lincoln, Abraham, 3, 35, 152–53
Lincoln, Evelyn, 100
Lindsay, John, 10, 183
Lippmann, Walter, 44, 164
Locke, John, 47
Lodge, Henry Cabot, 10, 192, 204
Loewe, Frederick, 69
Logevall, Fredrik, 211
Lovett, Robert, 45
Lowell, Abbott Lawrence, 43
Luce, Clare Boothe, 92, 157
Lucy, Autherine, 58

MacArthur, Douglas, 202, 203
MacBird (Gershon), 18

Macdonald, Dwight, 143, 144
Macmillan, Harold, 63, 82, 111–12, 114, 212–13
Madison, James, 159
Mahomet, 2
Making of the President, 1960, The (White), 71
Malaysia, 205, 212
Malenkov, Georgi, 115
Malory, Thomas, 20
Manchester, William, 97
Mann, Arthur, 171–72
Mansfield, Mike, 92, 157, 188
Mao Zedong, 3, 114, 225
Marcelo, Carlos, 110
Marcus, Stanley, 53
Marder, Murray, 117
Marsh, Charles, 63, 65
Marshall, Burke, 33, 143
McCarthy, Eugene, 177
McCarthy, Joe, 87
McClendon, Sarah, 30
McCloy, John J., 45, 113
McCone, John, 97, 118, 122, 192
McCormack, John, 153, 165, 204
McCulloch, William, 152
McHugh, Godfrey, 99–100
McKeldin, Theodore, 175
McNamara, Robert S., 38, 76, 80, 132, 136, 186, 188, 198, 211; during Cuban missile crisis, 119, 121, 126, 129; guilt over Vietnam of, 185; on JFK's Vietnam plans, 187; Kennedys' closeness to, 97, 103; military service of, 75
McNaughton, John, 206, 210–11
McPherson, Harry, 12, 15, 78, 93, 175, 180; on JFK's civil rights views, 151–52; on LBJ's civil rights views, 59; on LBJ's persuasiveness, 61; LBJ's upbraiding of, 64–65; on Texas politics, 56
Means, Marianne, 63
Medicaid, 6, 23, 170, 177
Medicare, 6, 23, 137, 151, 168–71, 177, 179, 215

Melbourne, William Lamb, Viscount, 46
Meredith, James, 16, 143
Mesta, Perle, 92
Mexico, 212
Meyer, Karl E., 79–80, 117
Meyer, Mary Pinchot, 81
Meyer, Sara, 80
Miller, Jack, 155
Mills, Wilbur, 139, 142, 168, 169–70, 179
Minikus, Lee, 175
Mitchell, Clarence, 154
Mitchell, Joseph, 141–42
Mobilization for Youth, 141, 145
Molotov, Vyacheslav, 115
Mondale, Walter, 214
Morgenthau, Robert, 96
Morte d'Arthur (Malory), 20
Moses, Bob, 183
Moss, Frank, 156
Moyers, Bill, 15, 78, 93, 150, 151, 164, 166, 182; on LBJ's friction with Kennedys, 98–99; LBJ's selection and, 88, 89
Moynihan, Daniel Patrick, 12, 78, 101, 145, 147, 175, 180–81, 220
Moynihan, John, 78
Moynihan, Liz, 78
Moynihan, Maura, 78
Moynihan, Timothy, 78
Mundt, Karl, 155
Murray, James, 167
Mussolini, Benito, 203, 204, 225
Myrdal, Gunnar, 136

NAACP, 154
Napoleon Bonaparte, 3
National Broadcasting Company (NBC), 29–30
National Institutes of Health, 169
National Organization for Women (NOW), 162–63
National Service Corps, 141
National Youth Administration, 16, 52, 136

Nation of Immigrants, A (Kennedy),
   171–72
Negro Family, The (Moynihan), 175
Nehru, Jawaharlal, 212, 225
Nelson, Gaylord, 78
Neuberger, Richard, 58
Neustadt, Richard, 138, 228
New Deal, 7, 11, 52, 72, 161, 164, 196, 219,
   221, 222, 223, 229
New Frontier, 80, 164
Newsweek, 29, 30, 79
New York Times, 30, 32, 57, 114
Nhu, Ngo Dinh, 10, 189, 192, 210
Night Comes to the Cumberlands (Cau-
   dill), 141
Nixon, Richard, xi, 6, 19, 95, 215, 224, 226;
   blandness of, 34; as congressional can-
   didate, 63; conservative ascendancy
   represented by, 11, 219, 229; Demo-
   cratic split planned by, 58; election as
   president of, 193, 220; elites resented
   by, 49, reelection of, 222
North Atlantic Treaty Organization
   (NATO), 127, 129
Novy, Jim, 51
nuclear testing, 111, 112, 114, 124, 131–33

Obama, Barack, x, xi, 221
O'Brien, Larry, 86, 89, 153, 166, 214;
   cautiousness of, 138, 142; JFK assassi-
   nation and, 101; LBJ respected by, 85,
   103, 187
O'Daniel, W. Lee, 54
O'Donnell, John, 28
O'Donnell, Kenneth, 33, 86; cautiousness
   of, 137–38; LBJ disdained by, 13–14, 85,
   89, 96, 99, 100, 101; loyalty to JFK of,
   186; military service of, 38; resignation
   of, 102
Ohlin, Lloyd, 136, 141, 145
Olds, Leland, 56
Onassis, Aristotle, 20, 70, 193
O'Neill, Thomas P. "Tip," 43, 90

1,000,000 Delinquents (Fine), 136
Organization of American States, 121
Ormsby-Gore, 5th Baron Harlech, 81
Oswald, Lee Harvey, 18, 110
Other America, The (Harrington), 134,
   143–44
Oufkir, Mohamed, 27
Owen, Geoff, 77

Panic of *1907,* 66
Parr, George, 54
Peace Corps, 133, 141
Penkovsky, Oleg, 118, 208–9
Philippines, 11, 205, 212
Phillips, Kevin, 21
Pinchot, Tony, 81
Piven, Frances Fox, 145
Political Education, A (McPherson), 78
Pol Pot, 3
Post, Marjorie Merriweather, 78
poverty, 134–49, 174–77, 179
Powell, Adam Clayton, 166
Powell, James, 160
Powers, Dave, 33, 70, 84, 186
Pretzel, Raimund (pseud. Sebastian
   Haffner), 71
Price, Don K., 43
Pringle, John, 81–82
Profumo, Jack, 82, 94
Prouty, Winston, 166
Public Interest, 181

Quayle, Oliver, 169

Raleigh, Walter, Sir, 42
Raskin, Marcus, 183
Rauh, Joseph, 154
Rayburn, Sam, 56, 65, 87, 89, 90, 138–39
Read, Ben, 78, 182, 214
Read, Nan, 182
Reagan, Ronald, x, 4, 11, 222, 226–27
Reedy, George: on LBJ's centrism, 15; on
   LBJ's class resentments, 49; on LBJ's

Reedy, George (*continued*)
contradictions, 50; on LBJ's drinking, 63; on LBJ's frustrations as vice president, 92; on LBJ's legislative achievements, 60; on LBJ's reputation among Jews, 53; LBJ's taunting of, 64; as press secretary, 62; on Robert Kennedy and LBJ, 86; on Texas energy industry, 56
Reeves, Richard, 16, 35
Reston, James, 117
Reuther, Walter, 91
Ribicoff, Abraham, 177
Ricks, Willie, 176
Roberts, Chalmers, 117
Roche, John, 185
Rockefeller, Nelson, 162, 224
Roe v. Wade (1973), 162
Rometsch, Ellen, 82, 94
Roosevelt, Franklin D., ix, 28, 35, 72, 78, 159, 189, 225, 229; bureaucratic pressures on, 191; effectiveness of, x–xi, 178; fireside chats of, xi; health insurance plan abandoned by, 167; internal struggles of, 54; JFK inspired by, 48; LBJ consoled by, 55; LBJ inspired by, 6, 12, 15, 52, 65; privileged background of, 36; southern economy examined by, 67
Roosevelt, Franklin, Jr., 70
Roosevelt, James, 167
Roosevelt, Theodore, 3, 36, 73, 229
Rose, Earl, 101
Rostow, Walt, 14, 75, 190–91, 194, 197, 198, 206, 208, 209
Rowe, James H., 176
Rowen, Harry, 80
Rusher, William, 162
Rusk, Dean, 45, 94, 132, 181–82, 192, 198, 214, 215; during Cuban missile crisis, 122, 126, 127; as Far East specialist, 203; military service of, 38; Sino-Soviet split ignored by, 207; Vietnam escalation recommended by, 211; on World War II, 204

Russell, Richard, 50, 56, 179, 222; LBJ's closeness to, 14, 55, 65, 155; racism of, 16, 151; Southern Manifesto signed by, 58
Rustin, Bayard, 176, 213

Salinger, Pierre, 29, 89, 100, 115, 117, 124
Sampson, Anthony, 71
Samuelson, Paul, 101
Scali, John, 124
Schlafly, Phyllis, 162
Schlesinger, Arthur M., Jr., 4, 17, 43, 75, 80, 81, 90, 187; as biographer, 3, 5, 21, 32, 47; at Harvard lunch, 101–2; LBJ disparaged by, 85; resignation of, 102–3
Schlesinger, Marian, 81, 101
Schultze, Charles, 145, 147, 176
Scott, Richard, 1
Search for JFK, The (Blair and Blair), 20, 33–34
Seigenthaler, John, 143
Serov, Ivan, 209
Shapley, Deborah, 185
Sheppard, Morris, 54
Shesol, Jeff, 89, 98
Shriver, Sargent, 36, 97, 136
Siegel, Jerry, 78
Sieverts, Frank, 78
Simpson, Thacher and Bartlett, 52
Sinatra, Frank, 36
Sino-Soviet Conflict, The (Zagoria), 208
Smathers, George, 84, 152
Smith, Alfred E., 37
Smith, Howard, 138, 152, 153–54
Smith, Steve, 36, 99
Smith, Walter Bedell, 205
Social Security, 137, 140, 167, 168, 170
Sombart, Werner, 36
Sorensen, Theodore, 21, 132, 147, 174, 218; as biographer, 3, 5, 32; civil rights bill viewed by, 152; during Cuban missile crisis, 124, 126; LBJ grudg-

ingly admired by, 103; racial conflict recalled by, 17; rhetorical flair of, 4, 7, 12

Southern Manifesto, 15, 56, 58

Soviet Union, 7, 8, 39, 45, 49, 108, 158, 190, 207, 213; American inequality attacked by, 140; during Berlin crisis, 110–16; Chinese relations with, 207–9; during Cuban missile crisis, 116–30; nuclear test ban accepted by, 133

Spalding, Charles, 70, 80

Spellman, Joseph, 210

Stalin, Joseph, 3, 111, 204, 206, 207, 225

Stennis, John, 14, 159

Stern, Isaac, 80

Stern, Larry, 79

Stevenson, Adlai, 17, 49, 87

Stevenson, Coke, 55

Stimson, Henry, 76

Sukarno, 212, 225

Sulzberger, C. L., 114

Swindal, James, 100

Symington, Stuart, 87

Taft, Robert, 222

Taft-Hartley Act (1947), 91

tax policy, 103–4, 139

Taylor, Maxwell D., 38–39, 97, 119, 191, 198, 200

Tennyson, Alfred Tennyson, Baron, 69

Thieu, Nguyen Van, 215

Thirteen Days (Robert F. Kennedy), 116–17, 126

Thirteenth Amendment, 153

Thomas, George, 16

Thompson, Llewellyn "Tommy," 126

Thomson, James C., 202

Till, Emmett, 58

Time, 29, 30

Tito, Marshal, 113, 212, 225

Tobin, James, 138

Tojo, Hideki, 120

Trenchard, John, 47

Trotsky, Leon, 71

Trueman, Peter, 77

Truman, Harry, 119, 150, 167, 191, 202, 204

Turing, Alan, 38

Turkey, 125, 127, 128, 129, 130

Uncertain Trumpet, The (Taylor), 39

unemployment, 104, 161

United Auto Workers, 135

United Nations, 30, 95, 121

United Press International (UPI), 29, 30

University of Michigan, 13, 163

University of Mississippi, 16–17, 94, 143, 158

US News & World Report, 29, 30

Valenti, Jack, 63, 150

Vietnam War, 2, 5, 6, 181–82, 201–10, 213–14; civil rights intertwined with, 183–84; Democratic Party riven by, 13, 19; divining JFK's plans for, 23, 116, 184–93, 197, 198–200, 215–16, 218–19; LBJ's escalation of, 116, 177, 186, 189–90, 195–200, 211–12, 218–20, 229; opposition to, 221–22; Tet offensive, 180; three phases of, 193–94, 200

Vinson, Carl, 56

Virtual JFK (Blight and Lang), 186, 187–88

Voting Rights Act (1965), 9, 12, 182

Wagner, Robert F. (senator), 167

Wagner, Robert F., Jr. (mayor), 141

Wallace, George, 17, 143, 160, 161, 174, 220

Wallas, Graham, 164

Walters, Herbert, 155

Walton, William, 101, 192

Warren Commission, 110

Washington, George, 36

Washington Post, 30, 32, 73, 117, 120

Watergate scandal, 11, 66, 79, 222

Wattenberg, Ben J., 40

Watts riot, 174, 175

Weaver, Robert, 140

Weber, Max, 22, 37

Weisl, Ed, Sr., 52

Welch, Robert, 162

Westmoreland, William, 195, 200

Whalen, Richard J., 34

Wheeling and Dealing (Baker), 93

Whigs, 45–48

White, Lee, 147

White, Theodore H., 3, 4, 8, 18, 20, 32, 69–70, 71

White, William S., 4, 63

Whitehead, Phillip, x

Whiting, Allen, 203

Why England Slept (Kennedy), 48

Wickenden, Elizabeth, 136

Wicker, Tom, 4, 5, 60

Wiggins, J. Russell, 79

Wiley, Mary Margaret, 63

Wilkins, Roy, 154

Wilson, Harold, 212–13

Wilson, Henry Hall, 142

Wilson, Woodrow, 13, 44, 130, 159, 164, 229

Wirtz, Alvin, 55, 65

Witte, Edwin, 167, 168

Wofford, Harris, 143

Wolfe, Tom, 79

Woods, Randall, 4, 53, 58, 163

Woodward, Bob, 79

World War II, 7, 8, 21, 38–39, 41, 68, 203

Wright, Zephyr, 16

Wriston, Walter B., 76

Yarborough, Ralph, 95, 96, 156

Yarmolinsky, Adam, 136–37, 147

Ylvisaker, Paul, 141, 145

Young, Milton, 155

Young Americans for Freedom (YAF), 162, 224

Yugoslavia, 114, 212

Zagoria, Donald, 208